PUBLISHED ON THE
LOUIS STERN MEMORIAL FUND

THE RHYTHM OF
BEOWULF

THE RHYTHM OF
BEOWULF

An Interpretation of
the Normal and Hypermetric Verse-Forms
in Old English Poetry

BY

JOHN COLLINS POPE
ASSISTANT PROFESSOR OF ENGLISH
IN YALE UNIVERSITY

... True musical delight ... consists
only in apt numbers, fit quantity of syllables, and the sense variously drawn out
from one verse into another ... Milton

NEW HAVEN
YALE UNIVERSITY PRESS
LONDON · HUMPHREY MILFORD · OXFORD UNIVERSITY PRESS
1942

English

53445

FEB 18 1948

PR
1588
P82

42-2647
1/27/48

TO
ROBERT J. MENNER

PREFACE

THIS book presents in greatly expanded form the theory that I outlined in 1936 at a meeting of the Old English Group of the Modern Language Association. I thought then that I should be able to present it more briefly and much sooner; but my predecessors in the field had seen to it that I should not dispose of them in any summary fashion, or present my own idea in its mere naked simplicity.

The very thoroughness imposed upon me by those with whom I ventured to disagree has brought with it an increased sense of indebtedness to them. I have spoken of my special obligation to Leonard in my discussion of his theory. My obligation to Heusler, both for his treatment of Old English versification and for his analysis of rhythm in general, may readily be inferred. What may not be so clear is that I owe most of all to Sievers. I have spoken more harshly of him than of the others, because I believe that his theory has led people farthest from the truth; but I am none the less convinced that he was the greatest of them all. His false theory did not prevent him from being the first and the best of guides toward a sound theory. If my own theory proves unsound, it will still be true that Sievers must be reckoned with before any other theory can be set up.

For the general principles of rhythm I have leaned heavily on the greatest book on the subject that I know, William Thomson's *The Rhythm of Speech* (Glasgow, 1923). It is only fair to add, however, that I was unfamiliar with this book when I developed my own theory, which sprang rather from a study of Sidney Lanier's pioneering work, *The Science of English Verse*, first published in 1880. Lanier's book has many faults of detail—faults which have made it impossible for me to cite it in my footnotes—but he grasped, without quite correctly stating, the fundamental notion that rhythm depends on the temporal relations of accents, and he expounded this and other fundamental notions with an imaginative pregnancy that sometimes goes farther than accuracy. Thomson has superseded Lanier, but it was Lanier and not Thomson who showed me how to analyze my habitual reading of *Beowulf* and so led me to what I hope is a fruitful reconstruction of that reading.

I have incurred countless obligations of a more personal nature through the generous assistance of my friends and my family. I cannot hope to repay any of them by the doubtful notoriety of a preface, but there are a few who must allow me to mention their names. Chief among these is Professor Robert J. Menner, who once taught me the rudiments of Old English and has continued to assist me at every turn. He has read the book in various stages of its growth, and is largely responsible for whatever traces of sound scholarship it contains. To Professors Frederick A. Pottle and John Archer Gee I am indebted for careful reading of manuscript or proof and for many valuable suggestions. To all three, and to many other scholarly friends, especially to Professor Chauncey B. Tinker and to Dean William C. DeVane, I owe various offices of kindness and constant encouragement.

One final group of acknowledgments remains. This has been an extraordinarily difficult and costly book to print. That it appears in so handsome and readable a form must be attributed in the first place to Mr. Carl P. Rollins, Printer to the University, who expended a great deal of time in studying the problem of the musical notation and a great deal of skill in working out the design. Equal praise is due to the unremitting effort of the staff of the Yale University Press, and to the craftsmanship of the J. H. Furst Company of Baltimore, the printers who executed the design. That the book could appear at all must be attributed to the funds that were made available through the Yale University Press.

J. C. P.

Silliman College, Yale University,
  November, 1941.

CONTENTS

PART I. THE NORMAL LINE

PART II. THE HYPERMETRIC VERSES

PART III. SPECIMEN NOTATIONS

APPENDIX

CATALOGUE OF RHYTHMIC VARIATIONS IN THE NORMAL VERSES OF *BEOWULF*

PART I

THE NORMAL LINE

INTRODUCTION

METRICAL studies of ancient poetry have at least two immediate aims, the establishment of the text and the recovery of the pleasure inherent in verse. We have gained much if we can feel reasonably certain that the words are the poet's own, but unless we know also the rhythm to which he set them, half their glory has departed. It is regrettable, therefore, that there has never been general agreement among scholars about the proper reading of Old English, or indeed any of the ancient Germanic poetry. Even the system of Sievers, which has been of immense service in the establishment of texts, and threatened for a time to displace all others, has been frequently challenged—most recently by Leonard and Heusler—and was partially rejected by Sievers himself. All three of these men came to recognize what Sievers' original system appeared to deny, a fundamental relation between the rhythm of verse and that of music. Nor have Leonard and Heusler lacked converts. Prominent among these, though perhaps not wholly persuaded, is Klaeber, who has included praise of Leonard and a summary of Heusler's system in his third edition of *Beowulf*.[1] Nevertheless, in spite of the advances that these two scholars have made, we shall find that there are grave obstacles in the way of an acceptance of their theories. When one considers the learning and ingenuity that have been bestowed on the problem and the instability and discordance of the results, one is likely to conclude that Germanic poetry was a very queer and unintelligible thing, or else that some vital clue has been lost.

[1] Fr. Klaeber, *Beowulf and the Fight at Finnsburg* (3rd. ed., New York: Heath and Co., 1936), p. 282. Klaeber's third edition has been used throughout this book. A detailed statement concerning the few textual changes that I have ventured to recommend will be found at the head of the Appendix, p. 232 below.

This book is founded upon the latter assumption, because a hitherto unexploited device—one that is altogether natural under the circumstances yet hardly to be discovered except by accident—has proved of amazing efficacy in producing the metrical order and expressiveness which we associate with competent poetry. If this device is illusory, then the problem remains in its present state of confusion; but if not, then Old English poetry must receive credit for a technical proficiency far beyond what has usually been attributed to it, and the art of its masterpiece, *Beowulf*, can for the first time be fully apprehended.

By right of age, length, and excellence, *Beowulf* has been the traditional testing-ground for theories of Germanic versification. It has once more been chosen as the center of attention, primarily for its own sake, yet also for this larger and indeed inescapable relationship. Old High German, Old Saxon, and especially Old Norse had, to be sure, certain minor peculiarities, but the fundamental verse-forms were so remarkably similar throughout the ancient Germanic world that a discussion of the rhythm of *Beowulf*, besides embracing nearly all the phenomena of Old English poetry, has still larger implications. In treating the so-called hyper-metric form in Part II, I have found it necessary to include other Old English poems, because the eleven lines of this sort in *Beowulf* are too few for the establishment of a theory. Our primary business, however, is with the normal form, of which the other three thousand lines of *Beowulf* are abundantly representative. A brief description of this form will show something of the problem with which we are to deal.

It is well known that the great majority of lines in Germanic alliterative verse, widely as they appear to differ among themselves, have certain features in common, and may be classified as normal lines against the much smaller array of those which, by reason of their conspicuously

greater bulk (to judge by the average number and weight
of their syllables), have been called expanded, or swelling,
or hypermetric. Characteristic of both classes is a division
into two more or less equal parts, called half-lines or verses.
This division is usually marked by phrasing, but even when
that is not the case, the two halves are recognizably distinct,
because the syllabic patterns repeat themselves within the
half-lines, and the pattern of the first half appears to have
little or no effect on that of the second. The two verses are
bound together by a consistent pattern of alliteration, which
may be defined without reference to particular theories. In
the normal verses we find regularly two syllables which, on
grounds of logic and grammar, should be more heavily
stressed than the others. The first of these in the second
half-line alliterates regularly with the first, or second, or
both, in the first half-line. So far, with minor exceptions,
all normal lines are the same.

Unfortunately for the metrists, however, the syllables
of the half-lines differ widely in number, in relative position
of the two strongest, and in the extent to which others call
for subordinate but still perceptible stresses. In the unemended text of *Beowulf*, for example, a normal half-line
contains from two to ten syllables, and although editors
have usually emended the few that contain only two or three
syllables, with the plausible idea that four was the regular
minimum, the variation remains wide enough to be troublesome. It is largely in consequence of this and the other
variations noted that so many different, mutually contradic-
tory theories have been evolved about how the lines should
be scanned. Of the multitude, only three need excite our
attention now, those of Sievers, Leonard, and Heusler. By
examining at the outset the peculiar virtues and defects of
these three theories, we shall reach an understanding of the
problem in all its complexity.

PREVIOUS THEORIES

SIEVERS

THERE is small difficulty in accounting for the popularity of the five-type system of scansion, which reached its fullest expression in 1893 with the publication of Sievers' *Altgermanische Metrik*.[2] Against the metrical defects of this system was set an array of statistical information that could not be denied. The characteristic sequences of syllables, long and short, stressed and unstressed, were established once for all, and were classified in a convenient if not altogether indisputable form. Indeed, the descriptive portion of Sievers' work is fundamentally sound, and must always be of service. It is even possible that the names of the five types, A, B, C, D, E, long so familiar to students of Germanic verse, will be retained for their convenience, even though they do not include quite all the known forms, and though their rhythmic significance must be completely changed. However this may be, one must grant that Sievers' work has indestructible elements, and that it has been helpful not only in the study of language and grammar, but in the amendment of many a faulty text. A few lines, to be sure, may have incurred censure by Sievers and his followers without just cause; but visual patterns of syllables are often a sufficient guide for editors of texts, and on the whole the work of these men has been beneficent. It is only when one comes to the major problem of verse—its

---

[2] For *Beowulf* the most important of Sievers' treatises is the earlier article, "Zur Rhythmik des Germanischen Alliterationsverses I," *Beiträge zur Geschichte der Deutschen Sprache und Literatur* 10 (1885), 209-314. The "Erster Abschnitt, Die Metrik des Beowulf" begins on p. 220. Also important is the sequel in the same volume, "Sprachliche Ergebnisse," pp. 451-545. Hereafter, these articles are referred to by the short title *Beiträge* 10, with page number.

effect on the ear—that the influence of Sievers becomes truly damaging.

Here, indeed, it is hard to overestimate the extent of the damage. To Sievers' theory may be attributed many an infelicitous, clumsily rhythmized performance that could yet call itself faithful to the original. To this theory likewise, and to these readings, may be attributed the widespread notion that the ancient Germanic people had a sense of rhythm all their own, one not to be understood by those whose verse had learned manners from the Greeks and Romans. Thus, while *Beowulf* has had many admirers among those who looked chiefly to the beauty and dignity of its language, the majority of students have been prone to believe what is almost inconceivable—that artistry in expression is here associated with a crude, "barbarous" rhythm. There is irony in this, for Sievers himself would have been the last to subscribe to such a notion, and his own reading, to judge by reports of enthusiastic auditors, must have been vastly superior to his theory. But the theory, if taken literally, can lead to no other conclusion.

To understand the shortcomings of this theory, we must be careful to distinguish it from the simple description of facts on which it rests. It is a fact to say that the verse, *sīdra sorga,* consists of four syllables, the first and third grammatically long and stressed, the second and fourth grammatically short and unstressed. If we decide, then, to mark all syllables that do not require stress with an ×, and to mark the others with appropriate accents (acute for primary, grave for secondary stress) and with signs of grammatical length (macron for long, breve for short), it is a fact that this sequence of syllables may be represented in notation as –́ × –́ ×. It is theory, on the other hand, though here correct, to divide the verse into two feet thus: –́ × | –́ ×. It is theory, and wrong, to assume that –, ⏑, or × indicates any specific metrical quantity. Actually,

as we shall see, these signs can indicate only certain ranges
of quantity, and the verse in question is to be read thus:
$\acute{r}\,\acute{r} \mid \acute{r}\,\acute{r}$, or what is rhythmically the same thing, $\acute{r}\,\acute{c}\,,\mid\acute{r}\,\acute{c}\,,$.
(If we let an eighth-note equal 1, and an eighth-rest equal $\wedge$,
we can express the same result thus: $\acute{2}\,\acute{2} \mid \acute{2}\,\acute{2}$, or $\acute{2}\,\acute{1}\,\wedge \mid$
$\acute{2}\,\acute{1}\,\wedge$.) Again, it is a fact that the verse, *hēah Healfdene,*
may be described thus: $\perp \perp \smile \times$. It is theory, and correct,
to divide it so: $\perp \mid \perp \smile \times$. It is theory, and wrong, to appor-
tion temporal values such as these: $\acute{r} \mid \acute{r}\,\acute{c}\,\acute{c}$. It is theory,
and right, to read $\acute{r} \mid \acute{r}\,\acute{c}\,\acute{c}$, or, again the same thing rhythmically, $\acute{r}\,^\times \mid \acute{r}\,\acute{c}\,\acute{c}$. Finally, it is a fact that the verse, *hū ðā*
æðelingas, may be described thus: $\times \times \smile \times \perp \times$. It is theory,
and wrong, to divide it so: $\times \times \smile \times \mid \perp \times$. It is theory, and
plausible, though not correct, to divide and measure it so:
$\acute{c}\,\acute{c} \mid \acute{c}\,\acute{c}\,^\times \mid \acute{r}\,\acute{r}$. It is theory, and correct, to divide and measure it so: $^\times\acute{c}\,\acute{c} \mid \acute{c}\,\acute{c}\,\acute{c}$. But the last example has taken us
into the heart of the new theory that is soon to be described,
and we must not anticipate. It is enough at present to
recognize that Sievers, like every other investigator of the
problem, was compelled to interpret the facts with reference
to certain theoretical assumptions. To the weakness of these
assumptions we can trace the essential defects of the entire
system.

Thus, the two chief errors in Sievers' theory are the
assumptions, first, that the signs −, ◡, and × have sufficiently definite metrical significance; and secondly, that so-
called rising and falling feet are interchangeable and equally
valid units of rhythm. The first error proceeds from the
notion that rhythm can exist without strict temporal rela-
tions: that a sequence $\perp \times \times \times \times \mid \perp \times$ can be substituted
for a sequence $\perp \times \mid \perp \times$ without any adjustment of quantities. Simple experiment in reading is enough to show that
we do not feel any equivalence here, or any rhythm, for that
matter, unless we make the sequence $\perp \times \times \times \times$ equal in

time to the sequence ´ × .[3] This means that we must either crowd four unstressed syllables into the time occupied elsewhere by one, or alter the quantities of the stressed syllables as well. Actually, we shall find that neither −, ˘, nor × can have a fixed duration, though each of them will have a normal quantity and a limited range within which this can be compressed or extended. Take, for example, the three verses of *Beowulf, lēof lēodcyning* (54a), *eald enta geweorc* (2774a), and *Oferswam ðā sioleða bigong* (2367a). The first, according to Sievers, would be scanned ´ | ´ ˘ × ; the second, ´ | ´ × × ´ ; the third, × × | ´ × | ˘ × × × × ´. Were we to assume that these signs indicate fixed quantities, we should be at a loss to produce a rhythm. Suppose, for example, we let − equal 2, ˘ equal 1, and × equal 1. The first verse would then be 2 | 2 1 1, the second 2 | 2 1 1 2, the third 1 1 | 2 1 | 1 1 1 1 2. The quantitative sums of the two feet of each verse (we may disregard the anacrusis preceding the third) would then be 2 and 4 for the first, 2 and 6 for the second, 3 and 6 for the third. The remedy for this absurdity is easy. Guiding ourselves by the accents, we shall read the first verse 4 | 2 1 1 (or, letting a caret represent a rest equal to 1, 2 ∧ ∧ | 2 1 1), the second 4 | 1 ½ ½ 2, the third ½ ½ | 2 2 | ½ ½ ½ ½ 2. The sum of the quantities in every foot is now 4, and we have a consistent rhythm; but we have found three values for −, 4, 2, and 1; two values for ˘, 1 and ½; and three for ×, 2, 1 and ½. As soon, therefore, as we rule out these equivocal signs, and fix the quantity

---

[3] For the sake of simplicity, I have here omitted certain hypothetical possibilities. It is true that, as William Thomson has maintained in *The Rhythm of Speech,* p. 183 and *passim,* the measures of verse are not always isochronous. Besides the minor irrationality produced by change of tempo, we sometimes encounter unequal but rational relations of measures (e. g. as 2 is to 3). Isochronous measures are the rule, however, and it is easy to produce them in *Beowulf* by means of limited quantitative variation. The assumption of fixed quantities, on the other hand, whether for all syllables or only for those that are heavily stressed, leads to changes of time that even prose would not tolerate.

of each syllable according to its position in the verse as well as its vague grammatical potentialities, we can record a rhythm, and, what is more, read what we have recorded. Otherwise we have chaos.

If this were the only error that Sievers had made, no great harm would have been done, because the quantitative adjustments here indicated are made unconsciously by every good reader, and the looseness of Sievers' notation would not have prevented correct reading of the verse. Much more serious was the error in his theory of feet. Rhythm is apprehended, not by the eye, but the ear. The bar has therefore no power—it cannot be heard. Unless it is used to indicate that the syllable following it is more heavily accented than its neighbors, it has no meaning whatever. Thus, in types B and C, the notations × ´ | × ´ and × ´ | ´ × indicate divisions that can be seen but not heard. The whole problem of the rhythm of the verse is ignored by such a notation as this. Such a scansion may be of service to an editor; to a reader, it is either a command to do the impossible, or a failure to say anything at all. What wonder, then, that such students of rhythm as Leonard and Heusler have refused to accept Sievers' theory, or that Sievers himself, as will be shown presently, was forced to abandon it?

It is perhaps worthy of note in passing that this absurdity in Sievers' system was the natural consequence of the theories of modern versification that were current at the time when he devised his own. We still find it convenient to scan certain poems by pseudo-classical feet, iambic, trochaic, and the like; and we are taught that a poem that is iambic in character may contain substitutions of trochees, or anapæsts, or spondees, etc. For instance, Tennyson's line,

Far on the ringing plains of windy Troy,

is conventionally scanned thus:

> Fár on | the ríng- | ing pláins | of wín- | dy Tróy,

and we are told that a trochee has been substituted for an iambus as the first foot. The division ´ × | × ´ is just the reverse of Sievers' C-type, × ́⌣ | ́⌣ ×, and equally absurd; for the ear always measures by accents. What is called trochaic substitution leads to several different rhythmic consequences. Here we find the commonest of them; everyone will read the line very nearly as follows:

> Fár on the rínging pláins of wíndy Tróy.[4]

The metrist, or the poet himself, may think of this phenomenon as trochaic substitution; but what has really happened is that the anacrusis with which iambic lines usually begin has been omitted, and the first three syllables are spoken in the time usually allotted to two. There is no change in time (i. e. basic structure and total quantity of the measure); the five chief accents are all present and recur at the usual intervals; there is simply a minor variation in the rhythmic pattern within the bounds set by these accents.[5] In fact, the rhythmic variation introduced by the rapid pronunciation of the first syllable of *ringing* (♪ ♪) is just as remarkable. All this is obscured by the notation ´ × | × ´ | × ´ | × ´ | × ´, where the bar marks divisions apparent only to the eye, and the quantities do not appear at all. (The conventional quantitative notation, − ⌣ | ⌣ − | ⌣ − | ⌣ − | ⌣ −, is even worse, because it gives false information about the quantities.) Because of confusions like this, the term " foot " has

---

[4] The quantity of the last syllable in any series is not fixed. It is here given a conventional value.

[5] Variation of tempo may, of course, be introduced at the discretion of the reader. He may wish to retard the first measure and hasten the fourth. Indeed, if he carries this tendency far enough, he may produce new rational relations of the measures; that is, he may actually change the time. Even so, the intervals between chief accents will remain the primary fact about the rhythm of the line,

acquired a hopeless ambiguity, so that metrists are now driven to use the unequivocal term " measure " to describe the only apprehensible unit of rhythm, the interval of time that begins with one principal accent and ends with the next.

It will be seen, then, that Sievers was only borrowing mistakes from contemporary metrical theory when he marked the " feet " of his five types. Unfortunately, the result was disastrous. Most people care little how modern verse is scanned, because tradition and rhythmic sense together have enabled them to read correctly in spite of incorrect analysis. In the case of the obsolete Germanic verse, however, tradition has disappeared, and rhythmic sense alone cannot solve the problem. That sense will, indeed, prevent anyone from reading in accordance with Sievers—it may be confidently asserted that Sievers himself could not have accomplished this; but it will not, unaided, lead to the true reading; for, as will presently appear, the old Germanic poets introduced a subtlety that does not reveal itself on the page except by inference. The key has been lost, and Sievers' doctrine, through the virtues that are mingled with its faults, has not only kept most scholars from seeking that key, but has given countenance to many a muddled reading and to the notion that the Germanic people had a queer sense of rhythm.

Sievers himself was wiser than his disciples. He came to recognize these faults in his system, and in his later years evolved a new one, one that was rhythmically sound. Concluding that verse is not verse unless it keeps time, he introduced proper temporal relations into his scansion of Germanic verse.[6] In order to do this, however, he thought that he was obliged to ignore the prose accentuation of many

---

[6] Sievers specifically retracts the rhythmic implications of his five types and outlines his new methods in " Zu Cynewulf," *Neusprachliche Studien, Festgabe für Karl Luick* (*Die Neueren Sprachen*, 6. Beiheft, 1925), pp. 61 ff.

words and the evidence of alliteration. Thus, he read the
first line of *The Fates of the Apostles,*

Hwæt, ic þisne sáng   sī·ðgiōmor fánd,[7]

which, in musical notation, runs thus:

Hwæt, ic þisne sáng   siðgiōmor fánd.

Instead of giving primary accent to the first syllable of
sīðgiōmor, which would require it in prose, and bears
alliteration in the verse, he attempted to signalize this syllable in a different manner, apparently by strong secondary
accent and elevation of pitch (marked with a point in his
notation),[8] while he transferred the primary accent to the

---

[7] *Ibid.,* p. 63. His three-stress lines, likewise illustrated on this page (hū ðā
æðelingas éllen cýþdon), which disturb the metre rather than the prevailing
time, come within an ace of my own theory. All that Sievers needed was an
initial rest in front of them.

[8] This is my interpretation of his term, "schwebende Betonung," or "hover-
ing accent." Pitch, as William Thomson has strenuously maintained, has nothing
whatever to do with rhythm, but one of its many functions is the heightening of
logical emphasis, for we frequently elevate the pitch of a syllable when we give
it heavy stress. In those cases, not altogether infrequent in modern English
verse, when we are obliged to reduce the stress of a logically emphatic syllable
in order to preserve the metre, we often allow it to keep the higher pitch, thus
saying, in effect: "I cannot stress this syllable as fully as its meaning requires,
because the metre demands that I give accentual precedence to its neighbor."
Take note, however, that it is logically superior." A good illustration is the end
of one of the lines in *Ulysses:* "He works his work, I mine." In prose, the
rhythm would run thus:

He works his work, I mine.

The metre, however, demands the following accentuation and quantitative
adjustment:

He works his work, I mine.

I observe this movement, allowing the secondary accents to be virtually as strong
as the primary, but much inferior to what they would normally be, and retaining a slightly elevated pitch on *He, his,* and *I.* (Monotone destroys the effect

second syllable. This procedure does indeed give a smooth and rhythmically sound reading; but, by disregarding the only visible clues to the rhythm, it must rest its claim to authenticity on the subjective evidence of " Schallanalyse " —on the assertion that this and only this reading will permit an unhampered recitation. If there were no other way to achieve a harmonious reading, one might accept the findings of even so questionable a method with thanksgiving. As it happens, however, there are two other rhythmic readings which adhere at once to alliteration and the possibilities latent in prose accentuation:

(1) Hwǽt, ic þìsne sáng siðgiōmor fánd,

(2) Hwæ̀t, ic þísne sàng siðgiōmor fánd.

The choice depends on the relative importance of *Hwæt* and *þisne* (which cannot be settled objectively), and on analogy with other lines. Since the first half-line has an unusual grammatical and alliterative pattern, there is perhaps no safe way to reach a decision. I prefer the first reading; Heusler, I think, would have preferred the second. What is important, however, is that both readings accord with the possibilities of prose accentuation, both respect the alliteration, and both are just as rhythmical as that of Sievers.

It is hard to believe that either of these readings can with justice be rejected by the elaborate but far too subjective tests of " Schallanalyse." By Sievers' own admission, " Schallanalyse " is not a subject for logical debate.

and obliterates either the meaning or the metre.) Probably because he has had to fight hard to prove the incontestable fact that pitch has nothing to do with rhythm, William Thomson gives up this line altogether as unmetrical. (See *The Rhythm of Speech*, pp. 268 and 391; but on p. 224, Thomson says exactly what I have said about pitch.)

One either believes or disbelieves.[9] Though I am disposed to think that there is some virtue in this occult analysis, and though I cannot speak as one of the initiate, I must express my disbelief in this instance. It is possible to reach what seems to my ear to be a splendid rhythm without sacrificing the objective evidence of alliteration and prose accentuation. It seems unwise, therefore, to abandon this evidence in favor of a system which demands a delicacy and an impartiality that few, if any, can hope to possess.

Thus, while Sievers' later theory testifies eloquently to the defects of the earlier, it appears as irreconcilable with the objective evidence of the lines themselves as did the earlier with rhythmic principles. We shall find that the earlier is really superior, because, in spite of its erroneous conclusions, it presents the evidence without which any theory is doomed, and presents it more fully and impartially than does any other work. We must proceed for the moment to examine other theories, but we shall return eventually to Sievers' analysis of syllabic sequences as the soundest point of departure for a new interpretation of their significance.

LEONARD

Of modern opponents of Sievers, the best known and most important are, in this country, William Ellery Leonard, and in Germany, the late Andreas Heusler. It is difficult to speak of a precise system in the case of Leonard, because he has never dealt with all the details, and still more because his views have changed somewhat since the publication of " Beowulf and the Niebelungen Couplet " in 1918,[10] approaching more and more closely to those of Heus-

---

[9] See, for example, Sievers' pamphlet, *Ziele und Wege der Schallanalyse,* Heidelberg, 1924.
[10] *University of Wisconsin Studies in Language and Literature,* No. 2, pp. 99-152.

ler, of whom he has expressed his approval.[11] In its inception, however, his theory was not like Heusler's. It rested on the modified " four-accent " theory of Kaluza.[12] The chief difference between this theory and Heusler's (if one ignores the temporally impossible divisions into feet recommended by Kaluza and substitutes the rhythmic divisions implied by both Kaluza's and Leonard's accentuation) is that Kaluza's accents produce four simple (ordinarily duple) measures in the half-line or verse instead of Heusler's two compound (quadruple) measures. Kaluza and Leonard grant that two of the four accents are strong, two weak, but they do not always follow the pattern strong-weak-strong-weak, which gives two measures of quadruple time. Sometimes the sequence is weak-strong-strong-weak (*in gĕardágùm*), sometimes weak-strong-weak-strong (*Hè ðæs frófrè gebåd*). Musically interpreted, Leonard's accentuation of Sievers' five types gives the following readings (I choose 2/4 rather than 2/8 for comparison with Heusler, but the tempo must be fairly rapid) :

A sīdrà sórgà
|♩|♩ |♩ |♩ |

Gewāt ðā ófer wæghólm
♩|♩ ♩ |♪♪ |♩ |♩ |

B Hè ðæs frófre gebåd
|♩ ♩ |♩ |♩ ♩|♩ |

C in gĕardágùm
|♩ |♩ |♩ |♩ |

[11] See his article, "Four Footnotes to Papers on Germanic Metrics," *Studies in English Philology, a Miscellany in Honor of Frederick Klaeber* (Minneapolis: Univ. of Minnesota Press, 1929), pp. 1-13, and the note on Heusler, p. 13. Those who do not understand Leonard's notation may find some enlightenment in his article, "The Recovery of the Metre of the *Cid*," *P. M. L. A.* 46 (1931). 289-306, which undertakes to establish a Germanic metre for the *Cid*.

[12] Max Kaluza, *Der Altenglische Vers: Eine Metrische Untersuchung*, Berlin, 1894.

D   frómum feóhgìftum

E   fýrenðèarfe ongéat

The gradation of accents here shown is possible so long as
we make four measures instead of two, because in all verse
the principal accents of consecutive measures tend to vary
in force. Nevertheless, while the readings given for type A,
where the sequence is strong-weak-strong-weak, are unmistakably correct, the others, with their various sequences,
clearly violate the natural movement of the words in two
ways. In the first place, the range of force between primary
and secondary accents is materially reduced by allotting a
separate measure to each accent, whether strong or weak.
In quadruple time, where the accentual pattern is strong-
weak-strong-weak, the secondary accent may be much
weaker than the primary, or of almost the same force,
depending on the exigencies of the words. In duple time, on
the other hand, where each of the four accents is theoretically independent, and no regular gradation can be predicted,
a greater uniformity tends to develop. Thus, in the B- and
C-verses just cited, the syllables *Hē, -fre, in,* and *-um,* and
similar syllables in the D- and E-verses, even though spoken
less forcefully than the others, will receive considerably
more emphasis than belongs to them by nature.[13] In the

[13] That this is no gratuitous conjecture of mine is established by Leonard's
own confession ("Four Footnotes," *loc. cit.,* p. 7) : "Theoretically my diagram
for *ofer hronrade* (C) is x̌ × x̌L × L × and for *fromum feohgiftum* (D) is
x̌ × x̌ L x̌ L × ; but the two cadences are in effect on the ear far more alike
than many so-called 'subtypes' of any of the orthodox five: *ofer* certainly had
practically as strong a stress as *fromum.*" (In his later explanations of his
theory, Leonard uses the sign L to indicate a brief rest at an unaccented point
in the verse, and L̦ to indicate one that takes the place of an accented syllable.
He calls the first a rest, the second a rest-beat.)

second place, the quantitative relations are sometimes distorted, most notably in the case of the short syllable *dag-*, which, when thus prolonged, assumes the sound of a long syllable. Such distortions as these sacrifice meaning to rhythm, so that the effect is sing-song; and though isolated parallels can be adduced from other verse in their defence, their presence in nearly half the verses of *Beowulf* casts a serious doubt on the authenticity of the system. To speak less technically of the matter, the reader who attempts to follow Leonard finds that, whereas in verses of type A every syllable fits so easily into its proper place that Leonard's rhythm fairly shrieks at him from the page, in most of the verses of other types he is often uncertain which of several minor syllables to dignify with stress, and always embarrassed by the feeling that he is forcing the words into an alien pattern. If he is content to do this, it is only because he is trying to make the best of a bad job.

Leonard, aware of these difficulties, has tended to remove some of them by a device unknown to Kaluza, the introduction of rests in place of either stressed or unstressed syllables. This device at once removes the distortions of quantity in the case of grammatically short syllables. Thus, though Leonard has not authorized this particular reading, his latest views would permit us to shorten -*dagum* in the offending C-verse:

in gēardagum [14]

They would also permit us to achieve the strong-weak-strong-weak sequence, and a persuasively natural treatment of syllables, in types D and E:

[14] In "Four Footnotes," p. 5, he suggests *in gear* ⌊ *dagum,* that is, marking a minor rest after *gear-* and none after -*dagum*; but I suspect that this odd notation is a mere slip. If he meant to indicate the reading given below, he left out the accent (⌊) with which he specifies a "rest-beat."

frómum feóhgiftum

| ♩ ♩ | ⁻ | ♩ | ♩ ♩ |

sécg weórce gefeh

| ♩ | ⁻ | ♩ ♩ ♩ | ♩ |

fýrenðearfe ongéat

| ♩ ♩ | ♩ ♩ ♩ | ♩ | ⁻ |

He has not yet done this consistently, however, and his reading of types B and C still shows a disproportionate emphasis on the unimportant preliminary syllables and an irregular order of accent. If, however, he has yielded to the persuasions of Heusler, he has seen that even these verses can be accommodated by the free use of anacrusis:

Hē ðæs frófre gebád

♩ ♩ | ♩ | ♩ ♩ | ♩ | ⁻ |

in gēar- dagum

♩ | ♩ | ⁻ | ♩ ♩ | ⁻ |

Thus, the principle of rests opens the way to both a natural accentuation of syllables and the establishment throughout the poem of the strong-weak-strong-weak sequence that is so imperiously prescribed by the verses of type A. If he is unafraid of extrametric anacrusis, which he has hitherto avoided, Leonard can follow Heusler in the establishment of two quadruple measures for each verse instead of the four simple ones which he inherited from Kaluza. He can also, by an extension of the same principle, use rests at a different place and achieve the perfect metre of the theory which will shortly be set forth. We may proceed, therefore, to an examination of the first of these alternatives, the system of Heusler.

A word of acknowledgment must be made before we

pass on to the latter. Despite the weaknesses of Leonard's published readings, and the new obstacles that he must face if he is consistent in his agreement with Heusler, his influence has been of great service to American students of the problem. He has, for one thing, been a fearless opponent of Sievers. For another, he has uttered most persuasively his conviction that *Beowulf* had a rhythm recognizable as such to a modern ear. Again, he has pointed out the rhythmic kinship of *Beowulf* with such otherwise dissimilar poems as the *Nibelungenlied*, Meredith's *Love in the Valley*, and *Sing a Song of Sixpence*. The *Nibelungenlied*, like his translation of *Beowulf*, is written in simple, only casually compounded time, the other two in quadruple (in the language of the older prosody, the first two are predominantly monopodic, the last two dipodic) ; but the resemblances are apparent none the less. Finally, he reads *Beowulf* with real feeling, and though a better scansion would lead to still finer results, what he has accomplished is of great value. It was my privilege to hear him read the opening lines of the poem in 1931, and though I was then too ignorant to profit fully by what I heard, the dim beginnings of my own theory are to be traced to that occasion.

HEUSLER

By far the best system that has so far been devised is that which Heusler elaborated in the first volume of his *Deutsche Versgeschichte*.[15] Indeed, it may be said that, if some unforeseen objection should prevent acceptance of the new theory here presented, Heusler's provides the only sound alternative. Common to both theories is the assump-

[15] Andreas Heusler, *Deutsche Versgeschichte, mit Einschluss des altenglischen und altnordischen Stabreimverses* (Paul's *Grundriss der Germanischen Philologie,* 8), Berlin und Leipzig, 1925-9. The first volume, published in 1925, includes a valuable introduction (Teil I), and a treatment of the ancient Germanic verse (Teil II: *Der altgermanische Vers*).

tion that the normal half-line or verse contains two measures of quadruple time, so that the multitude of rhythmic
forms may be viewed as so many variations of the type,
.. | × × × × | × × × ×, where × represents the time nor-
mally occupied by a grammatically short, accented syllable,
and the dots denote possible anacrusis (according to Heusler, not limited in number of syllables). In Heusler's system, but not in mine, this × represents a quarter-note, so
that the time is 4/4; and the ample measures thus provided
enabled him to include within their bounds the hypermetric
as well as the normal verses.

In conformity with this theory of the time, and with
what he conceived to be the requirements of the alliteration,
Heusler postulated a number of rules for Germanic versification, of which the chief may be summarized as follows:
Every verse must contain two syllables capable of bearing
primary accent. These are placed at the head of each measure. At the middle of each measure there is normally
another syllable bearing secondary accent, but the place of
this syllable may be filled by a rest, or, what is rhythmically
the same thing, by the prolongation of a preceding syllable.
As many additional syllables may be included between these
strongest points as can be spoken in the time allotted to the
measure. Finally, any number of syllables may precede the
first primary accent. These syllables of anacrusis, if their
number does not exceed one or two, can be given specific
quantities and reckoned as part of the last measure of the
preceding verse; but ordinarily they must be regarded as
extrametric preludes to the strictly measured verse that they
introduce. Hence follows the corollary that each verse must
be regarded as an independent rhythmic unit, capable of
separation from its neighbors by an indefinite interval,
which may or may not be filled with sound.

Experiment shows that all verses can thus be reduced to
order. The syllables taking primary accent are determined

by the logic of the phrase or sentence and, in the case of polysyllables, by the rules of pronunciation governing the entire Germanic family of languages—in other words, on precisely the same grounds as those on which Sievers erected his five types. Sometimes these rules, which may be called those of prose accentuation, must be modified by the exigencies of the rhythm. What might receive no accent in prose may receive secondary accent in the verse; what might receive secondary accent in prose may be elevated to primary accent in the verse. In no case is it necessary to pass beyond the limits of accentual adjustment that verse-rhythm everywhere allows. Indeed, the varying rhythms of prose itself are capable of producing just such accentual modifications as are admitted into the verse. And the testimony of grammar and logic is reinforced by the alliteration, which always introduces syllables which on these other grounds are to be adjudged the strongest. Since the second half-line contains by rule only one alliterating letter, and this at the beginning of the first of the two strongest syllables, Heusler reasonably (though, as will be seen, not necessarily rightly) concluded that this " chief letter " marked the beginning of the first measure, and relegated all preceding syllables to the position of anacrusis. The rhythmic forms thus evolved from the second half-line give additional evidence for the interpretation of the first, in which alliteration is sometimes confined to the second measure. So far as the determination of primary accents is concerned, all this accords with Sievers; but Heusler, by a right understanding of rhythm, produced, instead of the amorphous types of Sievers, consistently metrical variations of a single basic pattern. He illustrated the contrast between his readings and those of Sievers by the following analysis of five verses from the Old Saxon *Heliand*: [16]

[16] *Deutsche Versgeschichte,* 1. 139. Here and elsewhere, I have replaced Heusler's special signs by the musical symbols for which they stand.

Sievers   Heusler

B   an bōmin treo

                sō liof sō lēð

D   fast forðwardes

E   stēnwerco mēst

C³   an lioht godes

A   skeppien mid ēnoro skālon

Consecutive reading of these verses in their contexts would require, of course, the filling out of the final measures with rests wherever they were short. The only passage from Old English poetry that Heusler presented in this consecutive fashion is Cædmon's Hymn: [17]

Nū sculon herigean heofonrīces weard,

meotodes meahte, and his mōdgeþanc,

weorc wuldorfæder, swā hē wundra gehwæs,

ēce drihten, ōr onstealde.

Hē ǣrest sceōp eorðan bearnum

---

[17] *Ibid.*, 1. 143 f. Heusler's text is that of MS. Tanner 10, Bodleian Library. (See E. V. K. Dobbie, *The MSS. of Cædmon's Hymn and Bede's Death Song*, Columbia University Press 1937, p. 24.) My own reading is given below, p. 214.

3

heofon tō hrōfe,   hālig scyppend;

þā middangeard   moncynnes weard,

ēce drihten,   æfter tēode,

fīrum foldan,   frēa ælmihtig.

Two observations should be made about the notation here given, which is an exact reproduction of Heusler's except for the substitution of musical symbols for the arbitrary equivalents that he employed. First, Heusler recognized that a long accented or an enclitic syllable may be held beyond the time that it would normally occupy, so that the rests noted above may be filled if a legato reading is desired. Just as he himself read *and his mōdgeþanc* with a three-quarter note for *mōd-* instead of a half-note and rest, and *þā middangeard* with a half-note for *-dan-* instead of a quarter-note and rest, so we might read *frēa ælmihtig* with a whole note for *frēa* instead of a half-note and rest, or *eorðan bearnum* with half-notes for the two enclitic syllables instead of quarter-notes and rests. These substitutions would neither change the rhythm nor violate any principles of speech. Secondly, we may notice that whenever verses begin with unstressed syllables, like the first two in *and his mōdgeþanc*, these syllables are treated as anacrusis and are included within the time allotted to the last measure of the preceding verse.

This treatment of anacrusis is by no means characteristic of Heusler's theory, however, for Cædmon's Hymn is one of the very few poems in which such a treatment of it is possible. Heusler's usual practice is to treat the anacrusis

as an unmeasured prelude to the verse proper. This peculiarity, which will be discussed at length in the ensuing
pages, is illustrated in Klaeber's convenient summary of
Heusler in his third edition of *Beowulf* (p. 282). The
summary will serve admirably to bring out this and other
details of the system that are scattered through Heusler's
long work, and to show their application to *Beowulf,* from
which Heusler himself supplied very few illustrations. It is
reproduced below, with the following modifications: (1) the
substitution of musical symbols for Heusler's arbitrary
signs, (2) the addition of extra accents (double acute and
double grave), which Heusler often employed to distinguish
the most emphatic syllables from those that were accented
mainly because of their position in the metrical scheme, (3)
the omission of the hypermetric lines, which will be dealt
with later, and (4) the inclusion of the corresponding notations of Sievers. Klaeber emphasizes the extrametric character of the anacrusis by using a double bar to separate it
from the rest of the verse.

gomban gyldan,

|♩ ♩ 𝄽 |♩ ♩ 𝄽 |

A   ⌣ × | ⌣ ×

11 þæt wæs gōd cyning

♩   ♩   ‖♩⁻|♩ ♩ ⁻|

C ×   ×   ⌣ |⌣×

swā fela fyrena

♩ ‖♩♩⁻|♩ ♩♩ 𝄽

C   ×   ⌣⌣× |⌣× ×

164 fēond mancynnes

|♩ ⁻ |♩ ♩ ♩|

D ⌣ |⌣ ⌣ ×

æþelinga bearn

| ♩♩♩ ♩ |♩ ⁻

E   ⌣× ⌣ × |⌣

3170 ealra twelfe

|♩ ♩𝄽 |♩ ♩ 𝄽 |

A ⌣× |⌣ ×

eahtodan eorlscipe

|♩ ♩♩ |♩ ♩♩|

A [18] ⌣ ⌣× |⌣ ⌣×

3173 ond his ellenweorc

♩   ♩ ‖♩♩𝄽| ♩ ⁻|

B ×   × ⌣|× ⌣

So far, we have only a rough outline of a system that is worked out consistently to the smallest detail and might appear to be unassailable. Nevertheless, closer study reveals two obstacles, one comparatively unimportant, the other grave. The less important one will be considered first.

1. *The Tempo*

If we take the implications of Heusler's 4/4 notation seriously, we shall find ourselves embarrassed by the slow pace at which the normal verses must be read. Experiments with watch and metronome alike have convinced me that these admittedly quadruple measures ought to be called 2/4 (or more exactly 4/8), not 4/4. In the normal lines of *Beowulf*, I read between 50 and 70 measures in a minute. This means that, if we call the time 4/8, there will be between 100 and 140 quarter-notes to the minute—about the same num-

---

[18] Sievers was in some doubt whether this verse should belong to type A or to the expanded D, where some of his followers have placed it (e. g. Klaeber). For his discussion of the problem, see especially *Altgermanische Metrik*, p. 209. With a proper reading, the distinction is not of the slightest importance.

ber that we find in musical compositions of medium tempo. A 4/4 notation for the same reading would give between 200 and 280 quarter-notes to the minute, a range of tempos well beyond the bounds of those ordinarily employed by musicians. Doubtless one cannot dogmatize about the pace at which the old poetry was read. Thus, although fifty measures to the minute is as slow a pace as I can set without feeling that the longer syllables are being held beyond endurance, a still closer approach to song than my own reading might make still slower tempos endurable. But surely not a tempo twice as slow!

Is it certain, however, that we ought to take Heusler's tempo seriously? At one point, he remarks that it makes little difference whether one calls the time 2/4 or 4/4, so long as one recognizes that the two quadruple measures of a Germanic verse have the same extent as four duple measures of the more modern rime-verse.[19] Whether this statement is strictly accurate or not depends on what rime-verse we select. In English rime-verse—I do not venture to speak of German—the measures, if genuinely duple, are properly recorded as 2/8, and the statement holds good. Most rime-verse, however, is really triple, 3/8, mixed freely with what William Thomson calls dupletic—that is, the 3/8 measure is frequently divided in half, each half having the value of one and one-half eighth-notes.[20] Owing to fluctuation in tempo, however (the eighth-note has no absolute duration, only a customary range of durations), Heusler's statement may be allowed to stand even here. Let us admit that the two-measured Germanic verse occupies approximately as much time as the four-measured rime-verse. It might seem, then, as if there were no argument. Heusler called the time 4/4, I call it 4/8, but both readings have virtually the same pace.

[19] *Deutsche Versgeschichte*, 1. 136: "Ob man den Langtakt als 2/4-oder als 4/4-Takt schreibt, tut nichts zur Sache. Das Entscheidende ist die Einsicht, dass zwei solche Takte gleiches Volumen haben wie der viertaktige Reimvers."
[20] See William Thomson, *The Rhythm of Speech*, p. 94 f.

Unfortunately, Heusler introduced a further complication which makes this easy solution impossible.

The difficulty arises because of Heusler's attempt to include so-called hypermetric verses in the same scheme as the normal ones. As soon as we adopt a 4/8 notation for the normal verses, we discover that this cannot be done. When a 4/8 notation is applied to the normal verses in *Beowulf*, a grammatically long syllable taking either primary or secondary accent is often reduced in quantity to the value of an eighth-note, a short or unaccented syllable to that of a sixteenth; but quantities shorter than these do not occur. The reason for this restriction is obvious. At a pace of 100 quarter-notes to the minute, a syllable, however short, could not be pronounced in the time of a thirty-second note, and a long accented syllable would require awkward slurring to be compressed into the time of a sixteenth. Even the Old Saxon poetry, in which the measures often contain such an abnormal number of syllables that the tempo must be slightly retarded (perhaps to a pace of 90 quarter-notes to the minute), requires only minor modifications of this rule, which appears to be applicable without reserve to all other normal Germanic verses. A 4/8 notation of the hypermetric verses, on the other hand, would exhibit serious violation of the rule. Those in *Beowulf*, to be sure, would not quite break it, though they would come close to doing so. But in other poems there would be no doubt about the infraction. Two of Heusler's examples,[21] reduced to 4/8 notation, are these:

Gn. Ex. 175: bétre him wǽre þæt hē brōðor ǽhte

Heliand 3497: grímmes than lángo, the he mōste is júgutheo neóten

---

[21] *Op. cit.,* 1. 185.

Even allowing for the fact that the *Heliand* elsewhere transgresses the limits of Old English quantities, such a reading as the last is past belief. The fact is that 4/4 time really belongs to these hypermetric verses; they are twice as long as the normal ones. Any attempt to employ the same time for both must result either in altogether too great a variation of tempo, or in undue retardation of the normal verses, or in clumsy slurring of the hypermetric ones, or, finally, in frank breach of rhythm.

It has been necessary to anticipate here some of what belongs to a separate discussion of the hypermetric verses. These will be fully treated in Part II, and other reasons for regarding them as 4/4 verses will be adduced. Here we need only recognize that, if we leave them out of account, 4/8 becomes the proper time for the normal verses; and that there is really some point in making the distinction. On paper, 4/4 time for all verses seems more consistent because, if we employ it, we are never faced with so awkward a sign as a thirty-second note, and can thus make it appear that a single measure will include all variations. Experiment, however, will show that the uniformity can exist only on paper: that the tempo fixed by normal verses is much too rapid for the hypermetric ones; and, conversely, that the tempo fixed by hypermetric verses is much too slow for the others.

Hereafter, then, all readings of normal verses will be recorded in 4/8 time, and this time may be understood to represent a range of tempos very close to the middle of those employed by musicians. That is, there will be, in general, between 100 and 140 quarter-notes to the minute.

2. *Anacrusis*

The distinction just made between 4/8 and 4/4 time, important as it is for a proper reading of the poetry, involves no radical change in Heusler's system, for the accentuation and the relative quantities of syllables within a given verse remain the same. We must now proceed, however, to a more fundamental objection, one which has to do with the adjustment of syllables to the measures, however long or short these may be.

In the outline of Heusler's system given above,[22] it was stated that " any number of syllables may precede the first primary accent. These syllables of anacrusis, if their number does not exceed one or two, can be given specific quantities and reckoned as part of the last measure of the preceding verse; but ordinarily they must be regarded as extrametric preludes to the strictly measured verse that they introduce. Hence follows the corollary that each verse must be regarded as an independent rhythmic unit, capable of separation from its neighbors by an indefinite interval, which may or may not be filled with sound." Again, we have seen that Klaeber's specimens of Heusler's scansion,[23] in accordance with this doctrine, show extrametric anacrusis separating the two halves of single long lines.

As it happens, these specimen lines exhibit no more than dissyllabic anacrusis, and Heusler himself might have permitted us to read them without breach of rhythm. Let us rewrite here those in which the second half-line begins with anacrusis, in 4/8 time now, and with the anacrusis included in the time of the preceding measure. We shall follow Heusler in using a colon to separate the two halves. This is a mark of phrasing, and indicates that we may pause indefinitely, afterwards resuming the rhythm at the point where it was interrupted.

2247   heald þū nū, hrūse,   nū hæleð ne mōstan

1963   gewāt him ðā se hearda   mid his hondscole

26 him ðā Scyld gewāt   tō gescæphwīle

11 gomban gyldan,   þæt wæs gōd cyning

3173 eahtodan eorlscipe   ond his ellenweorc

No real difficulty arises here, though in the last two
lines we must take full advantage of the pause provided by
the phrasing in order to prevent an awkward jumble of syllables. Heusler would certainly not have objected to these
readings, taken by themselves, for we have seen above that
he scanned the whole of Cædmon's Hymn, where anacrusis
does not exceed two syllables, in precisely this fashion.[24]
What forced Heusler to his singular doctrine of extrametric
anacrusis is not only that even two syllables are sometimes
excessive, but that by his scansion we often have to reckon
with three or more. In *Beowulf*, the limit is five; in other
poems, still higher.

Let us now examine a few groups of consecutive lines in
Beowulf in which Heusler's scansion would produce this
extrametric anacrusis beyond any doubt. We may follow
Heusler in designating extrametric syllables by the sign °,
and Klaeber in using a double bar to mark the first measure
of each verse.[25]

Lines 64-7a.

þā wæs Hrōðgāre   herespēd gyfen,

wīges weorðmynd,   þæt him his winemāgas

[24] P. 23 f.
[25] Because of Heusler's general practice of citing verses one by one, and his
summary treatment of *Beowulf*, I am obliged to invent these scansions for him;
but similar scansions of OHG. and OS. will be found in *Deutsche Versgeschichte*
1. 143 and 166.

georne hȳrdon,   oðð þæt sēo geogoð gewēox,

magodriht micel . . .

Lines 178b-183a.

          Swylc wæs þēaw hyra,

hǣþenra hyht;   helle gemundon

in mōdsefan,   Metod hīe ne cūþon,

dǣda Dēmend,   ne wiston hīe Drihten God,

nē hīe hūru heofona Helm   herian ne cūþon,

wuldres Waldend.

Lines 720-724a.

Cōm þā tō recede   rinc sīðian

drēamum bedǣled.   Duru sōna onarn

fȳrbendum fæst,   syþðan hē hire folmum (æthr)ān;

onbrǣd þā bealohȳdig,   ðā (hē ge)bolgen wæs,

recedes mūþan.

Heusler argued eloquently in favor of the curious readings that the notation just given prescribes, and it would
be unfair to proceed without stating his case. First, then,
he imagined that there ought to be a distinction between
strophic, singable verse, and stichic, unsingable verse. According to him, strophic and singable verse includes its anacrusis within the temporal scheme, allotting it to the close
of the preceding measure; whereas the unsingable and
unstrophic sort can treat the individual verse more independently, so that its anacrusis is not subtracted from its
predecessor and not reckoned in the total time. In such a
case, he concluded, the anacrusis can have so many syllables
as to become a veritable prelude to its verse.[26]

Now this argument is not wholly unreasonable. Nevertheless, setting aside the question whether the distinction
between singable and unsingable verse is rightly taken, and
also whether *Beowulf* should be assigned to the latter class,
we may still ask whether there is any parallel to this unlim-
ited anacrusis in other than Germanic poetry. The answer
is no. It is true that minor freedoms are by no means uncommon, for it seems to be a fact that a pause, such as that
which often occurs at the end of a verse, tends to weaken
our sense of time and permit the overcrowding of measures. William Thomson formulated a " law " to cover this
peculiarity, which he found to be common in both English
and Greek verse. " A silent pause," he said, " indefinite in
duration, occurring within a line of verse or at its end,
affords, as a breach of rhythm, an opportunity, without
offending the rhythmical sense, of packing the respective
measure with syllabic material to the extent of a complete

---

[26] " Sangbare und strophische Dichtung rechnet den Auftakt in das Zeitmass
der Taktkette ein; er füllt den Schluss des voraufgehenden Taktes. . . . Un-
sangliche und unstrophische Dichtung kann den einzelnen Vers selbständiger
behandeln, so dass sein Auftakt dem Vorgänger nicht ' abgezogen,' nicht in die
Gesamtzeit eingerechnet wird. Und dann können die Auftakte silbenreich
werden wie eigne Vorspiele ihres Verses." (*Deutsche Versgeschichte* 1. 36.)

measure before the pause, and a measure after it minus its accented syllable, however short." [27] This looks at first sight like a justification for Heusler, but the examples cited by Thomson [28] are widely scattered in the first place, and in the second have simple rather than compound measures, so that the extra syllables are only one, or at most two. There is nothing anywhere else that approaches the abandonment of time that Heusler introduced into Germanic verse.

Heusler's second argument was designed to offset this weakness. After stating that the syllables of anacrusis, like those within the measures, increase in number as we turn from the Old Norse Edda (where the maximum is four) to Old English (where *Beowulf* admits five and other poems seven) and Old High German (where the *Hildebrandslied* admits six), and finally to Old Saxon (where, if we include hypermetric verses, we find that the *Genesis* admits eleven, the *Heliand* on one occasion fourteen, and five syllables are very common), Heusler asked us to regard these phenomena in the light of historical development. Supposing that the common Germanic point of departure had been fairly conservative, he maintained that extra syllables had gradually been appended to established forms until the number had reached the astonishing proportions of the Old Saxon poetry. He argued, moreover, that this increase had been accelerated by the tendency to break the originally unified long line into halves of a more independent rhythmical character, a tendency which had begun, he thought, in secular poetry, but reached its full development only in the run-on style of the religious writers. Yet he ended this argument with so earnest a plea against any attempt to measure the offending anacrusis, or to make it partially metrical by hurrying over it, that he once more reminds us of the strangeness of his doctrine.[29]

---

[27] *The Rhythm of Speech*, p. 217.
[28] *Ibid.*, p. 258 f.
[29] " Das befremdliche an den (ae. und) as. Auftaktriesen muss man in

On the face of it, indeed, this doctrine is so dubious that it can be accepted only if we are certain that there is no alternative. First, the rhythm that is established by the parts of the verse that Heusler measures, with its heavy primary and lighter but still noticeable secondary accents, is so striking and so imperious that these conspicuous interruptions seem even more disturbing than they would in other verse. Secondly, though extrametric pauses may always be inserted without impairing rhythm, and though the phrasing does generally coincide with the limits of the half-line, there are so many run-on lines in Germanic poetry that, if it were not for this theory of anacrusis, one might assume that the rhythmic flow was continuous for line after line. If we carry Heusler's theory to its limit, and break the rhythm after every verse, we shall achieve a hopelessly jerky movement that is entirely out of keeping with the progress of the sense. If, on the other hand, we accept his proffered compromise, including anacrusis within bounds where we can, and pausing between lines only where the sense forces us to do so, we shall be all the more disturbed when we reach those spasmodic, extrametric additions from which his system cannot escape.

A different objection, and a weighty one, was raised many years ago by Sievers, when he was attempting to dismiss

geschichtlichem Lichte sehen. Der gemeingerm. Ausgangspunkt lag wohl noch etwas unter dem Beow., etwa auf der Staffel des Finnsb.; und dann führt es schrittweise, von Stufe zu Stufe, in sonst übereinstimmenden Füllungstypen zu jenen erstaundlichen Steigerungen. . . .

" Möglich war diese Steigerung, weil man die Geschlossenheit der Langzeile auch syntaktisch preisgab: der Bogenstil der Geistlichen, vorbereitet schon im weltlichen Liede, lockerte den Zusammenhang zwischen An- und Abvers und machte den Kurzvers sprachrhythmisch selbständiger. Die langen Auftakte, schon die vom Masse des Hild., wirkten in gleicher Richtung. Sie bedingen an den Versgrenzen breite Zwischenräume, die nicht mehr in die Taktkette einzurechnen sind. Diese Auftakte sind nicht mehr ' gemessen '; an bestimmbare Zeitwert ihrer Silben ist nicht mehr zu denken. . . . Es sind *Vorspiele* zu ihrem Verse, wahrscheinlich auch in der Stimmgebung abgehoben von dem Verskern, der mit dem stabenden Iktus markig einsetzt. . . . Ein Überhasten der Silbenkette, damit der Abstand vom letzten zum ersten Iktus halbwegs metrisch bleibe, steht gewiss ausser Frage." (*Deutsche Versgeschichte* 1. 165 f.)

Heusler's then incomplete theory along with those of others who believed in measuring Germanic verse.[30] The substance of this objection was that verses of the types that Sievers called B and C—that is, those in which, by Heusler's scansion, the two measures are most lightly filled—were the only ones that carried anacrusis to such extraordinary lengths. Verses of types A, D, and E, where by Heusler's scansion one or both of the measures are more heavily burdened, rarely take anacrusis at all, and if they do, they limit it to one or two syllables. Sievers did not evade the difficulty by his own scansion, for his notation of types B and C, × . . . . ´ | × . . ´ and × . . . . ´ | ´ ×, as has been stated, is purely a paper scansion, without any rhythmic meaning whatever; but his objection must be considered. In *Beowulf*, by my own count, the figures for anacrusis, if we follow Heusler's scansion but classify the types according to Sievers, are as follows: [31]

Type	No. of Verses	Syllables of Anacrusis				
		1	2	3	4	5
A	2851	78	5	—	—	—
D	853	32	5	—	—	—
E	446	—	—	—	—	—
B	1047	104	633	258	43	9
C	1118	263	623	186	43	3

This table shows clearly that, in types A, D, and E, where Sievers' division into feet corresponds to Heusler's division into measures, anacrusis is either avoided altogether or limited to a number of syllables (ordinarily one, rarely two) that can be included in the time of a preceding measure; whereas types B and C, when divided as Heusler divided

[30] *Altgermanische Metrik*, p. 14 f.
[31] The evidence for this table will be found in the Appendix. Excluded, of course, are the 9 verses in Group F, the 22 hypermetric verses, and 18 purely conjectural or illegible verses, the addition of which brings the total to Klaeber's 6364.

them, not only have anacrusis in every instance, but emphasize the more difficult number, two, and introduce very often
the necessarily extrametric combinations, three, four, and
five. Why, we may well ask, should types B and C be the
only offenders against the rule established by most verse,
and supported by types A, D, and E, that anacrusis should
be included in the time of a preceding measure?

In reply, Heusler could only say that, when the measures are lightly filled (i. e. in types B and C as he divided
them), anacrusis is required; when, on the other hand, they
are heavily filled (i. e. in the other types as both Heusler
and Sievers divided them), it is avoided.[32] Although the
principle of compensation here invoked is reasonable in
itself and is supported by the apportionment of syllables to
the measures in other types of verses, it can account only
for the presence or absence of metrical anacrusis. As a
justification of the extrametric sort, it is worthless.

The real reason for Heusler's doctrine of anacrusis is
that he regarded it as inevitable; and if his interpretation
of the alliteration is correct, then that is indeed the case.
If the alliteration must always introduce the first measure
of the second half-line, we must accept extrametric anacrusis whether we like it or not. Examination, however, will
show that this so-called rule is an unnecessary though
plausible assumption; that there is good reason to believe
that the alliteration often introduced the *second* measure;
and that all these troublesome, anti-metrical readings can be
dismissed at once and forever. The grounds for this assertion form a part of the argument on behalf of the new
theory, to which the way is now open.

---

[32] *Deutsche Versgeschichte,* 1. 173 and 189 f.

THE NEW THEORY

VERSES OF THE TYPES CALLED B AND C

In the foregoing discussion, we have found the crux of the problem of Germanic versification in the types that Sievers called B and C. The other types, A, D, and E, point unmistakably to the unifying principle, two quadruple measures to each half-line. Moreover, when they contain any anacrusis—and that is seldom—it is usually monosyllabic, never more than dissyllabic, and can always be read in the time allotted to the last measure of a preceding verse. These types, therefore, not only suggest a uniform rhythmic structure within half-lines, but allow this to be maintained from line to line, broken only by such pauses as are needed to mark the phrasing. If all verses were of these types, the rhythm of the Germanic poets would long ago have yielded up its secret; for, although Heusler's analysis of them depends upon recent advances in rhythmic theory, the movement which he prescribes is simply that which any good reader would achieve by letting the words before him take command of his voice. But when this hypothetical reader is faced with types B and C, he is at a loss. Sometimes, if the verses in question begin with only one or two unimportant syllables, he will succeed. Again, if they begin with four or five such syllables, and he has stayed away from the theorists, he will succeed. But in the middle range—and this is the common one—where he has two or three syllables to deal with, he is almost certain to stumble.

A few years ago, having suddenly realized that, if verse keeps time, one ought to be able to beat time to it, and that if one can beat time, one can record the rhythm in musical notation, I undertook to test my habitual reading of *Beo-*

wulf, in those days an unreasoned compromise between the principles of Sievers and what feeling for rhythm I possessed. I discovered that whenever I kept time I was producing two quadruple measures in each verse, and that I always did keep time in reading verses of types A, D, and E. I did not then know Heusler's work, but I was reading these verses just as he read them, only perhaps a little faster. When I reached types B and C, however, I found myself in evil ways. Sometimes I maintained the time, but my records showed that this was achieved at the expense of consistency and occasionally of meaning. Sometimes, especially in less familiar passages, I was changing the time in a spasmodic fashion, thus producing rhythms alien to the context. Then suddenly, as I tried this shift and that, a reading that I had hit upon by accident and regarded as a freak revealed itself as the clue to the whole problem. Without knowing what I was doing, I had substituted a rest for the first beat of a B-verse. I had read,

egsode eorlas,   syððan ærest wearð

(musical notation)

feasceaft funden.

(musical notation)

How natural it had sounded!—perhaps too natural for such an ancient poem. There was a natural pause after *eorlas,* hence a good opportunity to measure this pause and make a rest out of it. It was also natural to give a slight accent to the first syllable of *syððan,* and to give *ærest* greater prominence than *wearð.* Finally, it was natural to proceed at once, without pause, to the predicate introduced by *wearð.* The alliteration, moreover, was signalized by primary accent, though this belonged to the second measure instead of the first. Proceeding from this point, I discovered that the appearance of ease was no accident. The same rule, applied

4

to similar verses, gave equally satisfactory results, so that it remained only to extend the principle to *Beowulf* as a whole, and thence to other poems. The use of what I shall call an initial rest had made possible the otherwise impossible task of including all the syllables of Germanic verse, together with the stresses that reveal their meaning, within the limits of a strict metre.

The initial rest provides the clue to the reading of types B and C, and is the most significant feature of the new theory, but because of the great variation in number of syllables within these types, it cannot be used with all B- and C-verses. In order to reach a full understanding of these verses and of the new readings to which the initial rest opens the door, we must study the variations in some detail.

First of all, however, let us reach an agreement about the terms B and C. Though Sievers' full notation of these types has been shown to be inconsistent with rhythmical theory, the names B and C are still useful as descriptions of syllabic sequences. In general, we shall call B any verse having the pattern × . . . . ´ × . ´, C any verse having the pattern × . . . . ´ ´̆ ×, where × is a syllable that does not demand stress, ´ and ̆ are grammatically long and short syllables that demand stress, and the dots represent the possibility of extra syllables of the type marked ×. If we add that ̆ × may replace any ´ in the pattern, we have a provisional description of all B and C verses in *Beowulf*, for the dots are carefully counted. We must remember, however, that these signs do not prescribe any rhythm. Rather, they indicate roughly the rhythmic potentialities of the syllables. We may find that one or two of the syllables marked × will require some stress when we have discovered the rhythm, and we may find that those marked ´̆ are not to be uttered with equal force. We have as yet no measures, and therefore neither definitely graduated accents nor any fixed quantities. So long as we concede all this, we can continue to speak of types B and C.

Examination of these types as they occur in *Beowulf* will lead us to additional information. We shall find that the first of the two syllables marked with accents is always at least as strong as the second and usually stronger, and that it regularly bears alliteration. In the second half-line, it is the only syllable that alliterates; in the first half-line, the other accented syllable may alliterate likewise, but more often than not the first alliterates alone. Cases in the first half-line where the second syllable alliterates and the first does not are so rare that they must inevitably be regarded as exceptions to the rule, if not as violations of the law. It is an easy conclusion, therefore, that the first of these prominent syllables ought to receive primary accent in our rhythm, and we can safely place a bar in front of it to indicate this. Our schemes will now be × .... | ́ × . ́ and × .... | ́ ́ ×. As yet, however, we cannot tell whether another bar should precede the second accented syllable or not. We want two measures, but all that our evidence can predict with certainty is the point where one of the two begins. In order to know more, we must examine the individual cases. We shall find that the position of the other bar depends on the number and nature of the syllables that precede the bar we have just drawn. Accordingly, the first main section of the ensuing discussion emphasizes these preliminary syllables and is subdivided in accordance with their number. Not until the second section will the treatment of the important syllables be fully defended.

I. The Readings Dictated by Preliminary Syllables

1. *Verses with Five Preliminary Syllables:*
Accent and Alliteration

Let us start with the few verses of *Beowulf* in which five syllables precede the bar that was tentatively drawn in the last paragraph. In the second half-line we find,

Type B

Hwæþere him on	ferhþe grēow 1718
þæs ðe hire se	willa gelamp 626
Ðē hē ūsic on	herge gecēas 2638
syþðan hē hire	folmum (æthr)ān 722
Hwæþere hē his	folme forlēt 970
þone ðe hēo on	ræste ābrēat 1298
þāra þe hit mid	mundum bewand 1461
tō ðæs þe hē on	ræste geseah 1585

Type C

þonne hē on þæt	sinc starað 1485
þāra þe hē him	mid hæfde 1625

In the first half-line we find,

Type B

Mæg þonne on þǣm | golde ongitan 1484

Type C

þæt ic wið þone | gūðflogan 2528

With these verses before us, we shall not be long in decid-
ing where the second bar should be placed. If we place it
before the last accented syllable, as Heusler would have
done, we shall have extrametric anacrusis to deal with. If,
on the other hand, we place it at the beginning of the verse,
we shall have no anacrusis, and a smooth rhythm. Why not
choose the smooth rhythm?

Heusler might have objected to this decision on two
grounds: first, because the last stressed syllable, to which
we now wish to assign secondary accent, is clearly more important than any of the five in the first measure, to one of
which we wish to assign primary accent; and secondly, because he believes that alliteration must introduce the first
measure of the second half-line, and (if double, as in 1484)
both measures in the first half-line. Both these objections

are plausible, but I think it can be shown that they are both unsound.

To answer the first, we may begin by recognizing the simple fact that five syllables in succession, no matter how unimportant, must not only fill most of the time allotted to a quadruple measure, but can hardly be spoken without differentiation of accent. In the verse,

Hwæþere him on ferhþe grēow,

the first syllable of *Hwæþere* must obviously be stressed in comparison with the other two, and *him* must take precedence of *on*. Consequently, we are virtually compelled to form a measure with these syllables, whether we wish to or not. If we insist on alloting two measures to *ferhþe* and *grēow*, we shall come out, not with two measures plus anacrusis, but with three full measures, whereas the established metre prescribes two! On the other hand, if we yield to common sense and confine *ferhþe grēow* to a single measure, the second, we can still regard these two words as the most important in the series, and express this importance by accenting the second measure more heavily than the first. Heusler himself recognized that some measures were more heavily accented than others by employing two sets of signs for primary and secondary accents, the single acute and grave for the light ones, the double acute and grave for the heavy. Although this is a very crude approximation of the wide range of accentuation in verse, it is so useful in the analysis of Old English verse that I have adopted it both here and elsewhere.[32] The following notation, accordingly,

---

[32] My use of the double acute differs slightly from Heusler's. As shown by the notations above, p. 23 ff., Heusler employed it only for the alliterating syllables. It does not appear, however, that there need have been a distinction between the accentuation of *metodès meahtè,* where both words alliterate, and *ēcè drihtèn,* where only the first alliterates. On the other hand, it is important to note the accentual inferiority of the non-alliterating first word in *Nū scùlon herigèan.* Indeed, the only practical advantage of the double system of primary

shows both the temporal equality of the two measures and the accentual superiority of the second:

Hwǽþere hìm on férhþe grēow [33]

| ♪♪♪ ♪ ♪ |♪ ♪ ♪|

The very same gradation of accents may be found in a modern poem, the first half-line of *Love in the Valley*: [34]

Únder yònder beéch-trèe.

| ♪ ♪ ♪ ♪ | ♪ ♪ |

Nobody will object to this reading, which is the only natural one, or suggest that we regard the relatively unimportant words *Under* and *yonder* as anacrusis, while we devote two whole measures to *beech-tree*. This is certainly the most important word in the line, but the fact is not obscured by the reading given. Any further emphasis of these two syllables would be ludicrous. We can surely regard the first hypothetical objection to our proposed readings as unsound, and proceed to a consideration of the second.

According to Heusler, alliteration must introduce the first measure in the second half-line, and each of the two potentially alliterating syllables in the first half-line must begin a separate measure. Since our reading of the given

accents is to call attention to the weakness of a first measure that lacks alliteration. Hence I use the single acute for a non-alliterating first measure, but the double acute for the second measure whether it alliterates or not. This is inaccurate, but it serves all practical purposes. It would require many more gradations and inhuman accuracy to record the true differences in the strength of accents.—I follow Heusler in using the double grave for all secondary accents on syllables that demand stress independently of their position in the metrical scheme—the second members of compounds, medial syllables after long stressed syllables, and such independent words as nouns, adjectives, adverbs, and finite verbs.

[33] The question whether, in this series, / is greater or less than \ is unimportant, because these accents are too far apart for comparison; but it could well be less. Sometimes ◞ and \ are virtually equal.

[34] I owe the valuable analogy of this poem to Leonard, as I have stated above, p. 20.

lines would violate both these rules, we must see whether
there is any reason to regard them as correct. On what evidence, then, are they based? Simply on the fact that, everywhere in Germanic alliterative verse, the alliteration introduces the first of the two strongest syllables in the second
half-line, and one or both of the two strongest in the first
half. There is no possibility of denying this fact—indeed,
that is the reason why Sievers' late attempt to dissociate
accent from alliteration cannot be accepted; but we have
just seen that, because of the variation of accents from
measure to measure, we do not have to admit Heusler's
deduction. If the first measure of the second half-line is
weakly accented, the alliterating syllable can begin the second measure without ceasing to be the first of the two
strongest syllables in the line. Again, if the first measure
of the first half-line is weakly accented, two alliterating
syllables can be confined to the second measure without
ceasing to be the two strongest syllables in the line. We cannot suppose that the old poets were so far ahead of their
times as to base their theory of verse upon measures, any
more than we can suppose that they were so deaf to rhythm
as not to produce and hear them. They simply made it a
practice to alliterate one or both of the strongest syllables in
the first half-line, and the first of these syllables in the second half-line. If the two strongest were preceded by enough
insignificant syllables to fill a measure, their sense of rhythm
would have forced them to confine these two strongest to
the second measure, but they would probably have been
unaware that they were doing anything unusual, and would
very rightly have thought that they were adhering to their
rules. More recent verse will show, quite as effectively as
this, that when rules are formulated without regard to
rhythm, they are often reconcilable with more than one
rhythmic result.

The natural readings of the verses already cited will
therefore be as follows:

Second Half-Line

Type B

1718 Hwæþere him on ferhþe grēow

626 þæs ðe hire se willa gelamp

2638 Đē hē ūsic on herge gecēas

722 Syþðan hē hire folmum (æthr)ān

970 Hwæþere hē his folme forlēt

1298 þone ðe hēo on ræste abrēat

1461 þāra þe hit mid mundum bewand

1585 tō ðæs þe hē on ræste geseah

Type C

1485 þonne hē on þæt sinc starað

1625 þāra þe hē him mid hæfde

First Half-line

Type B

1484 Mæg þonne on þǣm gólde ongìtan

or better, perhaps,

Mæg þonne on þǣm gólde ongìtan

Type C

2528 þæt íc wið þone gúðflogan

or, less probably,

þæt ic wið þone gúðflogan

So easy, almost inevitable are these readings of verses beginning with five unimportant syllables that many people must have recited them in this fashion, though the metrists have been reluctant to scan them accordingly. Lines with five introductory syllables, however, are rare in *Beowulf*. More frequent are those with four, still more frequent those with three, and much the most frequent those with two. It will be of advantage to study the latter first, returning afterwards to those with three and four, and passing on finally to those with one.

2. *Verses with Two Preliminary Syllables:*

The Initial Rest

Of the 2,165 verses of types B and C in *Beowulf* (roughly one-third of the poem), 1,256 are introduced by two unimportant syllables, 367 by one, 444 by three, 86 by four, and 12 by five. Thus, our treatment of those with two will be of peculiar importance, for they will give a distinct character to the poem. Are we to follow the example set by those of five syllables, and divide these verses | × × | ⌣ × . ⌣ and | × × | ⌣ ⌣ × , or will the weakness of these two preliminary syllables force us to reverse our decision, and follow Heusler in dividing them × × | ⌣ × . | ⌣ and × × | ⌣ | ⌣ × ? The answer has already been given. Against Heusler's division stands not only the analogy of verses with three, four, and five introductory syllables, but the difficulty often experienced in fitting even two such syllables into the last measure of a preceding verse; so that with Heusler's reading even these verses would tend to produce extrametric anacrusis, or at best an awkward haste. On the other hand, to allot an entire measure to these unemphatic syllables would distort their meaning. If we should read, for example,

hū ðā æðelingas   3a

|♩ ♩ | ♪♪ ♪|

syððan ǣrest wearð   6b

|♩ ♩ |♪♪   ♩ |

hē þæs frōfre gebād   7b

|♩ ♩ |♩♪♪ ♩|

the deliberate enunciation of the first two syllables, by contrast with the rapid utterance of the important words which they introduce, would give them an almost ludicrous prominence. We might tolerate such an effect on rare occasions, but if it were repeated as often as it would have to be in *Beowulf*, rhythm would seem to have taken undue command of language, and the whole poem would degenerate into sing-song. Looking at these verses without regard to their place in the rhythmic scheme, we see that the two pre-

liminary syllables should be subordinate to those that follow; that they are truly of the nature of anacrusis. We
seem, then, to be faced with a dilemma. But fortunately
there is a way out; for anacrusis derives its effect, so far as
meaning is concerned, from being placed in the up-beat or
arsis (the relatively unaccented portion) of a measure, and
all measures have an up-beat. We can reconcile rhythm and
meaning, therefore, by assigning each of these pairs to the
up-beat, not of the last measure of a preceding verse, but of
the first measure of its own verse, while we fill the down-
beat or thesis of this measure with a rest. We must read,[35]

$$\text{hū ðā æðelingas}$$
$$| \; \mathsf{C} \;\; \mathsf{C} \; | \mathsf{C} \;\; \mathsf{C}\mathsf{C}\,\mathsf{C} \; |$$

$$\text{syððan ǣrest wearð}$$
$$| \; \mathsf{C} \;\; \mathsf{C} \; | \mathsf{C} \; \mathsf{C} \;\;\; \mathsf{r} \; |$$

$$\text{hē þæs frōfre gebād}$$
$$| \; \mathsf{C} \;\; \mathsf{C} \; | \; \mathsf{C} \;\; \mathsf{C}\,\mathsf{r} \;\; \mathsf{r} |$$

By this means, we have not only produced a reading that
conforms to our treatment of the verses with five preliminary syllables (and incidentally shows us what to do in the
case of those with three or four), but we have preserved the
character of anacrusis that belongs by nature to the two
syllables without letting this anacrusis impede the rhythm.
It remains only to see whether there is any justification for
introducing a rest in place of the down-beat.

Rests in general are no novelty. Their existence in Germanic verse has been assumed by both Leonard and Heusler, and they are common enough in more recent poetry to

[35] In order to produce the required effect when, as here, the verses are
removed from their context, some external means of marking the beginning of
the first measure must be employed. The easiest method is to beat time, once
down and once up for each measure, or to tap the primary and secondary accents.

be accepted without hesitation.[36] It must be admitted, however, that the substitution of a rest for the down-beat of a
measure, frequent as it is in music, is very rare in the verse
with which we are familiar. The only place in which such a
substitution occurs regularly is at the end of a verse containing three spoken measures, when neighboring verses
contain four. In such cases (ballad-verse is full of them)
an entire measure is supplied by a rest. Cases where down-
beats are omitted at the beginnings of lines are so rare, however, that I have not been able to find any certain examples.[37]
The best I can do is to show what *might* be done by a
capricious reader of *Love in the Valley*:

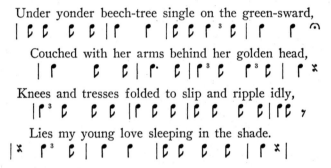

> Under yonder beech-tree single on the green-sward,
>
> Couched with her arms behind her golden head,
>
> Knees and tresses folded to slip and ripple idly,
>
> Lies my young love sleeping in the shade.

It is easy to read the fourth line so, because it is easy to
pause after *idly*, and to convert this pause into a rest by
reading the words *Lies my* rapidly, on the up-beat, subordi-
nating them to the more important words, *young love*.
Nevertheless, such a reading must be considered an accident, especially since no other line in the entire poem can be

---

[36] Ten Brink actually suggested the use of initial rests before a small number of C-verses like *gewaden hæfde* as a consequence of his rigidly mechanical
interpretation of the " four-accent " theory mentioned above, p. 16. (See Paul's
Grundriss der Germ. Phil., II[1] [1893], 519 f.) The present theory is entirely
unrelated and forbids rests before these verses.

[37] Only verses that customarily open with primary accent (e. g. trochaics
and dactylics) can be considered. The suppression of an opening syllable in
an iambic line does not count, because it would not receive primary accent if
present.

adduced as a parallel. Meredith's intention was pretty
certainly not this; he would probably have read,

Lies my young love.

| r᛫   c | r   r |

A diligent search might reveal a few more persuasive instances of initial rests in modern verse, but certainly not
enough to warrant our accepting them in *Beowulf* without
further question. Indeed, a good reason for their avoidance
by modern poets will appear when we come to discuss the
relation of Old English poetry to music.[38] We must abandon
the hope of a familiar analogy, therefore, and depend on the
old poetry itself for the decisive evidence. Are we to believe
in the initial rests merely for the negative reason already
advanced, that they offer a means of escape from excessive
anacrusis on the one hand and violent distortions of accent
and quantity on the other? This alone would be much, but
it is not all; for I think it can be shown that the rests con-
tribute in a positive fashion to both the meaning and the
beauty of the poem.

Thus, it is notable that wherever the metre demands an
initial rest the sense readily admits or even demands a pause
to clarify its phrasing. For example, in the first 500 long
lines of *Beowulf* (1000 half-lines or verses) I introduce some
311 verses with rests.[39] Of these 311 verses, 67 originate
sentences, 52 co-ordinate clauses without conjunctions, 28
co-ordinate clauses with conjunctions (I have here included
a few cases where co-ordinating conjunctions bind compound subjects or predicates rather than clauses), 103 subordinate clauses, 52 prepositional phrases, 8 appositional
phrases, and 1 a genitive phrase (*ðīnra gegncwida* 367a).
In all cases but the last, then, the tendency to mark the

---

[38] See the section called "The Harp," especially p. 90.

[39] This figure includes a few verses of type A3 (which will be discussed
later), and may be incorrect by a small number, because there is a handful
of verses of which the proper reading is doubtful.

phrasing by a pause is very strong, and even in the last the two words stand together in contrast to their neighbors. To convert the pause into a rest by leaving the first part of the opening measure vacant serves the double purpose, therefore, of bringing out the meaning and allowing the rhythm to continue unchecked. Moreover, this expedient seems more desirable in *Beowulf* than in a good many poems, because of the particular sort of rhythm which it employs.

The verses of *Beowulf* about which there is general agreement—those of types A, D, and E—have what we might loosely describe as a marching rhythm. The primary and secondary accents alternate like left foot and right, and are in general rather strong because of the high concentration of meaning that accompanies the elaborate inflections and the frequent composition of words. At the same time the rhythmic phrases, the half-lines (which coincide usually with the grammatical phrases), are both short and easily apprehended. If they are set off from one another too often by extrametric pauses, the effect will be jerky, because there exists in this strenuous rhythm itself the impulse to continue its motion for a longer period than a half-line. Yet some sort of pause is necessary both for definition of the phrase and for catching one's breath. In such a situation the use of a measured pause or rest becomes vitally important. When every third verse, on an average, begins with a rest, both metre and verbal phrasing become unmistakably plain, while the rhythm sweeps on imperiously for line after line. The initial rest, therefore, while it rescues the metre from the alternative evils of extrametric anacrusis and over-emphasis of unimportant syllables, is far from being an evil—even a lesser evil—in itself. Through its positive virtues, the enhancement of meaning and of rhythm, it proclaims its authenticity.

Nevertheless, one objection may persist. It may be said that this line of argument, though it might do well enough for rests in general, cannot justify such extraordinary rests as these, which, coming at the beginnings of verses where we expect primary accent, are hard to produce and still harder for a listener to recognize. A little practice with these unfamiliar rests will convince anyone that the objection is overstated. So long as a steady movement is maintained elsewhere, they can be produced and recognized with comparative ease. Still, there is enough weight in the objection, and in others not yet suggested, to make us grant the helpfulness of some external means of keeping time. As soon as we postulate a musical accompaniment, that of the harp, the peculiar position of the rests is explained, and their difficulty altogether disappears. It will be advisable, however, to reserve discussion of the harp until all the evidence is before us. Let us return, therefore, to the verses of types B and C, taking up first a less common variety of verses with two preliminary syllables, and proceeding thence to those with three, four, and one.

In most of the verses with two preliminary syllables, the first syllable requires greater accent than the second. Consequently, this first syllable takes the secondary accent of the opening measure, and the initial rest fills half a measure, as in

hū ðā æðelingas

| ᵡ ℓ ℓ | ℓ ℓ ℓ ℓ |

and the other verses already cited. In some thirty cases, however, the order of accentuation either must or may be reversed, and this reversal will alter the quantities. Among the clearest examples are these:

264a   gebād wintra worn

| ⌐ ℓ ℓ | ℓ ³ ℓ   ℓ |

452a   Onsend Higelāce

| ⌐ ℓ ℓ | ℓ ℓ ℓ ℓ |

926b   geseah stēapne hrōf

1201b   gecēas ēcne rǣd

2260b   Ne mæg byrnan hring

3010b   Ne scel ānes hwæt

There is no need to comment on so obvious a variation as this. We may proceed at once to the next section, where we shall find analogies for the two kinds of opening measure thus illustrated.

3. *Verses with Three or Four Preliminary Syllables*

Parallel to the arrangements of two preliminary syllables are the two ordinary arrangements of three. If the first of the three takes precedence, it will receive secondary accent, and the entire group will be confined to half a measure. If, on the other hand, the second syllable is the most prominent, this will take secondary accent, and the group will occupy three-quarters of a measure. Not infrequently, to be sure, the three syllables are separate words, no one of which is clearly superior to the others, so that either arrangement will serve; but this ambiguity is of no consequence. According to my judgment, the two forms are about evenly represented in both halves of the line. A few examples from the second half will make the distinction clear:

56   oþ þæt him eft onwōc [40]

---

[40] Only the two strongest syllables in a verse take part in the alliterative

3003 þone ðe ǣr gehēold

83 ne wæs hit ienge þā gēn

1672 mid þīnra secga gedryht

In very rare cases, where the first and third syllables are markedly superior to the second, or the first is unusually prominent, the three syllables may perhaps be allowed to fill a whole measure. I have adopted this variation in only four verses, all of which belong to type C and the first half-line, but I would not insist upon treating them so, nor deny the possibility of admitting a few others. The four which I have selected are these:

1363 ofer þǣm hongiað

2148 ðā ic ðē, beorncyning

671 Ðā hē him of dyde

3169 þā ymbe hlǣw riodan [41]

Four unimportant syllables usually fill a measure as readily as five. Commonly, the first and third of these syl-

scheme, so that the vowel of *oþ,* not to mention that of the still weaker *on-,* is purely fortuitous. No doubt this may have some effect on the general euphony of the verse, but none whatever on its basic structure.

[41] The last two cases are obviously less persuasive. Nevertheless, the *ðā* in both marks a new stage in the narrative, and like the similar introductory *then* in modern English, can very readily be given a good deal of prominence.

5

lables receive the stronger accents; rarely, the first and fourth or the second alone:

1809b   sǽgde him þæs léanes þànc   (63 times)

1751b   þǽs þe him ǽr Gód sealde   (twice)

609b   gehýrde on Béowulfe   (21 times)

It would be possible to read some of the verses included under the last variant with anacrusis instead of a rest: for example,

gehýrde on Béowulfe

38a   ne hýrde ic cýmlícor [42]

but the temptation to read them in this fashion is so seldom strong that such an arrangement can be ruled out entirely. We must always bear in mind, however, that although a series of relatively unimportant syllables will always show some gradation of accent, the choice often depends upon a speaker's momentary decision. Any reading, therefore, which preserves the established metre may be considered acceptable.

Thus far, we have been dealing with the B- and C-verses in which two, three, four, or five unimportant syllables precede the first strong accent. In all these cases, the unimportant syllables occupy a part or the whole of the first,

[42] In both these verses, the more rapid reading with initial rest, which I prefer, would probably induce partial or complete elision, so that the four syllables would become three.

lightly accented measure, while the two strongest syllables are confined to the second, heavily accented measure. A minor exception to this rule in the case of two unimportant syllables may be admitted, but we must prepare the way for it by a consideration of the verses with only one such syllable.

4. *Verses with One Preliminary Syllable*

There are 367 B- and C-verses (about one sixth of the two types and one seventeenth of the poem) which are introduced by a single unimportant syllable. Here the principles already established will force us to admit two different readings.

In many cases, these verses bear so strong a resemblance to those with two or three preliminary syllables that the same treatment must be accorded to them. There is conspicuous need for a pause, so that a rest is desirable, and the single syllable is capable of bearing light secondary accent and filling half a measure. We can and should read,

4a   Òft Scýld Scȇfing

364b   Hȳ bēnan sẏnt, etc.

On the other hand, there are a good many verses in which the first syllable is a prefix, usually verbal, like *ge-*, *on-*, or *be-*, so that it could not fill half a measure or receive even a light grade of secondary accent without gross distortion. Moreover, in almost every case, a rest is unthinkable, because the sense runs on too closely from the preceding verse.[43] The second halves of the following long lines

---

[43] There are six exceptional verses, all in the first half-line. These are peculiar, in that they begin with unstressed prefixes, but, since they introduce sentences, are particularly amenable to rests: 34 *ālēdon þā*, 620 *Ymbēode þā*,

will illustrate the point, together with the inevitable reading, very clearly:

220   wundenstefna   gewaden hæfde

990   blōdge beadufolme   onberan wolde

       or (elision)

1535   þonne hē æt gūðe   gegān þenceð

2497   symle ic him on fēðan   beforan wolde

    or (elision)

Such verses as these admit of no doubt. The first syllable must always be assigned, temporally, to the conclusion of the preceding verse, and the two strongest must introduce separate measures.

Hardly less clear are certain verses in which the first syllable is a monosyllabic preposition—not because this would be incapable of extension and secondary accent after a rest, but because a rest is undesirable. In such a line as

652 [Ge]grētte þā, 1870 Gecyste þā, 2516 Gegrētte þā, 3156 Geworhton þā. Ought we to read these with rests, as the phrasing suggests, or with anacrusis, like the other verses with unstressed prefixes that are under discussion at this point? Ordinarily, it seems undesirable to admit an initial rest longer than half a measure, because to do so would involve the omission of the secondary accent as well as the primary, and would thus weaken the rhythm considerably. Except for these six verses, indeed, there is no need to insert longer rests, because in every other instance where a rest is desirable the first syllable is a separate word, and even the least important monosyllable can assert enough independence to justify secondary accent and half-measure quantity, provided an antecedent rest preserves its subordinate relation to the succeeding word. A mere prefix, however, is too weak for even this minor dignity. If we are to use rests to introduce the verses in question, we shall be obliged to let them occupy three quarters of a measure. For the sake of uniformity, therefore, I have chosen to read these verses without rests, using extrametric pauses to set them off from their predecessors (as also in such A-verses as Gewāt þā ofer wægholm 217). Nevertheless, what would be a bad rule may constitute a pleasant exception, so that I cannot vouch for the propriety of my decision.

28   hī hyne þā ætbǣron   tō brimes faroðe

the prepositional phrase follows directly after the verb on which it depends, and of which it closely restricts the meaning, so that no pause is desirable, and one long enough to constitute a half-measure's rest would greatly injure the sense.

Between the two extremes, however, there stand a considerable number of verses of which the proper reading is debatable, depending mainly on the exact shade of meaning that seems most appropriate to the passage, and also, perhaps, but to a slighter degree, on whatever abstract superiority one of the two possible rhythms appears to possess. Normally, no such intimacy exists between a prepositional phrase and the preceding words as that which has just been illustrated, so that the introduction of a rest is usually possible and sometimes preferable. In the third line of the following passage, for instance, I prefer the use of a rest, because the prepositional phrase appears to gain force by close association with the ensuing rather than the preceding words; but it would be entirely possible to omit this rest in the interest of a more deliberate reading of *land Dena*:

251b-254a   Nū ic ēower sceal

frumcyn witan,   ǣr gē fyr heonan

lēasscēaweras   on land Dena [44]

furþur fēran.

[44] Note, incidentally, the verse, *þē on land Dena* (│ ⅹ Ϲ Ϲ │ Ϝ Ϲ Ϲ │), only a few lines above (242a). Without the rest, the third line would be read, │ Ϝ ⅹ │ Ϝ ᴗᴗ ⌒ Ϲ │ Ϝ │ Ϲ Ϲ ⅹ │, the sign ⌒ indicating the possibility rather than the necessity of a slight extrametric pause.

It is apparent, therefore, that not all B- and C-verses with a single preliminary syllable are to be read in the same fashion. Of the 367 verses of this sort in *Beowulf,* I read some 150 with initial half-measure rests, while I read the other 217 without rests, treating the first syllable as ana-crusis, to be reckoned temporally with the preceding verse and assigned eighth- or sixteenth-note quantity. The indis-putable examples on each side, however, are few—I have counted 45 of the first sort (beginnings of sentences or co-ordinate clauses), 67 of the second (verses in which the first syllable is an unstressed prefix, incapable of filling half a measure even after a rest, and in which a rest is undesirable anyway because of the continuity of the sense). Less posi-tive evidence will lead to a reasonable choice in many other cases, but some 50 or 75 verses remain truly ambiguous, because, although a choice will always affect the meaning to a slight extent, the precise shade of meaning intended by the poet cannot easily be determined. Readers are sure to differ here, just as they are sure to differ about certain verses that could belong almost equally well to type D or type E,[45] and for that matter, about countless verses in modern poetry. The important thing to remember is that both rhythms are equally metrical.[46]

[45] For instance, the verse *Godes yrre bær* would normally be classified as type E (|♪ ♪ ♪ ♪ | ♩ |), because the two interdependent nouns ought to stand together against the verb; but the verb is so unimportant in comparison with either of the nouns that the verse may seem more expressive when read as type D (|♪ ♩. |♪ ♪ ♩ |). For other examples, see Appendix, II D 18, p. 363.

[46] That the same verse may have two different rhythms according to its relation to its neighbors need not surprise us if we remember that a given word often changes its rhythm according to its position in a verse. Thus *umborwe-sende* fills the whole of verse 46b, but in 1187a, *umborwesendum ær,* the dative of the same word is limited to one measure. Again, *hilderince* fills the whole of verse 1495a, but in 1307a, *hār hilderinc,* the two strongest syllables of the

5. *Exceptional Verses with Two Preliminary Syllables*

Having admitted the need for two different readings of verses with one preliminary syllable, we must reconsider briefly the case of those with two such syllables. Is there ever any reason to read these without rests, treating the two syllables as anacrusis? Ordinarily there is not, because in almost every instance the phrasing points clearly to the need for a rest. In the interest of consistency, therefore, we might decide that all verses of this syllabic pattern should be read with rests. Nevertheless, I believe that such a decision would be wrong; for here and there we encounter pairs of verses that should not be separated by any pause, the first of these having only one long or two short syllables in its final measure, the second being of the type under discussion. In these cases, and these alone, it seems proper to regard the two unimportant syllables of the second verse as anacrusis, filling the second half of the last measure of the preceding verse. Out of the 1257 verses with two introductory syllables, only four seem clearly to demand this unusual treatment. All four belong to the first half-line and to type C:

303b-304a   Eoforlic scionon

ofer hleorber[g]an

same word are limited to one measure. So it is with types B and C whenever a single preliminary syllable makes two rhythms possible. If a rest is wanted, the words of the verse are compressed into the remaining time. If not, the first syllable is treated as anacrusis, and the remainder of the verse spreads itself over two measures.

2539b-2540a   híorosércean bǽr

under stǎncleofu

2559b-2560a   bordránd onswǎf

wið ðām gryregíeste

2906b-2907a   Wīglǎf siteð

ofer Bīowulfe

In all these sequences, a verb at the end of the first verse
is followed by a prepositional phrase which so closely restricts its meaning that a rest would be disturbingly artificial, splitting into two distinct parts what is virtually a
single long phrase. There may be three or four other
sequences in the poem that deserve the same treatment,[47] but
it is not so important to determine the exact number of
instances as to recognize the principle involved. We shall
find that whenever we are inclined to read the first two

---

[47] I have considered the following: (1) 1404b-1405a, [*swā*] *gegnum fōr* /
ofer myrcan mōr, (2) 1405b-1406a, *magoþegna bær* / *þone sēlestan,* (3) 1980b-
1981a, *Meoduscencum hwearf* / *geond þæt healreced,* and (4) 1316a-1317b,
fyrdwyrðe man / *mid his handscale,* but none of these appears at all certain,
even apart from doubts about the text in nos. 1 and 3. Thus in no. 3 the verb
has another modifier in front of it, which weakens the connection with the subsequent phrase. This is also true of no. 1, where the decision really hinges on
the treatment of the speculative syllable *swā.* I prefer to read it with an
antecedent rest, and this necessitates a rest before the next verse. No. 2 is
dependent on no. 1, which it directly succeeds, and it does not settle the problem
for no. 1, because *þone sēlestan* may be even more closely connected with the
following verse (*sāwollēasne*) than with the preceding, and hence the more
readily admit an initial rest. The closeness of the connection in no. 4 depends on
the shade of meaning desired.

syllables of a B- or C-verse as anacrusis instead of assigning them to the first measure after a rest, it is because the verse is so closely bound to its predecessor that it has lost its independence, and we wish to make one long phrase out of two short ones.

Similar combinations among verses of other types are by no means uncommon in *Beowulf*, and one group in which the union is particularly close furnishes an instructive counterpart to those under consideration. In these other pairs, a verse of type B, C, or D is followed by one of type A, and the last two or three syllables of the first verse (*fela* or *swā fela*) are more closely bound to the second than to their own. In accordance with verbal phrasing, they ought to form anacrusis, but the rhythmic pattern demands that they be associated with the first verse. Thus, they are pulled both ways with almost equal force, and we must reckon the two verses as a single long phrase:

1265b-1266a   Þanon wōc fela

geōsceaftgāsta

591   þæt næfre Grendel swā fela   gryra gefremede

1525b-1526a   ðolode ǣr fela

hondgemōta

1837b-1838a   hē mæg þǣr fela

frēonda findan

2511b-2512a

Ic geneðde fela

guða on geogoðe

2738b-2739a

ne me swor fela

aða on unriht

If such intimacy between verses can exist in these sequences, we ought not to be surprised by the comparable intimacy of the pairs under discussion, where the second member is a verse of type B or C with two preliminary syllables.[48] It is surely no accident that these rare combinations, where the sense dictates a perfect union, are made up of syllabic patterns that can be dovetailed so neatly. The first member —type E or the short form of type A—leaves vacant a half-measure at its close which can just be filled by the two introductory syllables of the second. Consequently, even though the overwhelming majority of B- and C-verses with two preliminary syllables must be read with rests, we can admit the few that seem to require anacrusis as exceptions that literally prove the rule.

6. *Summary*

We can now sum up our conclusions about the unimportant syllables with which B- and C-verses begin. When there is only one such syllable, it may be treated either as anacrusis or as the up-beat of the first measure, after a rest,

[48] I do not attach any great importance to the fact that the instances in *Beowulf* seem limited to type C in the first half-line. At any rate, *Deor* 1. 8 furnishes a persuasive instance where type B in the second half-line is involved: *Beadohilde ne wæs / hyre broþra deaþ.* Perhaps *Beowulf* itself can furnish an example in 2048, *þone þin fæder / to gefeohte bær.*

the choice depending mainly on the degree of intimacy with the preceding verse. Since mere prefixes cannot be made to fill half a measure even after a rest, these should always be read as anacrusis. (In only six cases could rests before prefixes be justified.) Two unimportant syllables may be treated as anacrusis if the connection with the preceding verse is so close that the two verses together form a single long phrase. (Such intimacy occurs only six or eight times in the course of the poem, and in each case the last half-measure of the preceding verse is vacant.) With this minor exception, two or more unimportant syllables are to be assigned to the first measure, and unless they are so numerous as to fill the whole of this measure without effort, they must be supplemented by an initial rest. If we add that a fifth syllable may sometimes form monosyllabic anacrusis, we shall have included all the variations of *Beowulf*. It remains only to repeat that, whenever the first measure is thus filled, in whole or in part, by unimportant syllables, it is lightly accented in comparison to the second measure, to which the important syllables are confined.

II. The Crowded Second Measure:
Analogy of Type D

Hitherto, in order to focus attention on the preliminary syllables of types B and C, it has been assumed rather than proved that the important syllables—those that follow the alliteration—could always be confined to the second measure if the need arose, so that the choice between the two possible readings of these types depended entirely on the nature of the preliminary syllables and the degree of intimacy with neighboring verses. It is now time to put this assumption to the test by a more systematic study of the important syllables than the examples already given have made possible. Fortunately, we shall discover not only that these syllables are never too weighty or too numerous to be packed into a single measure, but that most of the measures that result from this packing are authenticated by an exact analogy.

Some time ago, Kaluza observed that verses of types B and C terminated in the same way as the two kinds of D-verses.[49] The significance of his discovery was lost, because he scanned the D-verses improperly, but it was a real discovery none the less. Theoretically, the second measures of B- and C-verses, when they contain both the important syllables, have exactly the same structure as the D-verses; and in fact the parallels are very numerous. The D-verses, however, show fewer crowded measures on the one hand, and on the other a small number of measures (belonging to the sub-type D3) that are too scantily filled for types B and C, so that rare variants exist on both sides that cannot be exactly matched. No doubt the difficulty of matching some variants of B and C can be attributed to the smaller number of D-verses, or to pure accident; but there is reason to believe that the slight tendency toward conservatism on the part of the D-verses is not accidental. A principle of compensation seems to be at work everywhere in the poem; what one measure gains, the other loses. Now the first measure of the D-verse, though it ordinarily contains only one or two syllables, is very heavily accented, whereas the first measure of the B- or C-verse is very lightly accented. By the principle of compensation, therefore, we should expect precisely the difference in the second measures that we actually find. Nevertheless, this difference is apparent only in extreme cases; normally, the second measure of the B-verse is identical with that of type Db (Sievers' D4), and the second measure of the C-verse with that of type Da (Sievers' D1 and D2). In order to prove this, examples of all forms will now be given.

[49] Max Kaluza, *Der altenglische Vers: eine metrische Untersuchung* (Berlin, 1894), Theil I, pp. 57 ff. and 72 ff. I did not arrive at my interpretation of the B-

Types B and Db

1. The commonest form of the second measure of type B contains three syllables, the first grammatically long and stressed, the second unstressed, the third long and stressed. We may express this syllabic sequence by the signs $\bar{\times} \times \bar{}$, where grammar is the sole test of length, and the macron and breve express tendencies toward certain durations, not specific rhythmic quantities. If the middle syllable is an enclitic, it will be attracted toward its predecessor; if a proclitic, toward its successor. At one extreme, therefore, we shall have the rhythm |♪ ♪ ♩|, at the other |♪. ♪ ♩|. When syllables are spoken at this rapid pace, however, their relative burden (that is, the number and difficulty of the muscular movements that are needed to produce them) often counteracts the principles of phrasing, so that the extremes meet at the half-way point indicated by the notation |♩ ₃♪ ♩|, which I have used throughout for the proclitic variant and sometimes for the enclitic as well.

Of the form |♪ ♪ ♩| or |♩₃♪ ♩|, then, there are 698 B-verses (out of a possible 1007),[50] and 176 D-verses (out of a possible 205). We may readily compare the following:

B(89b)   þǣr wæs hearpan swēg

D(2513a)   frōd folces weard

B(40b)   him on bearme læg

D(1131a)   holm storme wēol

and C-verses by way of Kaluza, but I might have done so if I had had the wit to see the meaning of his parallels.

[50] This figure excludes the 40 B-verses that I read with anacrusis instead of rests, but their syllabic patterns are exactly the same as the others.

B(2137a)   þǣr unc hwīle wæs

D(496b)   Scop hwīlum sang

B(852b)   þǣr him hel onfēng

D(2609b)   hond rond gefēng

B(1587b)   swā him ǣr gescōd

D(2777b)   Bill ǣr gescōd

B(2289b)   hē tō forð gestōp

D(210a)   Fyrst forð gewāt

2. The form $|\flat\ \sqcap\ \rfloor|$ (syllabic sequence $\acute{-}\ \times\ \times\ \grave{-}$), is found 157 times in B-verses, 22 times in D-verses. Examples for comparison are:

B(7b)   hē þæs frōfre gebād

D(494b)   þegn nytte behēold

B(756a)   sēcan dēofla gedræg

D(2774a)   eald enta geweorc

B(74a)   Đā ic wīde gefrægn

D(390b)   word inne ābēad

Two B-verses in this class require elision:

517b   hē þē æt sunde oferflāt

525a   Đonne wēne ic tō þē

or perhaps

These and one other, to which we shall come presently, are the only B-verses in the poem that break the rule restricting unstressed syllables to two between the stressed syllables when the first of these is grammatically long, to three when it is grammatically short. The reading *wēn' ic* is supported by the manuscript in two verses of type A (338a, *Wēn' ic þæt gē for wlenco,* and 442a, *Wēn' ic þæt hē wille*), and is equally necessary in another verse of type A,

1184a   wēne ic þæt hē mid gōde.

or perhaps

While it is true that a slovenly stretching of the measure would enable one to read all these verses without elision, the case for the shorter forms seems to me to be unassailable.

3. What Sievers called resolution of the first stress (the substitution of two syllables, the first short, for one long) produces two additional forms, of which the shorter has the syllabic sequence ⌣ × × ×. Depending on the burden

of the unstressed syllables, this sequence will give one of
two rhythms, | ♫ ♪ ♩ | or | ♫♩ ♩ |. (I employ the liga-
ture between eighth-notes whenever it is convenient to show
that the first is grammatically short. It has no rhythmic
significance, except to indicate that the burden of the first
syllable is very slight, so that its quantity might be still further reduced. Long stressed syllables, on the other hand,
when compressed to eighth-note quantity, have such great
burden that they threaten to extend themselves.) The sequence occurs 62 times in B-verses, 4 times in D-verses.
Examples for comparison are:

B(326b)   wið þæs recedes [51] weal

D(341a)   wlanc Wedera lēod

B(1844a)   þū eart mægenes strang

D(1870b)   cyning æþelum gōd

4. The longer form with resolution of the first stress
has the syllabic sequence ⏑⏑ × × ⏑, and the rhythm
| ♫ ♫ ♩ |.[52] This is found 13 times in B-verses, only once
in a D-verse, which provides, happily, a very close parallel:

B(362a)   ofer geofenes begang

---

[51] The late Southern pronunciation of palatal *c* as *tʃ* would make the first
syllable grammatically long, but the Anglian and early Southern would leave
it short, and such syllables are treated as short in all the poetry.

[52] By rule, unstressed syllables may be either long or short, but in these
rapid forms, they are almost always short.

D(2367a)   Oferswám ðǎ síoleða bigóng

To this class also belongs the other overcrowded B-verse to which reference was made above, p. 69. Here we must substitute the archaic form *ðon* for *ðonne*: [53]

469b   sě wæs bétera ðonne ic

The same formula appears in other poems, and in three instances a consonant follows *ðonne*, so that mere elision would be impossible: [54]

Juliana 100b   sě is bétra þonne þǔ

(where the form *betra* suggests a further shortening for the preceding verse), and with precisely the same rhythm, *nǣfre furður þonne nū* (*Elene* 388b), *Hwylc wæs māra þonne sē* (*Guthlac* 400), *hī bēoð swīþran þonne ic* (*Riddle 16,* 5b), and *ic bēo lengre þonne ǣr* (*Riddle 23,* 7b). Another verse, of type E, requires the same treatment, thus removing any suspicion that the scansion rather than the word is at fault:

Juliana 324b   géornfulra þonne ic

5. Resolution of the second stress gives us two other sequences, of which the shorter is ⏗ ⏑ ⏗⏑ , rhythmically

---

[53] The older form *þon* is recorded once in *Beowulf* (44b, *þon þā dydon*). That it is not found elsewhere in the MS. is probably due to scribal blundering. Not only in all the verses cited here, but as a rule elsewhere, *þonne* was abbreviated to *þoñ*. Hence, if a scribe saw a genuine *þon* in the MS. from which he was copying, he would be likely to supply a mark of suspension, thus emending the unfamiliar but metrically essential form out of existence.

[54] Line references are to Krapp and Dobbie, *The Exeter Book,* and for the *Elene* to Krapp, *The Vercelli Book.*

6

either | ♪♪♪♪| or | ♩₃ ♪♪♪|. This is a very easy movement, but, oddly enough, though it occurs 62 times in B-verses, it appears only once indisputably, and twice doubtfully, in D-verses. We may compare the following:

B(853a)   þanon eft gewiton

D(128b)   wōp up āhafen

B(1101a)   nē þurh inwitsearo

D(1162a)   win of wunderfatum

B(49b)   him wæs geōmor sefa

D(570a)   beorht bēacen Godes

The last two D-verses are doubtful, because both *wunder-* and *bēacen* are often treated as monosyllables (*wundr-* and *bēacn*). Such a treatment is partly mere convention, for it is usually hard to prevent the final consonants from becoming vocalic, but nevertheless it may be safer to call the rhythm of the second measure | ♩ ♩ ♩ |, like that of the majority of C-verses. Several of the B-verses that I have included here are open to the same question and might be better described as C-verses.

6. The longer form with resolution of the second stress has the syllabic sequence ´ × × ´⌣× , and the rhythm | ♪ ♫ ♪ ♪ |. This is found only 11 times in B-verses, and once, doubtfully, in a D-verse:

B(800a)   ond on healfa gehwone

D(1747a)   wom wundorbebodum

Here it may be noticed that, if we prefer to regard *wundor-* as monosyllabic, we at least gain another example for the preceding form.

7. If both stresses are resolved two more variants arise, of which the shorter has the syllabic sequence ‿‿ ⸝ ‿‿ , and the rhythm | ♫ ♪ ♪ ♪ | or | ♫♪ ♪♪ | . This is found three times in B-verses, not at all in D-verses:

1181b   þæt hē þā geogoðe wile

2052a   æfter hæleða hryre

3005a

It seems curious that this form, easier than the preceding, should not be better represented. Probably the accidents of language rather than rhythmic principles are responsible.

8. The longer variant has the syllabic sequence ‿‿ ⸝ ⸝ ‿‿ , and the rhythm | ♫ ♫ ♪ ♪ | . It is found in one B-verse:

879b   būton Fitela mid hine

Though this can certainly be read without undue difficulty, we might well substitute *Fitla,* thus gaining another example of number 6 above.

We have now examined all the variations in the second measures of B-verses, when these measures include both of the important syllables. Consequently, it is plain that there is not a single B-verse in the poem that is unreadable by the new method, and that the majority are supported by the exact analogy of D-verses. Let us now turn to the C-verses and their parallels in type Da.

Types C and Da

1. Again the vast majority of verses has the simplest form—in this case a second measure containing three syllables, the first grammatically long and stressed, the second likewise stressed but either long or short, the third unstressed, which may be represented by the symbols $\underset{\sim}{\acute{\ }}$ $\underset{\smile}{\acute{\ }}$. This sequence produces the rhythm $|\,\jmath\ \jmath\!\!\!\jmath\ \jmath\!\!\!\jmath\,|$ or $|\,\jmath\ \jmath\!\!\!\jmath\ \jmath\!\!\!\jmath\,|$, according to the grammatical length or burden of the second syllable. Burden is the only distinction between these two forms, which are about evenly represented, and need not ordinarily be separated. Several considerations make the ligature useful, however, as an indication of the shortness of the first syllable of the pair. For instance, if the next verse has monosyllabic anacrusis, the ligatured form will be shortened to $\sqcap\!\!\!\jmath + \jmath$, or occasionally $\overset{3}{\jmath\!\jmath\!+\!\jmath}$; whereas that without ligature will become $\jmath\ \jmath\!\!\!\jmath + \jmath\!\!\!\jmath$. Again, some readers might produce $\jmath_{3}\jmath$ instead of $\jmath\ \jmath$, but they could not do this where the first syllable was long, for in the latter case the tendency would be towards the opposite variation, $\jmath_{3}\jmath$, excluded though it is by the rules of phrasing.[55] We must be careful to realize, however, both here and in the comparable D-verses, that the ligatured form does not represent resolution in Sievers' sense of the word, because in these verses $\jmath\ \jmath$ cannot be replaced by $\jmath$. The heavily

---

[55] Enclitic syllables are always attracted toward their predecessors, and where this attraction is reinforced by rhythmic phrasing, as at the end of a verse, it is strong enough to withstand all contrary influences. See William Thomson, *The Rhythm of Speech*, p. 155.

burdened form, ♪ ♪ , on the other hand, can be resolved, as we shall see, into ♫ ♪ or ♫♩ .

This simplest form, then, |♩ ♪ ♪| or |♩ ♪ ♪|, occurs no less than 791 times in C-verses, and 543 times in D-verses. (The total number of C-verses under consideration is 937,[56] of D-verses 631.) Examples for comparison are:

C(1899a)   ofer Hrōðgāres

D(826b)   sele Hrōðgāres

C(1371b)   ǣr hē in wille

D(1650b)   weras on sāwon

C(1420b)   syððan Æscheres

D(1323b)   Dēad is Æschere

C(640b)   ēode goldhroden

D(2025a)   geong goldhroden

C(1292b)   wolde ūt þanon

D(2545b)   strēam ūt þonan

[56] This figure excludes the 181 C-verses which I read with anacrusis instead of initial rests, but these have the same syllabic patterns as the others.

2. Resolution of the first stressed syllable produces the sequence ⌣⌣ ⌣́ , with the rhythm |♪ ♪ ♪ ♪|, rarely |♪ ♪ ♪ ♪|. This form occurs 138 times in C-verses, 88 times in D-verses. We may readily compare the following:

C(3a)   hū ðā æþelingas

D(906a)   eallum æþellingum

C(1082b)   on þǣm meðelstede

D(502a)   mōdges merefaran

(The subordinate form, ♪ ♪ ♪ ♪|, illustrated last, is very rare, occurring only once more in a C-verse, 190b *ne mihte snotor hæleð,* and we could rule out both this and the example given on the ground that *meðel-* and *snotor-* were regarded as monosyllables.[57] Type D admits 30 examples, but 25 of these are furnished by the same word, *maþelode,* three others by the more or less similar *hafenade, openian,* and *glitinian,* and one by the dubious *snotor guma.* Since the verbs may be survivals from a time when their penultimate vowels were long, the example given above begins to look decidedly exceptional.)

---

[57] One other C-verse, which I read with anacrusis instead of a rest, has the same syllabic pattern, if recent speculations about the quantity of *nosan* are correct: 2803b *æt brimes nosan* (♪|♪ ♩. |♪ ♩.). I think we should retain *nōsan,* but see the glossary of Klaeber's third edition of *Beowulf,* s. v. *nose,* and the references there given. In my Appendix, 190b and 1082b are treated as if *snotor* and *meðel* were monosyllables, and so classified with the second measure |♩ ♪ ♪|.

3. Resolution of the second stress, giving the syllabic pattern ⏑́ ⏑̆ ⏓ ⏓ and the rhythm $|\,\sqcap\,|$ or $|\,\sqcap\,|$, is exceedingly rare, occurring only three times in C-verses, once, doubtfully, in a D-verse. We may as well examine all four verses:

C(1946a)   þæt hīo lēodbealewa (*but perhaps* -bealwa)

(2096b)   Hē on weg losade

(2796b)   þē ic hēr on starie

D(2921b)   milts ungyfeðe

(In the D-verse, the stressing of *un-* may be questioned, because there is evidence on both sides. To read this verse as type A would therefore be legitimate, and the rhythm would be smoother. If we deprived *un-* of all its stress, the rhythm would become $|\,\bullet\,|\,\bullet\,\bullet\,\bullet\,\gamma\,|$. If we let it retain strong secondary stress, the rhythm would become $|\,\bullet\,\bullet\,|\,\bullet\,\bullet\,\bullet\,\gamma\,|$.)

4. Resolution of both stresses produces the syllabic sequence ⏑̆ ⏓ ⏑̆ ⏓ ⏓, and the rhythm $|\,\bullet\,\bullet\,\sqcap\,\bullet\,|$ or $|\,\bullet\,\bullet\,\sqcap\,|$. There are five examples in C-verses, none in D-verses. (The same sequence is found in seven other C-verses, but I read these with anacrusis instead of rests.) All five examples can be spoken with ease:

350b   Ic þæs wine Deniga

1603b   ond on mere staredon

2309b   wæs se fruma egeslīc

1260a   sē þe wæteregesan

164a   Swā fela fyrena

These are all the variations exhibited by the second measures of C-verses when they include both of the important syllables. Once again, as with the B-verses, it is clear that not a single example in the poem is unreadable by the new method, and that the majority are supported by the exact analogy of D-verses.

*

*   *

We have now examined both the preliminary and the important syllables, and so brought to an end our consideration of types B and C, which were the outstanding obstacle to a consistent rhythm. Anyone who has been patient enough to make trial of the suggested readings will admit, I am sure, that they are neither unduly difficult nor out of harmony with the meaning of the verses. If any further justification were needed, I might add that the initial rests characteristic of the first measure are not the only attractive feature of these readings. The crowding of important syllables in the second measure injects a strong excitement into the poem that it would otherwise lack. Supposing, for a moment, that there would be no objection to the anacrusis, let us set the tame

Hē ðæs frōfre gebād

beside the triumphant

Hḕ ðæs frȫfre gebā́d

and see whether, all other considerations apart, the second measure alone does not assure us of the superiority of the latter form. By this new reading of the B- and C-verses, the whole poem is transformed. We have escaped from the mere jumble that results from an effort to make sense out of Sievers' feet, from the indifference to alliteration and prose-accent that marks his later theories, from the undue emphasis of unimportant syllables and the inconsistencies of Leonard, and from the extrametric anacrusis of Heusler. In place of these have emerged, first, the initial rest, utilizing for rhythmic purposes the pauses that language requires; secondly, a seemly consideration for the less important syllables; and thirdly, the zest of a highly charged second measure. A further refinement will be proposed in the next section, but already we can discern in *Beowulf* not only a strict metre in which every syllable has its place, but some hitherto unsuspected rhythmic variations which add greatly to the vitality and expressiveness of the words. Any Germanic poem, however trivial, stands to gain by these changes. *Beowulf*, because of its other excellences, gains enormously. Its admirers can now claim for it that formal control and that harmony of rhythm and meaning which are among the foremost signs of great poetry.

THE VERSES CALLED A3

Among the verses that the new theory treats in a different fashion from that recommended by Heusler (altogether, about one third of the total number in *Beowulf*) there remain for consideration only a few of those that Sievers classified as a sub-type of A, A3.

In most of the verses of type A, as in those of types D and E, the alliteration, if single, introduces the first measure. In the third sub-type, however, it introduces the second measure; and parallel with this transference of the alliterative emphasis is a change in the logical prominence of the syllables. The other A-verses have strongly stressed syllables at the beginning of each measure, and if there is anything to choose between them, the first is the stronger.[58] In type A3, on the other hand, while the first measure may be introduced by a syllable of considerable importance, this is never superior to that which introduces the second, and often there is no syllable in the first measure that demands stress in its own right. In other words, the syllables of the first measure bear a close resemblance to those that, according to our new reading, fill a part or the whole of the first measure in types B and C. Not infrequently, they are identical.

Two important differences, however, will force us to be cautious in dealing with this point of resemblance to types B and C. In the first place, the second measures are radically unlike. Types B and C have two heavily stressed long syllables or their equivalent, either separated by one or two unstressed syllables or followed by one; whereas type A3 has normally one long stressed syllable or its equivalent, followed by a single unstressed syllable. Occasionally this final syllable is the second member of a compound and receives strong secondary stress, but even then the second measure is weaker than that of the B's and C's. To express the same thing in terms of syllables alone, without reference

---

[58] Occasional exceptions may be found where the alliteration is double. Where the first syllable is much weaker than the second, however, as in *oð þæt him ǣghwylc* (9a), or *oð þæt ymb āntīd* (219a), the alliteration may well be accidental. Several times the words *oð* and *oððe* would produce double alliteration in B- and C-verses of the second half-line if their presence were not discounted by the greater prominence of subsequent syllables. Accordingly, I have assigned the verses here quoted to type A3.

to measures, the B- and C-verses resemble most others in having two heavily stressed syllables, the first of which takes precedence in alliteration and, if there is a choice, in emphasis; whereas the A3-verse has normally only one, and this stands so close to the end of the verse that, if we seek to elevate a second from the ranks to keep it company, we shall choose one of those that precede it, thus causing the alliteration to fall on the last of the pair instead of the first. The only other verses that share this peculiarity with type A3 are a few irregular ones that Sievers did not classify and wished to emend, such as *þenden hē wið wulf* (3027a), and an occasional verse of type B in the first half-line, the only clear case being *hē is manna gehyld* (3056a, with alliteration of *h*).[59] Because of this peculiarity, type A3 is not admitted to the second half of the line, where the alliteration is always restricted to the first of the two strongest syllables.[60]

In the second place, the comparative weakness of the second measure is offset by a slight increase in the minimum requirements for the first, as well as by the admission of stronger and more numerous syllables as a maximum. There are some 309 verses of type A3 in the first half-line.[61] Of these, 9 have two syllables preceding that which alliterates,

[59] Though *-hyld* is heavily stressed, it is subordinate in my reading to *manna*, which takes the primary accent of the second measure. This makes the correctness of the verse even more doubtful than it would otherwise be, and I think we should read *hē is gehyld manna*. For full details concerning the two verses here cited and their possible analogues, see Appendix, I B 50-1 and I F 4, pp. 285 f. and 321.

[60] We might suppose that the rare form of A3 in which the final syllable takes strong secondary accent would fulfill the requirements for the second half-line, especially in view of the presence therein of such verses as 1134b *swā nū gȳt dēð*, but all these can be assimilated to type C by the substitution of archaic or analogical forms (*dōið* or *dē-eð*), so that no plausible example remains. Probably the final syllable of the A-verse was too strongly dominated by its predecessor to be reckoned as a separate stress (cf. *bānhūs* and *bānhūse,* the secondary stress being more marked in the second by contrast with the final syllable).

[61] I include the five verses with short endings listed in the Appendix, I A 104-7, p. 273 f.

107 three, 134 four, 49 five, and 10 six. Thus, there is a recognizable difference merely in numerical range between these verses and those of types B and C, where many have only one syllable before the first that alliterates, the majority two, only a few five, and none six. We might explain the difference in the minimum by Sievers' very persuasive theory that every verse—at least in the stricter poems—was required to contain at least four syllables; and again, we might set down the absence of six preliminary syllables in types B and C to mere chance, since six can be found here and there in other poems; but a comparison of the average numbers, combined with the not infrequent occurrence of a syllable of real importance in the first measure of type A3, makes it preferable to account for the difference in terms of compensation.

Because of these two points of difference, which go hand in hand, we must take care not to assume identical rhythms for the first measures of these divergent types in all cases— and there are a good many—in which the syllables involved are the same or similar. A syllable that takes secondary accent after a rest in type B or C may well receive light primary accent in type A3, because its petty dignity does not have to stand comparison with any overwhelming power in the second measure, and conversely, a little added emphasis at this point may be needed to give weight to the verse as a whole. It is true that the total weight of a verse, in terms of accent and burden, may vary enormously in accordance with the mood of its particular passage and its function therein, and that type A3 is employed very frequently as a light introduction to the weighty verses that follow; but nevertheless we can discern a tendency to avoid extremes, so that the total weight of most verses is very nearly the same. With due reservations, therefore, we may accept the principle that a gain for one measure means a loss for the other, while moderation in one means moderation in the other.

A few examples will illustrate these generalizations. We need not concern ourselves with those verses in which five or six syllables precede that which alliterates, because even in types B and C such a large number would fill the first measure (with rhythms like | ♫ ♫♩ | — and | ♫♩ ♫♩ |—), or overlap it to form anacrusis. Those with four syllables can likewise be taken for granted when the first is strong enough to receive light primary accent. If, on the other hand, the second syllable is superior to the first, the analogy of types B and C may tempt us to insert an initial rest (e. g. | ♪ ♫♩ |—) instead of treating the first syllable as anacrusis (e. g. ♪ | ♩ ♫ |—). We shall confine our attention, therefore, to these exceptional sequences of four, and to those of three and two, beginning with the last.

The nine verses with two syllables before the alliteration are in the first column below, with parallels from types B and C in the second:

391a	Ēow hēt secgan	1783b	unc sceal worn fela
1175a	Mē man sægde	{2155a	Mē ðis hildesceorp
		{2355b	þǣr mon Hygelāc slōh
941a	ðē wē ealle	15a	þē hīe ǣr drugon
2481a	þēah ðe ōðer [62]	2642b	þēah ðe hlāford ūs
2587a	þæt se mǣra	2059a	þæt se fǣmnan þegn
2977a	Lēt se hearda	702b	Cōm on wanre niht
632a	Ic þæt hogode	1345a	Ic þæt londbūend
2036a	on him gladiað	380b	on his mundgripe
262a	Wæs mīn fæder	476b	is mīn fletwerod
		1457a	wæs þǣm hæftmēce

[62] Klaeber prints the whole line thus: *þēah ðe ōðer his / ealdre gebohte;* but *his* belongs properly to the second half as anacrusis. Only by giving it secondary accent, which it does not deserve, could we force it to be associated with the first half. Klaeber himself suggests the alternative in his note. *Finnsburg* 47, *hū ðā wīgend hyra wunda genǣson,* which he there cites, is not quite the same, because dissyllabic *hyra* can be associated with both halves at once (| ♪ ♪ | ♪ ♪ ♪ ♪ | ♩ ♪ ♪ | ♩ ♩ | — B + A). See further p. 234 below.

Although the resemblances between the first two syllables of corresponding verses in these columns are striking, the principles already stated make it more imperative to insert rests before those that belong to types B and C than before those of type A3. In the first two examples of the latter, therefore, since the syllables seem a little heavier than elsewhere, I prefer to let them occupy the whole of the first measure (| ♩ ♩ |—). In the other examples, however, with the possible exception of 2977a and 262a, the two syllables are so unemphatic that I prefer to insert rests and limit their scope to half a measure (| ᛭ ♫♩ |—) ; and this treatment of them seems doubly natural in view of the fact that they all introduce new ideas, which reach their climax in subsequent verses. The analogy of the B- and C-verses, while it need not be pushed to the limit, does nevertheless make these seven surprisingly light A-verses more intelligible.

The large number of A3-verses with three syllables preceding the alliteration (107 in all) can be divided into two groups, those in which the first syllable is at least as strong as the second (this distinction is sometimes hard to make, but I count about 77), and those in which the second is the stronger (about 30). In the first group, the choice lies between | ᛭ ♪♪♪ |— and | ♩ ♪ ♪ |— or | ♪ ♪ ♩ |—; in the second, between | ꝯ ♪ ♪ ♪ |— and ♪| ♩ ♩ |—.

In most of the verses of the first group, the three syllables are decidedly stronger than the corresponding ones of types B and C, so that there is no question of their ability to fill the whole of the first measure. Characteristic of the group are the following:

118a Fánd þà ðǽr ínne

1888a Cwṓm þà tō flṓde

710a Ðā cōm of mōre

1896a þā wæs on sande [63]

559a Swā mec gelōme

There is a handful of verses, however, in which the three syllables are weak enough to resemble those of types B and C, and consequently to raise the question whether they should be limited to the second half of the opening measure:

Type A3		Types B and C	
106a	siþðan him Scyppend	1308a	syðþan hē aldorþegn
1508a	swā hē ne mihte [64]	3069a	Swā hit oð dōmes dæg
2305a	wolde se lāða	755b	wolde on heolster flēon (elision?)
		646b	wiste þǣm āhlǣcan
2797a	þæs ðe ic mōste	228a	þæs þe him ȳþlāde
3120a	Hūru se snotra	369b	hūru se aldor dēah
9a	oð þæt him æghwylc	56b	oþ þæt him eft onwōc
219a	oð þæt ymb āntīd [65]		

Just what to do in such cases as these is by no means certain. On the one hand we have the analogy of types B and C, together with the fact that the phrasing would be assisted

[63] All the evidence in the poem bears out the natural assumption that *ðā* meaning 'then' is more emphatic than *ðā* meaning 'when.' It constantly marks the stages of the narrative, like its modern counterpart, so that if it stands first in a clause, it can readily take primary accent. Although I would not deny the possibility of subordinating it to the verbs in these two verses (— , or less probably | —), the reading given seems to me far more expressive.

[64] A controversial verse, which may not be authentic. *Swā* here means 'so that,' not the slightly more emphatic 'so' of 3069a and 559a above. It would be possible to give precedence in stress to the pronoun ( ).

[65] As I have already remarked, p. 80 n., I consider the alliteration of *oð* in these two verses accidental.

rather than hindered by the use of rests. On the other hand we have the principle of compensation. Although I do not see any way to settle the question beyond dispute, I am inclined to favor the principle of compensation, especially since three syllables, however unimportant, can fill a measure more readily than two. With some misgivings, then, I have decided against the use of rests.

With the other group, however, that in which the second of the three syllables is stronger than the first, the probabilities are reversed, because if the first syllable is treated as anacrusis, the other two must fill the first measure, and in most cases they seem too weak to do this without considerable strain. Accordingly, I read all but one of the thirty with initial eighth-note rests, the sole exception being the problematical verse,

459a　Geslóh þìn fǽder,

which, except for the alliteration, and the possibility that we ought to read fǽddèr,[66] could pass for a B-verse of the sort that must be introduced by anacrusis instead of a rest. Even this verse, despite the more or less inevitable emphasis of the verb and the ease with which the pronoun can be elevated to the minor dignity of secondary accent and full quantity, could be reduced to | ♪ ♪ ♪ | ♪ ♩. | without much difficulty. A few characteristic illustrations will show that the latter rhythm is preferable for the other twenty-nine; provided, of course, I have not erred occasionally (as perhaps in the final example) by refusing primary accent to the first of the three syllables:

Type A3　　　　　　　　　　　　　Types B and C

71a　　ond þǽr on ínnàn　　　424b　ond nū wið Grendel
　　　　　　　　　　　　　　　　　　　　　sceal

[66] See Appendix I A 105, p. 273 f.

2714a þæt him on brēostum   1456a þæt him on ðearfe lāh

1661a ac mē geūðe   740a ac hē gefēng hraðe

1380a Ic þē þā fǣhðe   1220b Ic þē þæs lēan geman

Finally, we come to the eighteen verses in which the second of four syllables is stronger than the first. Judging by the fashion in which the first group with three syllables was treated, one might expect that all these would run more smoothly with anacrusis than with rests. This, however, is not the case. In ten of these verses, the syllables are so exceptionally insignificant that I prefer to limit them to three quarters of a measure. Inasmuch as all ten can be found in the appendix,[67] I will quote only two at this point:

Type A3	Types B and C
22a þæt hine on ylde	45a þē hine æt frumsceafte
3009a ond þone gebringan	1291b þā hine se brōga angeat [68]

All the important points of difference between my readings and those of other students of the problem have now been presented, except for the hypermetric verses, which are discussed in Part II. My readings of types D and E, the majority of type A, and a small minority of types B and C are substantially the same as Heusler's, except for a difference in tempo that would be unworthy of notice if it were

---

[67] Appendix, I A 74, 75, and 86. The other eight are listed under I A 89, 94, and 95.

[68] The small number of these verses makes exact parallels impossible.

7

not for the hypermetric verses. Concerning the majority of types B and C, however, I differ radically from Heusler, and produce by means of this difference a continuous rhythm—punctuated, to be sure, by frequent initial rests, and suspended on rare occasions by pauses — instead of a rhythm that is impeded at every third or fourth verse by extrametric anacrusis. Finally, I extend the principle of initial rests to a few of the verses of type A3, thus gaining for these a somewhat less artificial movement. The logical consequence of the changes that have thus been introduced, and their final justification, form the subject of the ensuing paragraphs.

THE HARP

Now that the new theory has been set forth, and its essential feature, the initial rest, has been justified as well as possible by reference to principles of phrasing and accent, we may turn our attention to a matter which has heretofore been disregarded—the musical instrument with which the Anglo-Saxons are known to have accompanied their songs. I have left the harp out of the discussion up to this time, because there has been much dispute about the possibility of its use as an accompaniment to *Beowulf*. Heusler and Sievers, for example, have asserted that the poems that were meant to be sung have disappeared, the only survivors being such as were intended for unaccompanied recitation.[69] It seemed best, therefore, to show what grounds there were for the new theory even if no accompaniment were assumed, especially since it was without reference to anything but the words themselves and the general principles of rhythm that

[69] See Heusler's *Deutsche Versgeschichte*, 1. 90 f., and Sievers' *Altgermanische Metrik*, pp. 186 ff. Heusler elaborates the point much more fully in his earlier work, *Die Altgermanische Dichtung* (Berlin, 1923), pp. 36 ff. He believes (p. 39) that Cædmon's Hymn was sung. Accordingly, his scansion of it in *Deutsche Versgeschichte* 1. 143 (above, p. 23) treats its limited anacrusis (monosyllabic and dissyllabic) as part of the metre. In my own reading, the hymn has no anacrusis at all. See below, p. 214.

this theory was evolved. Now, however, the harp must receive its due, for the assumption of its use is indispensable to a complete understanding of the initial rests.

We have seen that the only way to maintain an unbroken rhythm in *Beowulf* without doing violence to the meaning of the words or the alliterative pattern is to make use of initial rests before the majority of verses beginning with unimportant syllables, and that when we have adopted this principle, we encounter such rests very frequently—about once in every three verses—though not with any degree of regularity, some periods containing several rests in succession, others very few. This combination of frequency and irregularity appears to bespeak both a fondness for rests and an easy familiarity with them, as if there were neither any aesthetic objection to their use, nor any difficulty experienced in producing them; for infrequency of occurrence might suggest repugnance, and regularity the need for anticipation as an aid to the reciter, if not to his audience. How, nevertheless, are we to reconcile this evidence of ease and pleasure with the extreme rarity of initial rests in other verse? It is hard to believe that the taste of the entire Germanic world would have changed so suddenly and so radically that what was once a chief means of delight would, as it were over night, have become reprehensible; or that so striking a device as the initial rest, after being developed to a high degree of expressiveness by generations of poets, would have been completely forgotten in a moment. Yet the fact remains that even the alliterative verse of the fourteenth century, which stems, in however debilitated a form, from the older tradition, shows no acquaintance with rests of this character. Something more than the combined forces of human inconstancy, political upheaval, and modification of language is needed to account for the change. Moreover, despite all that has been said in praise of the initial rests of *Beowulf*, an unaccompanied recitation of the poem reveals a serious weakness in their use.

Initial rests are easy enough to produce and to hear so long as another verse precedes them. They cannot be produced, on the other hand, at the beginning of a poem, or after a considerable pause in the midst of it, unless some external means of marking the position of the latent accent is employed. Without the assistance of the preliminary stroke of a baton, or the tapping of a finger, or the sounding of an instrument, the listener will not recognize the presence of a rest. He will hear the syllables that follow it as anacrusis, the second measure as the first, and will declare that this opening verse is one whole measure short. If such rests were used at all in unaccompanied verse, or for that matter in unaccompanied song, they would have to be placed at the head of verses that were sure to have predecessors, certainly not at the head of stanzas, or fits, or verse-paragraphs, or entire poems. Yet these are precisely the places, among others, in which the rests of *Beowulf* occur. A great many of the numbered fits (whatever they may signify as points of division), most of the paragraphs that editors have marked, and a large number of sentences begin with rests, so that a reader would be hard pressed to find a stopping-place where he might resume without discomfort. Indeed, the opening verse of the poem, to which I have sedulously avoided any reference up to this time, has a rest! *Hwæt, wē Gār-Dena* belongs to type C, with the heaviest accents on *Gār-* and *Den-*. We could, to be sure, owing to the exclamatory nature of *Hwæt*, give it a primary accent with a rest after it, thus forcing it, despite the alliteration, into a somewhat irregular example of type D:

Hwæt, wē Gār-Dena,

and this is what we ought to do in the absence of any other means of marking the initial accent; but there is no use in denying that, if the verse occurred in the midst of the poem, we should read,

Hwæt, wē Gār-Dena,

just as we should read the following:

530a   Hwæt, þū worn fela   (w alliterates)

942b   Hwæt, þæt secgan mæg   (s alliterates)

2248b   Hwæt, hyt ær on ðē   (æ alliterates)

Nor is *Beowulf* alone in this respect. Most of the other Old English poems begin in the same way, and the long ones all contain initial rests at points where a reader might wish to resume after a pause.

From this evidence we must draw one of three conclusions: either that the hypothesis of initial rests is incorrect, or that verses with rests were modified rhythmically whenever they were recited without prologue, or that there existed some external means of keeping time. In refutation of the first of these, I can only offer the substance of this book. The second, though likely enough at times when verses were casually quoted (witness the rhythmic alterations that we habitually introduce into the words of songs when we quote them in conversation or read them without thought of the music), is unthinkable as a regular practice. The third conclusion thus appears inevitable, and in view of the fact that the harp was habitually mentioned as the proper accompaniment to poetry, it is just what we ought to have expected. If the harp were keeping time, the voice might omit the first accent of a verse at the beginning of a poem, or anywhere else, without causing the slightest confusion. In musical recitative, indeed, the voice so frequently begins off the beat that the effect is a commonplace.

Thus, the assumption of the harp dispels the only practical objection to the theory of initial rests by enabling us to postulate a regular beat, not merely imagined but heard, as a complement to the voice. But it does more than this. It also removes the historical doubts that have been raised by explaining both the origin of the rests and their disappearance. It explains their origin by showing us that they are not an isolated and somewhat mysterious phenomenon, but a natural development of accompanied song or chant, one which has plenty of analogies in music to make up for the lack of them in poetry. It explains their disappearance less directly, but no less clearly. If their strict observance depended on the harp, then it depended in large measure on a small class of trained minstrels who knew both the art of the instrument and the ancient traditions of poetry. This class, the foster-child of aristocracy and fashion, was bound to perish sooner or later. In England, it could not long have survived the Norman Conquest, if indeed it was not already extinct by that time. Shortly after its demise, the form of the verse by which it had lived would have followed it into oblivion. Those who remembered fragments of the verse or found it recorded in books would often have failed to observe the rests, distorting the original rhythms in order to fill in the gaps that these had left. Eventually, they would have mistaken these degenerate readings for the true ones, and all memory of the initial rests would have vanished. So, by accounting for this known result and yet justifying our belief in that strictly controlled form which the rests make possible, the harp becomes a kind of open sesame to the entire problem. It is inseparable from the theory of initial rests.

Indeed, the elaborate argument of the foregoing para-

graphs ought to have been unnecessary, for the burden of
proof lies squarely on the shoulders of those who have
sought to make us believe that the extant Germanic poetry
was unaccompanied. They have been led to this belief, not
by any historical evidence, but by the theories of Germanic
versification that they have invented. Leonard believes in
the harp, because his reading, however inconsistent in its
treatment of syllables, is consistently metrical. Sievers did
not, because the rhythms that his original system suggested
were mutually antagonistic. Heusler did not, because his
impeccably musical measures were separated by a host of
syllables that he was unable to include within their bounds.
To be sure, he advanced another reason—that only strophic
verse, with the opportunity that it offers for recurrent
melody, can be sung; but even if we go so far as to grant
that the accompaniment of the harp would entail a more or
less fixed melodic pattern for the voice, his statement is con-
tradicted by the testimony of living epic traditions.[70] Surely
it is better to suppose that the poetry that has survived is
representative of the sort that that poetry itself was given
to describing — " þær wæs hearpan swēg, swutol sang
scopes " — than of a modern sort, such as was never ex-
pressly mentioned by those who practised the art.[71] In an

[70] Through the courtesy of Mr. Albert Lord, of Eliot House, it has been my
privilege to hear some of the phonograph records of the extant Serbian epic
that were left to Harvard University by the late Milman Parry. These narrative
poems, which, though they often run to thousands of verses, are extemporized
by professional singers on the foundation of a traditional narrative and a number
of formulaic phrases, are stichic, not strophic; but this does not prevent
them from being sung. Each verse has a simple but complete melodic pattern,
which is repeated *ad infinitum,* or exchanged for another at will. The singer
usually accompanies himself with an instrument, but sometimes sings alone. He
never speaks the words, for they are born to a tune.

[71] I need scarcely remind the reader that the passage here cited from *Beowulf*
(89a-90b) is only one of several in that poem and in others of the Old English
period, all of which point in the same direction, or that there is strong corrobo-
rative evidence from contemporary historical writers both in England and on the
continent. For a good account of this evidence and a straightforward interpretation of it, see H. M. and N. K. Chadwick, *The Growth of Literature,* 1
(Cambridge, 1932). 572-7 and 588 f.

effort to find a degree of order in *Beowulf* that would allow it to pass as reasonably metrical spoken verse, we have been led to the establishment of a rhythm so strictly governed that it approaches the realm of music, and to the introduction of rests of a sort that musical accompaniment alone can fully justify. A complicated process of reasoning has thus taken us back to a belief from which common sense ought never to have allowed us to depart.

Just what the musical accompaniment was like, and what melodic patterns were employed by the voice, can probably never be known or even conjectured. That portion of the ancient art seems to be irrecoverably lost, and it is doubtful whether the fragmentary history of music on the one hand, or the temporally and racially remote analogies of Slavic practices on the other, can be of much service. We may be fairly certain that the small harp then in use kept the time with a minimum of harmonic variation, sounding the main beats and perhaps contributing a few flourishes by itself at points where the narrative could be briefly suspended. Although a plucked instrument leaves the voice free to preserve the inharmonic modulations of pitch that belong to ordinary speech, it seems likely that the *scop*, a practised performer, would have adjusted his pitch to the instrument, either producing a kind of level chant with more or less spontaneous variations, or making use of simple melodic phrases corresponding in length to the half-line and in rhythm to its few essential features. Those better instructed in music than I may be able to shed further light on this interesting subject, but much will inevitably remain obscure.[72] If, however, my interpretation of the rhythm of the words is correct, we may be sure that the harp would not have modified it in any important way. It is true that music frequently

---

[72] Heusler's speculations on the requirement for verse that could be sung to the harp are interesting and suggestive, despite his bias. See *Die Altgermanische Dichtung*, p. 39.

alters the rhythm that spoken words would assume by themselves, formalizing quantities and altering accents in order to avoid changes of time, extending verses in order to achieve the long final quantities or rests that may be needed to complete its phrases or give time for breathing; but these desiderata of music are already present in the rhythm of the words, and any serious modification of this would remove the very features that music demands. Despite all that we have lost, therefore, we can still be reasonably certain of the movement of the lines, and understand that, whatever else it was, Germanic verse as represented by *Beowulf* was a finely regulated and richly varied rhythmic achievement.

PART II

THE HYPERMETRIC VERSES

INTRODUCTION

Beowulf contains three groups of lines, 1163-8, 1705-7, and 2995-6, which do not conform to Sievers' five types, and strongly resist any effort to confine them within the metrical scheme that has just been advocated for the others. They have been called 'schwellverse' by the Germans, owing to their conspicuously greater weight and length, and will here be called, in conformity with the usual practice, hyper-metric. Verses of this sort are scattered through Old English and Old Saxon poetry, usually in well-defined groups, though sometimes in isolation, and therefore no metrical theory, whether of *Beowulf* in particular or of Germanic poetry in general, can rest unchallenged if it fails to offer some reasonable interpretation of their movement. The present theory, fortunately, while it insists upon a distinction between normal and hypermetric, can deal with both without changing its fundamental principles. Before approaching the solution that these principles suggest, however, we must gain a clear understanding of the problem. To this end, we must first determine the limits of the discussion, and then glance briefly at two previous theories, those of Sievers and Heusler.

Since there are only eleven hypermetric lines (twenty-two verses) in *Beowulf*, it seems advisable to extend the investigation to Old English poetry in general. We must exclude *Genesis B*, because it is translated from Old Saxon, and retains some of the peculiarities of the latter; but no further restrictions are necessary. Not, indeed, that all poems have the same weight. The Cotton and Exeter gnomes, for example, show certain tendencies that distinguish them from the epic tradition. Some poems, such as *Daniel, Christ and Satan,* and *Solomon and Saturn,* seem to exhibit more textual corruption than usual. Others, notably *Christ III*, may owe their occasional laxity to the author rather than the scribe. Many employ hypermetric forms so seldom that their authority is slight. In spite of these inequalities, however, the main characteristics of the form are the same throughout.

Sievers published a list of hypermetric verses in Old English at the beginning of his first article on them (*Beiträge* 12. 454 f.). The list, which includes approximately 850 half-lines, is reasonably accurate, though Sievers often omitted to specify whether the line-numbers referred to both halves of a line or only one, and more recent editors than Grein, whose text Sievers employed, have sometimes altered the divisions of lines. For the convenience of the reader, I present herewith a corrected list. It must be remembered, however, that, both because certain verses can be treated as normal or hypermetric according to the context, and because our texts are far from reliable, no list can pretend to perfect accuracy.

1. *Beowulf* (ed. Klaeber): 1163-8, 1705-7, 2995 f. = 22 verses.

2. *Judith* (ed. Grein-Wülker or Cook): 2-12, 16-21, 30-34, 54-62a (as line 62 stands, unemended, it forms a hypermetric first hemistich, without a mate), 63-68, 88-95 (96a should probably be emended, but is normal in MS.), 96b-99, 132, 272 f. (273b should conclude with the first word of 274: *Hogedon þa eorlas aweccan*), 287 f. (rearranged as one line, as in Kluge's *Lesebuch*: *mid niðum neah geðrungen, þe we sculon [nu] losian*), 289 (with last word of preceding line: *somod æt sæcce forweorðan*, etc.), 290-91, 338-49, 350 (if the following emendation be admitted: *[sæs] ond swegles dreamas þurh his sylfes miltse*) = 136 verses.

3. Poems in the Vercelli Book (ed. Krapp):
   a. *Andreas*: 51, 303, 795 f., 799, 801b-802, 803b, 1022 f., 1114a = 19 verses.
   b. *The Fates of the Apostles* (omitted by Sievers): 98 f., 102 = 6 verses.

c. *The Dream of the Rood*: 8-10 (for 9b, which is corrupt, we might perhaps read, *Beheoldon þær engeldryhta fela*), 20-23, 30-34, 39a (39b and 40a must be read as normal, but they are probably an interpolation), 40b-43, 46-49, 59-69, (71b is normal but corrupt; the best emendation is [*stefn*] *up gewat*, not the hypermetric *syððan* [*stefn*] *up gewat*), 75, (102a is barely hypermetric as it stands; read *miht* for *mihte*, as Kluge suggests), 133 (but by reading *worulddreamum* for *worulde dreamum* we have a normal line, which seems better) = 64-66 verses.

d. *Elene*: 163, 580b-582a (according to Trautmann's rearrangement: *þæt eow sceal þæt leas apundrad / / weorðan to woruldgedale. / Ne magon ge ða word geseðan / /*; i. e. three verses, followed by a normal line, 582b in Krapp, with emendation: *þe ge hwile nu* [*hyddon*] *on unriht*), 583-9, 609 f., (631b looks hypermetric, but makes no sense; I think 631a, *rice under roderum*, may have crept in through omission of *hyht* in 629b, and suggest, for the whole line, *ge he ða rode* [*rice*]*ne tæhte*; cf. 607 and 623), 667 f., 701a (probably not 701b, which begins a new sentence and can only be hypermetric by courtesy), 1102b, 1157b, 1159b = 31 verses.

4. Poems in the Exeter Book (ed. Krapp-Dobbie):

a. *Christ II*: 621 = 2 verses.

b. *Christ III*: 888 f., 892b(?), 921a(and perhaps b), 981b(?), 1049a(?), 1107a(?), 1162-3a (probably not b), 1208a(?), 1304b(?), 1359(?), 1377b(?), 1380b(?), 1381-5, 1409b(?), 1422-4, 1425b, 1426b-1427, 1460b(?), 1463b(?), 1467b(?), 1487 f. (but 1488a is doubtful), 1495 f., 1513 f., 1546, 1560a = 42-58 verses. Most of the isolated half-lines that are here questioned can be read as normal. It is simply a question how much license can be admitted in the normal line. In most cases, I prefer the effect of normal readings.)

c. *Guthlac I* (including the first 29 lines, which used to be assigned to *Christ III*; it is noteworthy that the style of the hypermetric verses speaks loudly for this arrangement): 1-3, 5, 25, 80, 88-92, 190 f., 239-42, 289-91, 363, 376-9, 465-9, 510, 636, 701 f., 741 = 70 verses.

d. *Guthlac II*: 1110, 1158, 1160b-62, 1294-5a, 1301-3 = 18 verses.

e. *The Phoenix*: 10, 29, 630 = 6 verses.

f. *The Wanderer*: 65a(? Probably a slightly irregular instance of normal, expanded D), 92a(? Sievers thought this normal B, but the unstressed syllables are too heavy for this type), 111-15 (entirely regular) = 10-12 verses.

g. *Precepts* (*Fæder Larcwidas*): 17b-19 = 5 verses.

h. *The Seafarer*: 23, 103, 106-9 = 12 verses.

j. *The Fortunes of Men* (*Wyrda*): 15 f. = 4 verses.

k. *Maxims I* (*Gnomica Exoniensia*): 1-6, 30b, 35-45, 46 (arranged as two lines by Grein, and not counted by Sievers; 46 can be regarded as a normal long line, supplemented by 46b, a hypermetric half with the same alliteration), 47-53, 56-59, 62-64 (the last is like 46 above), 65-70, 98, 100-105, 109-14, 116, 124, 144-6, 147b, 149b, 151b(?), 164 (like 46 above), 167, 174 f., 181 f., (183 is not one line, but it cannot be divided sensibly until the meaning is agreed upon), 184-6, 192 f., 196b-198a, beside a number of hypermetric halves with double alliteration that stand alone: 54 f.(?), 168, 178-80, 188-90, 191(?) = 145-152 verses.
(For the suggestion that some verses are grouped stanzaically, see Sievers, *Beitr.* 12. 478 and *Altg. Metrik*, p. 144 f.

l. *The Order of the World* (*Schöpfung*): 98-100, 101 (an isolated half-line; *sigan* should begin the next line, which becomes hypermetric throughout), 102 = 9 verses.

m. *The Riming Poem*: 80-83 = 8 verses.
(I think that all the other suspiciously full verses, 14, 45, 55 f., the last group of which was called hypermetric by Sievers, are merely irregular. The rime seems occasionally to have interfered with metrical niceties.)

n. *Wulf and Eadwacer* (formerly *Riddle I*): Sievers cites 9a, but I think this is normal.

o. *Riddle 16*: 1, 2b, 3-4 (but probably Holthausen is correct in making 2a hypermetric also) = 7-8 verses.

p. *Riddle 40*: Sievers cites 5b, but I think this is corrupt.

q. *Resignation* (Sievers' *Hymn 4*): 1 (an isolated half-line), 2, 79 f. (If the text is correctly divided, 79a and 80b must be hypermetric, 79b may be, and 80a should be rearranged to read *gewitnad for worulde pisse.*) = 7 verses.

r. *The Lord's Prayer I* (Sievers' *Hymn 5*): 1b-5 (the first half-line is partially destroyed) = 9 verses.

5. Poems in the Junius MS. (ed. Krapp):

a. *Genesis A*: 44-46, 155 f., 913, 1015-19, 1522b-23, 2167-70, 2174, 2328 f., 2406 f., 2411 f., 2855-57a (2857b should probably be emended), 2858 f., 2866-9 (but 2869a, *men mid siðian,* is neither hypermetric nor normal, and should be emended to *mannan mid siðian,* following Schmitz and Holthausen) = 64 verses.

b. *Exodus*: 570b-74 (but 570a is corrupt, and may have been hypermetric originally, 573a is somewhat irregular, and 574b requires the customary emendation, *syððan hie þam [herge] wiðforon,* in order to be properly alliterative and hypermetric) = 9 verses.
(Sievers cites 411, but this is merely corrupt, apparently the remnant of two normal verses, and is now spread over lines 411-12.)

c. *Daniel*: 59a (but since this can better be interpreted as two normal half-lines, there is probably corruption some-where), 106 (certainly 106a and possibly 106b), 203-5, 207-8 (which form, if properly arranged, the second half of one hypermetric line and the whole of another, the obscurity of the passage suggesting that something is lost), 224-5 (226a lacks alliteration, and seems hopelessly corrupt), 226b-27, 232-5, 237 f., 239 (a single hypermetric half with no mate), 240-44 (245a, 246a, and 247a could all be classified as hypermetric, but are probably normal), 261a, 262-70 (265 is corrupt, lacking proper alliteration, but was evidently hypermetric), 271-3 (two hypermetric lines, when properly arranged), 434-7 (432-3 could be forced into a hypermetric pattern, but only 432b resists normal treatment, and this should probably be emended, with Cosijn and Schmidt, to *swa him gecyðed wæs*), 440, 443-5a, 446b-47, 449 (with questionable alliteration), 451-7 = ca. 99 verses.

d. *Christ and Satan*: 201-4 (dropping out from 202 the words *in wuldre mid,* which are repeated in the next line, and thus making two good hypermetric lines in place of the present jumble: *ecne alra gescefta; ceosan us eard in wuldre // mid ealra cyninga cyninge, se is Christ genemned*), 230a (perhaps corrupt, like 225a), 604a (probably corrupt) = 6-8 verses.

6. *The Meters of Boethius* (ed. Krapp): 5, 45; 7, 23 (with ir-

regular alliteration); 10, 67; 16, 1; 17, 11-12 (one line, if the text is allowed to stand); 25, 45 f.; 26, 79; 29, 31 f.; 31, 8 = 22 verses.

7. *Gnomica Cottoniana* (ed. Grein-Wülker): 1-4, 42-45, 47a = 17 verses.

8. *The Runic Poem* (*Runenlied,* ed. Grein-Wülker): 25-28 = 8 verses.

9. *Psalm 50,* Cotton MS. (ed. Grein-Wülker): 31 = 2 verses.

10. *Solomon and Saturn* (ed. R. J. Menner, *The Poetical Dialogues of Solomon and Saturn,* Modern Language Association, Monograph Series, 1941): 303 f., 318-22 and perhaps 323a, 329 f. (not 328b, which is too long to be normal but is not properly hypermetric), 358-61, 427, 443-9, 478, and perhaps the isolated 480b = 44-6 verses.
    (Sievers omitted this poem from his list, and with some reason, since the text is corrupt in some places and illegible in others; but the 22 whole lines cited above seem fairly certain. Professor Menner's edition supplies several new MS. readings and differs from Grein-Wülker in the numbering and sometimes in the arrangement of lines. The corresponding lines in Grein-Wülker are: 310 f., 325-9 and perhaps 330a, 336 f., 365-9 (making two lines of 365-7), 435, 451-8a (making one line of 457-8a), 486, and perhaps 488.)

The total number of verses is thus about 903-935.

The preceding list, insofar as it goes beyond a mere catalogue of verses that exceed normal limits and implies the existence of another equally definite form, rests upon certain structural principles that have not yet been defined. It must now be our task to determine these principles. Many of them were clear to Sievers, certain others to Heusler. Consequently, a review of their theories will clarify the problem to some degree. On the other hand, since the present theory of the normal verse has been based upon principles that neither of these men accepted, a correspondingly new theory of the hypermetric must obviously be devised. This new theory will emerge bit by bit in the course of the analysis of its predecessors.

SIEVERS

Sievers first expounded his theory of hypermetric verses in the *Beiträge zur Geschichte der Deutschen Sprache und Literatur,* 12 (1887). 454 ff. Later, in *Altgermanische Metrik* (1893), p. 135 ff., he had slightly modified his analysis in deference to Luick; but the essentials remained the same, and indeed the first account, being somewhat simpler, will serve our needs better than the second. Accordingly, we shall begin with the first.

The fundamental idea in Sievers' theory was that the hypermetric verse had three main stresses, and consequently three feet, instead of the two stresses and two feet of the normal verse. Occasionally, indeed, he detected a fourth stress, but he was inclined to regard this as an exception, and his classification of types was governed by the notion of three. He did not insist that the three stresses need be of equal force, because it was evident that the first was sometimes strong (*gán under gýldnum béage, Beowulf* 1163a) and sometimes weak (*þằr þā gódan twēgen,* 1163b); but he thought that each of the three was, by position as well as by strength, sufficiently prominent to govern a foot. Dividing his feet in accordance with his theory of the normal verse, he made what will appear, I believe, to be an important discovery. The second and third feet, taken together, were regularly indistinguishable from normal verses of one of the five types. Most of them belonged to type A, but a few to types B, C, D, and E. This discovery led to his first classification of the hypermetric types. He represented the first foot merely by his customary signs, ´, ˘, ×, etc., adding to these in each case the appropriate letter for the remainder of the verse. For the sake of clarity, I shall reproduce here the various patterns in the order which he first assigned to them, with examples for each.

I. ´ × ... + A, D, E.

1. Type ´ × . . . . . || ´ × . . | ´ × (A). As the dots show, several variations are included. The simplest form is exemplified by *wéaxan wítebrógan* (*Gen.* 45a), the commonest by *grímme wið gód gesómnod* (*Gen.* 46a). The first foot may be further expanded, both by the admission of secondary stress, *árlèas of éarde þínum* (*Gen.* 1019a), and by inclusion of as many as six unstressed syllables, *bétre him wǣre þæt hē bróðor áhte* (*Gn. Ex.* 174a). Monosyllabic anacrusis may likewise be admitted, *ālǣten līges gánge* (*Dan.* 262a), and even dissyllabic occasionally, *oft mon féreð féor bi túne* (*Gn. Ex.* 145a), though Sievers later gave *oft* a fourth stress, as we shall see. Similarly, the second foot may be augmented, though this is more conservative, and rarely admits more than two unstressed syllables, *óðrum áldor oðþringeð* (*Gen.* 1523a). Three is the limit, *dól bið sē þe him his drýhten ne ondrǣdeð* (*Seaf.* 106a).[1]

The examples given so far belong to the first half-line, and contain alliteration in the first foot, which is correspondingly emphatic. Characteristic of the second half-line, though sometimes present in the first, are verses in which the alliteration is delayed until the second foot. In these cases, the same patterns are discernible, but the first foot is weakly stressed. In many cases, indeed, the syllables of the first foot are so weak that Sievers assigned a stress to one of them merely for the sake of the metre. Thus, for the simplest form, Sievers cites *þù scealt geómor hwéorfan* (*Gen.* 1018b); for the commonest, *hǽfdon hīe wróhtgetéme* (*Gen.* 45b); for the fullest, with six unstressed syllables in

---

[1] Sievers could find only three examples of this form. The one cited may be reduced by elision. Another, *Gn. Ex.* 146b, should probably be reduced, as Sievers suggested, by altering *wulfas* to *wulf*. The third, *forhwón āhénge þū mec héfgor* (*Chr. III* 1487a), remains the only really persuasive representative, and even this is rendered dubious by other irregularities in its neighborhood.

the first foot and two in the second, *hè ūsic wile þāra lēana gemónian* (*Gn. Ex.* 6b).

It is understood, of course, that a grammatically long stressed syllable may be "resolved" into two, the first of which is short and stressed: e. g., *súnu mid swéordes écge* (*Gen.* 2858a). This phenomenon need not be further illustrated, since it does not alter the fundamental patterns of the verses.

Endings of type A are by far the commonest. Sievers counted 673 out of 819, or more than 80 per cent (*Beiträge* 12. 475), and my own count of a slightly smaller number of verses substantiates this figure. Next in importance, not in frequency (for indeed there is little to choose among the other types in this respect), but in clarity of form, are verses with endings of types D and E.

2. Type $\perp$ × . . . || $\perp$ | $\perp$ $\asymp$ × (D). Among verses of the first half-line, with strong openings, the simplest form is illustrated by *béalde býrnwiggènde* (*Jud.* 17a), the fullest by *Júdas hire ongēn þingòde* (*El.* 609a, 667a), and, with anacrusis, *ālédon hīe þēr límwērigne* (*Rood* 63a). Among verses of the second half-line, with weak openings, the simplest form is illustrated by *spræc þā ides Scýldinga* (*Beow.* 1168b), the fullest by *siððan hīe þone brýne fándèdon* (*Dan.* 454b).

3. Type $\perp$ × . . || $\perp$ $\asymp$ × . | $\perp$ (E). Among verses of the first half-line, with strong openings, the simplest form is illustrated by *swéord ond swātigne hélm* (*Jud.* 338a), the fullest by *wélan ofer wídlònda gehwýlc* (*Chr. III* 1384a). Among verses of the second half-line, with weak openings, the simplest form is illustrated by *him þæs grim lèan becōm* (*Gen.* 46b), the fullest by *genàmon hīe þēr ǽlmìhtigne Gód* (*Rood* 60b).

II. Other less determinate types.

4. Type × ⟙ || ⟙ × . | ⟙ × (A). Sievers regarded this as a variation of the first type above, but he listed it separately because of the possibility of dividing it differently, × ⟙ | ⟙ × || ⟙ ×, and calling it C+ ⟙ ×. It will appear later that the former division is preferable. Sievers noted only eight examples, all from the first half-line, and one of these will suffice: *ne féax fy̆re beswǽled* (*Dan.* 437a).[2]

5. Type ⟙ || .... × ⟙ | ≚ × (C). This type usually has a strong opening in the first half-line. The simplest form is *hríncg þæs héan lándes* (*Gen.* 2855a), unless *héan* be regarded as dissyllabic, or *grétan gódfy̆rhtne* (*Andr.* 1022a). The fullest is *scéomiende mon sceal in scéade hwéorfan* (*Gn. Ex.* 66a). The weak opening, characteristic of the second half-line, is exemplified by *hwæt ēac sǽ cy̆ð́de* (*Chr. III* 1163b) and *hwònne him eft gebýre wéorðe* (*Gn. Ex.* 104b). It is clear from these examples that, as Sievers admitted, this type can readily be confused with certain forms of the normal verse. The shorter forms with strong openings have exactly the same patterns as normal expanded D; and even the longest with weak openings are indistinguishable from normal C. It seems necessary to admit the type as hypermetric, however, because it occurs in hypermetric passages; and indeed the reason for its ambiguity will shortly be apparent. The same reservation applies to the type that follows, which can seldom be distinguished by its syllabic pattern from normal expanded Db or normal B.

6. Type ⟙ × ... | ⟙ × . | ⟙ (B).[3] Strong openings of

---

[2] I think there is no reason to suspect the authenticity of this rare form, but two of Sievers' examples are dubious: *geséoð sórga mǽste* (*Chr. III* 1208a), which stands in the midst of normal lines and may be corrupt, and *on þǽs þéostran wórulde* (*Chr. III* 1409a), where the MS. has *weoruld,* and the stress attributed to *þás* seems unlikely.

[3] The inconsistency of this notation was apparent to Sievers. He explained that he did not write ⟙ || ... × ⟙ | × . ⟙ because the verses seemed to

the first half-line range from the simple *éorðan ́yðum þéaht* (*Riddle 16.* 3a) to the full *gebídan þæs hē gebǽdan ne mǽg* (*Gn. Ex.* 104a), with monosyllabic anacrusis. Weak openings, mostly of the second half-line, range from the simple *þǽr him stéarn oncwǽð* (*Seaf.* 23b) to the full *hwǽðre hē in brēostum þā g ́yt* (*Andr.* 51b).

These were the fundamental types of hypermetric verses as Sievers first conceived them. Later, however, in *Altgermanische Metrik* (p. 135 ff.), he introduced several modifications, two of which deserve our attention. The first was a change in nomenclature suggested by Luick, who wished to think of the hypermetric verse, not as a normal one with an extra foot at the beginning, but as an amalgamation of two normal verses. Thus, the sequence ´ × ´ × ´ × was not to be called ´ × +A, but AA, as if two verses of type A had been fused in the fashion indicated by the following diagram:

$$A \;´\; × \;´\; ×$$
$$+A \qquad\quad ´\; × \;´\; ×$$
$$\overline{AA \;´\; × \;´\; × \;´\; ×}$$

Similarly,

$$B \; × \;´\; × \;´$$
$$+A \qquad\qquad ´\; × \;´\; ×$$
$$\overline{BA \; × \;´\; × \;´\; × \;´\; ×}$$

$$C \; × \;´\;´\; ×$$
$$+A \qquad\quad ´\; × \;´\; ×$$
$$\overline{CA \; × \;´\;´\; × \;´\; ×}$$

The adoption of this nomenclature seemed advisable to Sievers, not because he believed that any such fusion had really taken place, but because it enabled him to classify the hypermetric verses more completely. Accordingly, he now labelled eighteen different sequences with various combina-

---

arrange themselves more naturally the other way (*Beiträge* 12. 471); and in his summary, he changed his formula for the preceding type to ´ × . . . | ´ | ⌣ × (C), thus unconsciously bringing both closer to the sort of formula dictated by rhythmic principles.

tions of the five letters, using A, B, and C for the first two feet, and A, B, C, D, and E for the last two.

What was gained in convenience, however, was lost in accuracy. The last two feet are invariably identical with the five normal types, so that the letters that Sievers applied to them have a precise meaning; but in many instances the first two feet are not identical, only vaguely similar. For example, the verse *þæt hē wèse prísthýcgènde* (*Gn. Ex.* 49b) is called CD; but whereas *prīsthycgende* would pass for a D just as it stands (´ | ´ ` ×), *þæt hē wese prīsthycg-* can only be regarded as a C (× × ´‿× | ´ ×) by a large stretch of the imagination. All that the label CD means in this case is that the first foot has the pattern × × ´ ×, and is directly followed by ´. Again, under A*A Sievers includes *glēawe mèn sceolon gíeddum wrixlan* (*Gn. Ex.* 4a); but *glēawe men sceolon gieddum* (´ × ´ × × × | ´ ×), though it could be read as an A* (Sievers used the asterisk to denote expanded types), has at least exceptional weight in its first foot, and stands in marked contrast to the characteristically conservative pattern of the second and third feet, *gieddum wrixlan*. One could multiply instances of this sort of confusion, for the fact is that only the last two feet are consistently similar to the normal verse.

We shall save ourselves a good deal of unnecessary trouble, therefore, if we disregard these misleading symbols, and substitute others that are simpler and clearer. Sievers' first foot always contains either a strongly stressed syllable with alliteration, or a more lightly stressed syllable without alliteration. Let us call the first sort a strong opening, and label it H, for hypermetric. We can then call the second sort a weak opening, and label it h. Thus we shall have HA, HB, HC, HD, and HE for the verses with strong openings, and hA, hB, hC, hD, and hE for those with weak openings. This system has the apparent disadvantage of telling us nothing about the structure of the opening, but at this stage

of the investigation that is really an advantage; for we shall
find that Sievers' tendency to regard it as a foot comparable
to the others was misleading.

The second important modification in Sievers' theory
shows us one of the difficulties in the classification of openings. Sievers now admitted that some hypermetric verses
appeared to have four feet, not three. The particular
verses that he cited by way of illustration (*Altgermanische
Metrik*, p. 144) were not very happily chosen, because some
of them may be merely corrupt. Thus, *éalle him brímu
blódige þúhton* (*Ex.* 573a), though it certainly looks as if it
had four stresses, might be questioned because of its abnormal alliterative scheme. Again, *behéoldon þæt énglas
drýhtnes éalle* (*Rood* 9b, where the MS. has *engel*) is un-
doubtedly wrong, for no other verse of the second half-line
places the alliteration at the end of the opening, or doubles
it.[4] On the other hand, Sievers suggested that a number of
verses already classified as having only three feet might
better be read with four; and he gave several plausible examples, among them the verse already questioned, *glēawe
men sceolon gieddum wrixlan,* which he would now read
⌐× | ⌐× × | ⌐× | ⌐× , splitting the opening into two
feet. A cursory examination will show that almost all the
longer openings can better be regarded as two feet than as
one. Even when only one syllable demands stress by its
logical importance, another would naturally receive it in
consequence of the number of still less emphatic syllables
that surround it: e. g., *bétre him wǽre þæt hē brōðor áhte*
(*Gn. Ex.* 174a). If, therefore, we follow Sievers in assum-

---

[4] I have already suggested, in the list at the beginning of this section, the
possibility of reading *behéoldon þæt éngeldrỳhta féla* (or *feala*), which might
easily have been corrupted by a scribe into the nonsense of the MS. It is true
that *engeldryhta fela* passes for an E with difficulty, but normal verses like
morgenlongne dæg (*Beow.* 2894a) might justify it. Otherwise, we shall have
to content ourselves with emending *engel* to *englas*, and omitting *ealle*. (I have
passed over as irrelevant the question whether MS. *þær* need be emended to
þæt.) See further below, p. 223, n. 14.

ing that the hypermetric verse usually has three feet, we shall welcome his admission that it may sometimes have four.

These are the main outlines of Sievers' theory. We must now try to see whether it can be modified to fit the scheme that has been evolved for the normal verse. In examining the latter, we have seen that it is a comparatively simple matter to convert Sievers' two-foot types into two-measure variations of a basic form │♪̂ ♪ ♪ ♪│♪̂ ♪ ♪ ♪│. In types A, D, and E, the feet and measures are co-extensive, so that, for example,

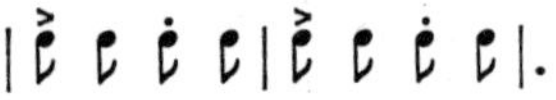

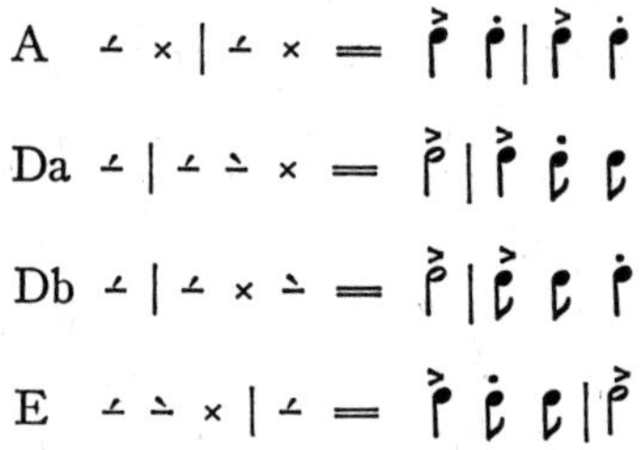

A � by musical notation⌟

$$ \text{A} \quad \angle \times \mid \angle \times \;=\; \hat{\text{♪}}\,\text{♪}\mid\hat{\text{♪}}\,\text{♪} $$

$$ \text{Da} \;\; \angle \mid \angle \; \angle \; \times \;=\; \hat{\text{♪}}\mid\hat{\text{♪}}\,\text{♪}\,\text{♪} $$

$$ \text{Db} \;\; \angle \mid \angle \; \times \; \angle \;=\; \hat{\text{♪}}\mid\hat{\text{♪}}\,\text{♪}\,\text{♪} $$

$$ \text{E} \;\; \angle \; \angle \; \times \mid \angle \;=\; \hat{\text{♪}}\,\text{♪}\,\text{♪}\mid\hat{\text{♪}} $$

In types B and C, on the other hand, we must shift the bars, so that, for example,

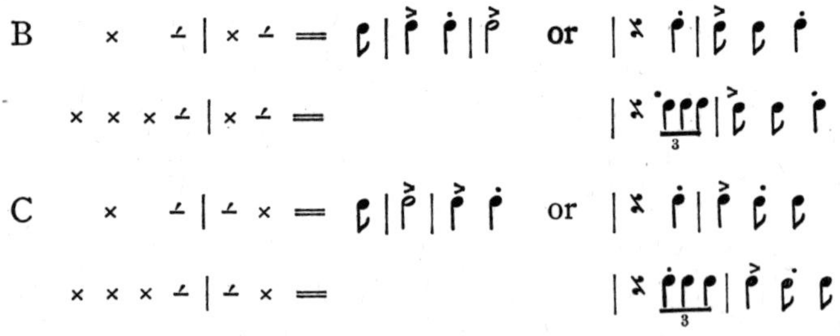

$$ \text{B} \quad \times \quad \angle \mid \times \; \angle \;=\; \text{♪}\mid\hat{\text{♪}}\,\text{♪}\mid\hat{\text{♪}} \quad \text{or} \quad \mid \times\; \text{♪}\mid\hat{\text{♪}}\,\text{♪}\,\text{♪} $$

$$ \times \; \times \; \times \; \angle \mid \times \; \angle \;=\; \mid \times\; \underset{3}{\text{♪♪♪}}\mid\hat{\text{♪}}\,\text{♪}\,\text{♪} $$

$$ \text{C} \quad \times \quad \angle \mid \angle \; \times \;=\; \text{♪}\mid\hat{\text{♪}}\mid\hat{\text{♪}}\,\text{♪} \quad \text{or} \quad \mid \times\; \text{♪}\mid\hat{\text{♪}}\,\text{♪}\,\text{♪} $$

$$ \times \; \times \; \times \; \angle \mid \angle \; \times \;=\; \mid \times\; \underset{3}{\text{♪♪♪}}\mid\hat{\text{♪}}\,\text{♪}\,\text{♪} $$

Extending the same principles to Sievers' three- and four-foot hypermetric verses, we find it a simple matter to read these with the corresponding number of 4/8 measures. A few examples will suffice:

Three Measures

HA   weaxan wītebrōgan   (*Gen.* 45a)

|ſ ſ |ſſ |ſ ſ |

grimme wið God gesomnod   (*Gen.* 46a)

|ſ ɕ ɕ |ſ· ɕ |ſ ſ |

HB   eorðan ȳðum þeaht   (*Riddle 16.* 3a)

|ſ ſ |ſ ſ |ſ ˟ |

HC   grētan godfyrhtne   (*Andr.* 1022a)

|ſſ |ſ |ſ   ſ |

HD   bealde byrnwiggende   (*Jud.* 17a)

|ſ ſ |ſ |ſ ɕ ɕ |

HE   welan ofer wīdlonda gehwylc   (*Chr. III* 1384a)

|ɕ ɕ ɕɕ |ſ ɕ ɕſ | ſ˟ |

hA   þū scealt geōmor hweorfan   (*Gen.* 1018b)

|ſ   ſ | ſ   ſ | ſ ſ |

Four Measures

HA   betre him wǣre þæt hē brōðor āhte   (*Gn. Ex.* 174a)

|ſ ɕ ɕ |ɕ ɕ ɕ   ɕ | ſ ſ |ſſ |

We shall not rest here; but it is clear that at least the
majority of hypermetric verses, taken singly, can be treated
as if one or two extra 4/8 measures had been prefixed to two
normal measures. Our new method of analysis shows, moreover, why the verses called HB and HC above can serve as
hypermetric or normal as occasion demands. Normal B and
C, when only one syllable precedes the alliteration, can be
read in two ways: ɕ|ſ ſ|ſ and ɕ|ſ|ſ ſ, or |˟ ſ|
ɕ ɕ ſ| and |˟ ſ|ſ ɕ ɕ|. In the former case, the three or
more syllables that begin with alliteration fill two measures,
in the latter only one. So, in HB above, the combination
ȳðum þeaht, which would pass for a B-verse minus its preliminary syllable, can fill two measures and form the close

of a hypermetric verse, or confine itself to one measure and form the close of a normal D-verse.

At first sight, therefore, the problem looks simple. Sievers, with his usual fidelity, has recorded the main stresses and the syllabic patterns, and we have only to substitute strictly defined measures for his feet in order to read the verses properly. Sometimes we shall have three measures, sometimes four, but the last two will always resemble those of normal verses. Unfortunately, there are a number of difficulties.

Chief among these is the fact that the transition from normal to hypermetric, when the two forms are interpreted in the way just now suggested, is almost painfully awkward. Probably Sievers did not feel such awkwardness, because his method of rhythmizing the normal verses, which was not exactly stated in his notation but may be inferred, was apparently very loose, more like prose than verse. Expecting in the normal verse, as a constant element, only two conspicuously prominent stresses, he did not feel that the transition from two to three, and from three to four, was at all troublesome. In the present theory, on the other hand, the normal verse assumes much greater formality, and the effect of this formality is to emphasize the idea of duality. The two verses that are paired to form a line consist of two measures each, and the measures themselves can be subdivided into two temporally equal parts. When, after a normal passage, we come suddenly upon a group of hypermetric verses, and try to produce three measures instead of two, we experience a considerable shock. The hypermetric passage seems incongruous. Moreover, the sense of incongruity is increased by the occasional intrusion of four measures, which in themselves would be compatible with two, but for that very reason mingle awkwardly with three.

In the second place, this mingling of threes and fours appears improbable. Hypermetric passages are seldom extensive. Why, then, should two forms rather than one have been employed? A change from the normal form to one equally definite, yet congruous, would add variety and at the same time preserve the sense of order. On the other hand, a change to an indefinite and only occasionally congruous form introduces a sense of confusion. It is almost as if we had come upon a section of prose.

In the third place, if we allot three measures to all verses except those that demand four, we shall find that we must set off most of these by extrametric pauses, because the measures themselves will generally be too full for rests. If we accept the theory of initial rests for normal verses, we ought to expect something similar in the hypermetric. Is it not possible, then, that what Sievers thought the exception was really the rule? Can we not allot two measures to each opening and two more to each close, and so not only make room for rests, but achieve a structure that is both uniform and congruous with the normal? Not quite; but I hope to show that this comes very close to the proper solution. We shall understand it better, however, by glancing briefly at Heusler's theory.

HEUSLER

In the previous criticism of Heusler's theory of the normal verse, his treatment of the hypermetric necessarily received some attention, because in his opinion the two forms were not to be distinguished.[5] To both he allotted two quadruple measures, to which he gave the same 4/4 time-signature. In his mind, therefore, the so-called hypermetric verses differed from the rest only by extra fullness, so that the syllables of which they are composed were spoken in a greater hurry. The ever-present difficulty and occasional impossibility of such readings at the tempo set by the normal verse have already been shown;[6] but we must look at another aspect of them, the way in which Heusler divided Sievers' three-stress verses into two parts.

Sievers had already suggested, for analytical purposes, a twofold division into opening and normal close, though in his scheme the opening was usually only half as long as the close. Moreover, we have seen that some openings carry alliteration and correspondingly heavy stress, whereas others lack alliteration and have correspondingly light stress. Heusler began by relegating these weak openings to the position of anacrusis—extrametric, as usual. Having thus disposed of them, he had nothing left to measure but the close, which, as already stated, is the exact equivalent of a normal verse—or, in the case of types B and C, of that portion of a normal verse which begins with alliteration. If one grants Heusler his extrametric anacrusis, there is no difficulty here, for these verses with weak openings become nothing but normal ones with more anacrusis than usual.

---

[5] Heusler's discussion of hypermetric verses will be found in *Deutsche Versgeschichte* 1. 180-7 and *passim*.
[6] Above, p. 28.

With strong openings, on the other hand, the case is different. Here, Heusler could not get rid of the extra sylla-bles by placing them outside the bounds of his measures. What he did was to allot one measure to the opening and one to the close. In Sievers' scheme the close has two equivalent stresses, and is treated just like a normal verse; in Heusler's, the second stress is subordinate to the first, and the whole close is restricted to half the time of a normal verse.

The results of this system can best be seen by applying it to a consecutive passage. Let us take the six hypermetric lines in *Beowulf* numbered 1163-8. Though Heusler em-ployed a 4/4 notation, we must reduce this to a 4/8 for the sake of comparison with the normal line. With this modifi-cation, then, Heusler's notation would run approximately as follows:

gān under gyldnum bēage   þǣr þā gōdan twēgen

sǣton suhtergefǣderan;   þā gȳt wæs hiera sib ætgædere,

ǣghwylc ōðrum trȳwe.   Swylce þǣr Unferþ þyle

æt fōtum sæt frēan Scyldinga;   gehwylc hiora his ferhþe trēowde,

þæt hē hæfde mōd micel,   þēah þe hē his māgum nǣre

ārfæst æt ecga gelācum.   Sprǣc ðā ides Scyldinga ...

Were it not for one vital suggestion, we might dismiss this reading as in every respect inferior to that of Sievers. Its weaknesses, indeed, are all too apparent. Heusler's extrametric anacrusis, troublesome enough in the normal verse, becomes so regular and cumbersome a feature of the hypermetric that it can only be described as preposterous. And even if we could accept this anacrusis, we should still be perturbed by the contrasts in pace within those portions of the lines that Heusler measured. His reading obliges us to pass without warning, and for no reason that appears in the spirit of the words themselves, from the leisurely movement of the close that follows a weak opening to the breakneck haste of the verse with a strong opening.

The one vital suggestion lies in the treatment of the verses with strong openings—and not in their pace, but in the relation between opening and close. Unlike Sievers, who regarded the strong opening as one of three (rarely two of four) equivalent members of the whole verse, Heusler regarded every strong opening as one of two equivalent members. The shortest and the longest of these openings were made to fill exactly the same amount of time as the normal close, and the corresponding division of the verse into two measures subordinated the duality of the close to the larger duality of the whole. It is clear that this structure, if we can assure ourselves of its correctness, will be preferable to that of Sievers; for it will be uniform in itself and at the same time consistent with that of the normal verse.

The proof of its correctness rests upon two characteristics of the verses, their logical structure and the position of the alliteration. Since the five verses with strong openings in the passage just quoted are typical in both respects, they will serve as models for the whole class. We see at once that each of these five verses has double alliteration, and that Heusler's structure accords perfectly with its position by placing it at the head of each of the two measures.[7] The logical phrasing is likewise clarified by this structure. If we draw a line in each of the five verses at the point where

---

[7] Single and triple alliteration are occasionally found in verses with strong openings, but these irregularities do not interfere with the established pattern. A full account of the alliteration will be found on p. 152 ff. below.

a logical phrase-division can most easily be made, we shall discover that this line always falls somewhere between the first syllable of the opening and the first syllable of the close:

gān / under gyldnum bēage
sǣton / suhtergefæderan
ǣghwylc / ōðrum trȳwe
æt fōtum sæt / frēan Scyldinga
ārfæst / æt ecga gelācum

We may notice also that *sǣton, æt fōtum sæt,* and *ārfæst* are at least as closely united to the phrases that precede them as to those that follow. Now it is regularly characteristic of the verses with strong openings to separate opening from close by placing a minor phrase-division at or near the end of the opening, and enjambment of the preceding verse is very frequent. Consequently, the logical duality of these verses is very strongly marked. Heusler's metrical structure emphasizes it by giving the same amount of time to opening and close, and only one primary accent to each.

In this one respect, therefore, Heusler apparently came nearer the truth than Sievers. The latter's triple division of *gān under | gyldnum | bēage* gives us three equivalent stresses and thus obscures the pattern suggested by dual alliteration and dual phrasing. Even the fourfold division that was suggested at the end of the analysis of Sievers' theory, *gān | under | gyldnum | bēage,* is inferior to the two-fold, because this fourfold division, though consistent with the phrasing, fails to emphasize it sufficiently. Besides, the infrequency of two strongly stressed syllables in the opening (note the weakness of *under*) offsets the regularity of two such stresses in the close (*gýldnum béage*), and shows us plainly that a consistently dual pattern can only be achieved by following the lead of the alliteration and sub-ordinating the second stress of the close to the first. Indeed,

9

there is an exact analogy for this procedure in type D of the normal line. *Lēof lēodcyning* has double alliteration, and, being composed of two words, a dual logical structure. Despite the disparity in number of syllables and stresses, therefore, we have been able to give this verse a correspondingly dual metrical structure. We do not set up three measures, *lēof* | *lēod-* | *cyning,* but two, *lēof* | *lēodcyning.* With precisely the same justification, Heusler set up the two measures *gān under* | *gyldnum bēage,* and we shall find that this structure supplies us with an important clue to the problem. We are now ready, therefore, to attempt its solution.

THE NEW THEORY

In the course of the preceding discussion, several important features of the hypermetric verse have emerged. From a study of Sievers, we have learned not only the syllabic patterns that these verses assume, but also two highly significant characteristics which they share in common: first, a close that is identical in structure with the normal verse, and second, two sorts of openings, strong with alliteration, and weak without alliteration. From a study of Heusler, we have learned that the verses with strong openings have a dual logical and alliterative pattern which can be matched by a dual metrical structure.

Certain desiderata have also become clear to us. The first and most obvious of these, perhaps, is a basic metrical uniformity—a uniformity which was partially denied by Sievers when he admitted four-foot verses by the side of three, and by Heusler when he refused to measure the weak openings and assigned to the closes that follow these openings a markedly different pace from that which he bestowed on the verses with strong openings. Other desiderata, however, become apparent when we consider the fact that the hypermetric verses, though they almost always occur in groups, are closely associated with the normal verses that surround them. On the one hand, we cannot feel that the hypermetric verses ought to have the same metre as the normal, because, in all but a few cases, they differ markedly from the normal in syllabic structure. Here Sievers is superior to Heusler. On the other hand, the metre of the hypermetric verses ought to be sufficiently similar to that of the normal to make the transition between one and the other easy. Here Heusler's dual structure is superior to Sievers' triple. Moreover, the normal close ought to have the same pace as the normal verse, because the two are structurally identical. Here Sievers satisfied the requirement always, Heusler only when he was dealing with verses that had weak openings. Finally, the new theory that has been advanced for the normal verse makes it desirable to introduce into the hypermetric the most conspicuous feature of that theory—the means by which the rhythm of a normal passage maintains an unbroken continuity without detriment to the half-line phrasing—the initial rest. All these desiderata can be obtained by what is now a fairly obvious interpretation of those features of the hypermetric verse that were mentioned in the preceding paragraph.

Let us start with the strong opening, and make one change in the scheme suggested by Heusler. Keeping his two measures, let us double the time of each of them, producing two measures of 4/4 time instead of two of 4/8.[8] Instead of

gān under gyldnum bēage,

| ♩ ♪ ♪ | ♪ ♪   ♪ ♪ |

we shall have

gān under gyldnum bēage.[9]

| ♩ˣ ♫ | ♩ ♩   ♩ ♪ ♪ |

The advantages of this reading are plain. We have a metre that is different from the normal, just as the syllabic pattern would lead us to expect, yet one that is sufficiently similar to the normal to make the transition easy. Indeed, that transition is really easier than in Heusler's reading, because, while

[8] Heusler, as I have said before, used 4/4 time for both normal and hypermetric, but for this reason his 4/4 is not the same as mine. In his system, the quarter-note is the maximum quantity for a short syllable; in mine, the eighth-note. My 4/4 time, therefore, is equivalent to what Heusler would have called 4/2.

[9] Or | ♩ ♩ ♩ | ♩ ♩ ♩ ♪ ♪ |, because the stressed syllable of *under* is long and can therefore be doubled like the others; but I think this word is too unimportant for the longer quantities, and the rest helps the phrasing. This is one of the consequences of the difference between Heusler's 4/4 and mine. See the preceding note.

the time of each measure is doubled, the range of quantities remains the same. The normal close occupies exactly the same amount of time as a normal verse. Thus we overcome every weakness of Heusler's reading while retaining its advantages. The desired uniformity of structure cannot be fully attained unless we can bring the weak opening into harmony with the strong, but in verses with strong openings we need expect no trouble, for by allotting a whole 4/4 measure to the opening we have left ample room for Sievers' four-stress variation. We must now see, therefore, whether the weak opening will adapt itself to the same scheme.

The problem is very simple at this stage. In order to fill two 4/4 measures with a verse that has a weak opening, we need only apply the principles that were set forth for the normal types B and C. Before every weak opening there is a phrase-division, and the opening itself leads up to the close. As with types B and C, therefore, we must insert an initial rest, assign the relatively unimportant syllables of the opening to the latter part of the first measure, and put the weighty close in the second measure. We must read,

þǣr þā gōdan twēgen.

| ♩ ♩ ♩ | ♩ ♩ ♩ ♩ |

We have now everything that was required. We have a uniform metre, two 4/4 measures to each half-line. We have a distinction between weak and strong openings, and a like treatment of the like closes that follow these openings. We have a duality that corresponds to both the logic of the verses and the structure of the normal metre. We have, therefore, an ease of transition between normal and hypermetric, which is further assisted by the fact that the syllables of the close occupy exactly the same amount of time as they would in a normal verse.[10] Finally, we have an initial

---

[10] The tempo of the hypermetric verse as a whole gives the effect of being slower, because the normal close is conservative in its admission of extra sylla-

rest before each weak opening, which means that, in general, every other verse is set off sharply from its predecessor, yet the rhythm proceeds without break as in the normal passages.

So far as the main principles are concerned, there is no more to be said. The two measures of 4/4 time, one for the opening and one for the close, the spreading of the syllables of the strong opening over the whole of the first measure, with internal rests if they are needed at the point where the phrasing breaks, the confinement of the syllables of the weak opening to the latter part of the first measure after a rest—these are the essentials. They will be sufficiently illustrated by the notation of a few characteristic lines. In view of the emphasis of this book, it seems proper to select the eleven hypermetric lines of *Beowulf*, which appear in three passages, the one already quoted as an illustration of Heusler's theory, and two others:

1163 gān under gyldnum bēage   þǣr þā gōdan twēgen

sǣton suhtergefæderan;   þā gȳt wæs hiera sib

ætgædere,

ǣghwylc ōðrum trȳwe.   Swylce þǣr Unferþ þyle

bles, and still more because the opening has often only two or three syllables. Thus, while the quantitative range is the same, long quantities are more frequently employed. This effect of slowness is entirely in keeping, I believe, with the spirit of the lines. I have avoided using this as an argument because it is easy to deceive oneself about the spirit of a line when one does not know its metre, and still easier when one thinks one does; but I am not alone in my opinion. Cf. Sievers, *Altgermanische Metrik*, p. 216 (§ 185), where he speaks of the hypermetric tempo as solemn and slow ("feierlich-langsam") and assigns as one reason for this opinion the specific employment of the form for the expression of solemn and emphatic moods ("zum ausdruck feierlicher und emphatischer stimmungen"). The average quantities of the syllables in Sievers' three-stress reading would hardly differ from the normal, so that he can be considered a relatively unprejudiced observer.

DESCRIPTION IN TERMS OF THE NEW THEORY

A full description of the hypermetric form would involve a classification of all the variants according to opening, close, and alliteration. Enough has already been said about the close, however, in the course of the presentation of Sievers' theory. We have learned that more than eighty per cent of the closes have the pattern of type A, and that the rest are about evenly distributed among the other four types. We must remember, of course, that the close always begins with a stressed syllable, so that it can resemble only that portion of type B or C which follows the preliminary syllables. Otherwise, the identity with normal types is exact, and there is no need to discuss the notation of the variants. The 4/4 measure to which they are invariably to be assigned fills exactly the same time and has virtually the same characteristics as two 4/8 (or 2/4) measures. It may be thought of as a compound of two such measures in which the first takes a slight precedence of the second in the strength of its primary accent. The close arranges itself, therefore, in the 4/4 measure with exactly the same quantities as it would have if it were a normal verse accommodating itself to two 4/8 measures. This being so, we can turn all our attention to the various kinds of openings and the alliterative patterns.

1. *Weak Openings*

Weak openings, though sometimes encountered in the first half-line, are typical of the second.[12] They are dis-

---

[12] There are some 439 weak openings in the second half-line against 36 strong, whereas the first half-line has about 381 strong openings against 80 weak. The various poems differ considerably in the frequency with which they admit weak openings into the first half-line. Thus *Beowulf* admits 1 out of 11, *Judith* 1 out of 67 (excluding line 2a, which should read *gifena in ðys ginnan*

æt fōtum sæt frēan Scyldinga;   gehwylc hiora his ferhþe

trēowde,

þæt hē hæfde mōd micel,   þēah þe hē his māgum nǣre

ārfæst æt ecga gelācum.   Spræc ðā ides Scyldinga...

1705   ðīn ofer þēoda gehwylce.   Eal þū hit geþyldum healdest,

mægen mid mōdes snyttrum.   Ic þē sceal mīne gelǣstan

frēode, swā wit furðum sprǣcon.   Ðū scealt tō frōfre

weorþan...

2995   landes ond locenra bēaga,—   ne ðorfte him ðā lēan oðwītan

mon on middangearde,   syðða[n] hīe ðā mǣrða geslōgon...

The full effect of these lines—the slow emphasis of the
strong openings, the relaxation, amounting sometimes almost to conversational garrulity, of the weak openings, the
even stability of the closes—can hardly be felt unless they
are taken in their context of normal lines,[11] to which they
present an interesting and agreeable contrast. Taken alone,
they show at any rate how easily they adapt themselves to
the proposed metre, and they furnish a good illustration of
the variations that are commonly found within the limits of
the form. But since there are, after all, a great many variations which they do not exhibit, a more detailed description
of that form in the light of the principles just set forth will
now be presented.

[11] The first six are so presented among the specimen notations in Part III,
p. 196 f. below.

tinguished from strong openings by two characteristics, the
lack of alliteration and the corresponding lack of heavily
stressed syllables. It is necessary to state both these characteristics, because neither of them is a sufficient guide by
itself. Thus, there are a few openings which rank as weak
despite the presence of alliteration. Conversely, some openings have syllables that are strong enough to be heavily
stressed, and only their lack of alliteration shows that
the poet wished to subordinate them. These trifling inconsistencies will be understood if we examine the details.

The scheme of the second half-line, whether normal
or hypermetric, calls for alliteration on the first heavily
stressed syllable and on that alone. In the hypermetric verse
with a strong opening, as in types A, D, and E of the
normal verse, this syllable comes at the beginning. In the
hypermetric verse with a weak opening, on the other hand,
as in types B and C of the normal verse, it comes at the
start of the second measure, the close, after a number of
preliminary syllables. Now it sometimes happens in the
normal verse of type B or C that one of the comparatively
insignificant syllables of the opening echoes the main alliteration of the line. In the verses *hū hit Hrĭng-Dĕne, ŏþ
þæt him ĕft onwŏc,* and even *ŏðer ĕarmscĕapen* (*Beowulf*
116b, 56b, 1351b), the most prominent of the preliminary
syllables picks up the alliteration in this way; yet however
much this supplementary sound may add to the euphony of
the verse, and however conspicuous it may seem, we must
not count it as a part of the structural scheme of the line,
because the first really important syllables are *Hring-, eft,*
and *earm-,* and it is on these that the structure of the line
depends. In all probability, the poet was either unconscious
of or indifferent to the correspondence of the preliminary

grunde), *Genesis A* 1 out of 31, *The Dream of the Rood* none out of 33; but
the *Exeter Gnomes* (*Maxims I*) 15 out of 77, *Daniel* 11 out of 51, and *Guthlac
I* 18 out of 35.

syllables. In just the same way, when we encounter such hypermetric verses in the second half-line as *swylce ēac sīde byrnan* (*Judith* 338b) or *gewītan him wērigferhðe* (*Judith* 291b) or *ōðer bið ēadig swīðe* (*Solomon and Saturn* 358b), we recognize that the structural alliteration is supplied by *sīde, wērig-,* and *ēadig,* and that we must disregard the correspondence of the subordinate words, *swylce, gewitan,* and *ōðer.* There are, indeed, only about twenty-five of the four hundred and thirty-nine verses with weak openings in the second half-line that show this correspondence, and in most of these the preliminary syllables are less conspicuous than in the examples cited. The comparative weakness of the syllables, combined with the unorthodoxy of double alliteration, is decisive. In the second half-line, therefore, the weak opening can always be recognized.[13]

In the first half-line, however, the alliterative pattern is more flexible. Double alliteration is the rule, yet both single and triple are occasionally found. It is sometimes hard, therefore, to decide whether an opening that contains alliteration and words of medium strength, neither as strong as those that follow nor altogether negligible, is to be considered strong or weak. Definitely weak, I should say, are the openings in *Forhwòn āhēnge þū mec hēfgor* (*Christ III* 1487a), *Ond èac þā èaldan wùnde* (*Christ III* 1107a), and *Swā cwæð snòttor on mōde* (*Wanderer* 111a). More doubtful is the opening of *oferdrēncte his dùguðe èalle* (*Judith* 31a), though I should much prefer to read the verse with an initial rest, giving *-drencte* secondary accent and so treat-

---

[13] That the poets were careful to avoid double alliteration on the two heavy stresses of the second half-line (that is, on the two primary accents in the case of strong openings, and on the primary and strong secondary of the close in the case of weak) is shown by the fact that I have found only one exception, and that in a technically inferior or corrupt poem: *swā mīn gewyrhto wæron* (*Resignation* 80b).

ing it like a weak opening.[14] Doubtful also is *Ic þec ofer eorðan geworhte* (*Christ II* 621a). The verse sounds more natural to me when read with an initial rest and a secondary accent on *þec*, but perhaps the Lord, who is speaking, was expected to confer an unusual dignity on *Ic*. In that case it would take primary accent, count as an alliterating syllable, and make the opening strong. Doubtful as these verses are, however, they are among the very few in which any conflict arises between the desire to stress an alliterating syllable and the desire to treat an opening as weak.

The second characteristic of a weak opening, its lack of heavily stressed syllables, requires further definition. In order to be weak, the opening must be less heavily stressed than the close. Consequently, the strongest class of words —nouns, adjectives, participles, and infinitives—is definitely excluded.[15] There is no other restriction, however. Such comparatively important words as finite verbs, adverbs, the correlative *ōðer* (the one . . . the other), and the indefinites *sum, ǣnig, fela, eall* (which do not rank with the ordinary noun-adjective group) are freely admitted so long as the close has words of the first group. But strong openings likewise admit this secondary group of words, especially finite verbs. Ultimately, therefore, where this group is in-

[14] Perhaps the first half-line admits a kind of compromise between strong and weak openings—namely, a semi-strong opening with heavy secondary accent and alliteration. See further under the description of strong openings.

[15] Three weak openings contain infinitives: *sēcan him ēce drēamas* (*Daniel* 440b), *gehēawan þysne morðres bryttan* (*Judith* 90a), and *ōðer him ongan wyrcan ðurh dierne cræftas* (*Solomon and Saturn* 443b). Only the first is a clear exception to the rule, and it is justified by the fact that *sēcan* introduces an amplifying variation of the previous half-line (*Ðā gewāt se engel up[þe]*), so losing its normal force and admitting an initial rest. Compare the normal B-verse, *sēcan dēofla gedræg* (*Beowulf* 756a). The second has to be read like a strong opening in spite of the lack of alliteration, because *gehēawan*, in order to follow directly upon *mōte* at the end of the preceding verse, must take primary accent. (Has *gehēawan* been substituted for some other word? I can think of nothing that would fit except possibly *gemearcian.*) The third has too many syllables for comfort, and I suspect that we ought to substitute *worhte* for *ongan wyrcan.*

volved, the distinction between strong and weak openings has to be made on the basis of the presence or absence of alliteration—or, in the rare cases when alliteration seems accidental, of the logical and syntactical structure of the passage.

The number of syllables in weak openings varies from two to eight. If there are only two syllables, the first is always long and stressed, the second potentially long. That is, the second syllable may be short if it is enclitic, and so capable of extension by an ensuing rest. If proclitic, on the other hand, it is always long—and never a mere prefix, but an independent monosyllable. Thus, *oððe* can be used, but not *on ge-,* nor even (apparently) *ond ðurh-.* Two monosyllables are most commonly employed.[16] The upper limit, eight, was presumably not fixed by any rule. Very few openings have more than five syllables, and the usual number is three or four.[17]

In order to adjust the weak opening to the 4/4 measure,

---

[16] The line between hypermetric verses with short weak openings and normal verses with anacrusis is fairly sharp. More than 80% of the hypermetric verses have closes of type A, and among these the two-syllable opening is by no means uncommon. On the other hand, type A in the normal line rarely admits anacrusis, and when admitted this is monosyllabic or (exceptionally) a short dissyllabic combination like *ofer.* In other words, the gap between normal ´ x | ´ x and hypermetric ` – | ´ x ` x is seldom filled. The pattern ` | ´ x ´ x is slightly irregular for a normal verse, impossible for a hypermetric. Three apparent exceptions (the only ones I have encountered) are easily emended: for *and swegles drēamas* (*Judith* 350a) we should almost certainly read *sǣs and swegles drēamas*; for *ond twēon swīðost* (*Elene* 668a), *ond on twēon swīðost*; and for *ond blōtan sylf* (*Genesis* 2857b), which as it stands can only be normal B, something like Holthausen's *ond hine blōtan sylfa.* There are no instances whatever in hypermetric contexts of two syllables of the forbidden sort.

[17] If we count a short stressed syllable and its successor as one, the range in *Beowulf* is from 2 to 5, with an average of 3.8; in *Genesis A* from 2 to 5, with an average of 3.1; in *Judith* from 2 to 5, with an average of 3.4; in *Daniel* from 2 to 6, with an average of 3.3; in *Christ III* from 2 to 6, with an average of 3.3; in *Elene* from 2 to 5, with an average of 3.6; in the *Exeter Gnomes* (*Maxims I*) from 2 to 6, with an average of 3.6; in *Guthlac I* from 2 to 7, with an average of 3.8; in *The Dream of the Rood* from 2 to 6, with an average of 4.5; and in *Solomon and Saturn* from 3 to 8, with an average of 4.4.

one must follow a procedure similar to that which has been advocated for the preliminary syllables of normal B and C. Since the weak opening introduces a new phrase and leads up to the close,[18] any rest that is needed to fill out the measure must come at the beginning. Initial rests are, indeed, the rule. When they are employed, the strongest syllable of the opening—usually but not necessarily the first—receives the secondary accent of the measure, and the other syllables adjust themselves as they best can. The second half of the measure, in consequence of the fact that two syllables of the pattern ´ ⁻ are the minimum, is always filled. Only rarely is there so large a number of syllables that the initial rest is omitted and the entire measure filled. Such instances do occur, however, just as in the case of preliminary syllables of normal B and C. Then the first strong syllable takes primary, the second secondary accent; but since no syllable in the opening requires as much emphasis as the first syllable of the close, the accentuation of the first measure as a whole becomes less vigorous than that of the second.

The principal variations in number and arrangement of syllables are illustrated by the following list:

Two Syllables

þū scealt geōmor hweorfan   *Gen.* 1018b

| ⁻ 𝄽 𝄽 | 𝄽 𝄽   𝄽 𝄽 |

oðþæt fīra bearnum   *Jud.* 33b

| ⁻ 𝄽 𝄽 |𝄽𝄽 𝄽 𝄽 |

oððe sundoryrfes   *Jud.* 340b

| ⁻ 𝄽 𝄽 |𝄽 𝄽 𝄽𝄽|

---

[18] The only exception is *Judith* 90a, *gehēawan þysne morðres bryttan,* already mentioned as an anomaly—in reality a strong opening that lacks alliteration.

Two Syllables Resolved [19]

hyre ðæs Fǽder on rŏderum   *Jud.* 5b

Three Syllables

Ongån þā rŏdera wăldend   *Gen.* 2406b

sǣgde him unlȳtel spĕll   *Gen.* 2407b

frǣgn hine dægrīme frŏd   *Gen.* 2174b [20]

þā hīe oðlǽded hăfdon   *Ex.* 570b

Three Syllables Resolved

þŏne sculon burhsĭttende   *Gen.* 2328b

Four Syllables

þĕah ðe hīe hit frĕcne genĕðdon   *Ex.* 571b

þurh þā heora bĕadosearo wǣgon   *Ex.* 573b

sĕnde him of hĕan rŏdore   *Dan.* 235b

þā hē wŏlde măncyn lȳsan   *Rood* 41b

---

[19] I have not troubled to illustrate the substitution of ⏑ × for – except at the point of greatest stress.

[20] The alliteration of the line is *d*. The *f* of the two secondary accents illustrates a rare, probably accidental phenomenon.

Four Syllables Resolved

hwæðere heora feorh generede   *Dan.* 233b

Geweotan ðā ðā wītigan þrȳ   *Andr.* 801b

Five Syllables

forðām þe hīe his cræftas onsōcon   *Dan.* 225b

sē ðe hīe of ðām mirce generede   *Dan.* 447b

curfon hīe ðæt of beorhtan stāne   *Rood* 66b

hwīlum hit wæs mid wǣtan bestēmed   *Rood* 22b

hnāg ic hwæðre þām secgum tō handa   *Rood* 59b

Five Syllables Resolved

gedyde ic þæt þū onsȳn hæfdest   *Chr. III* 1382b

Six Syllables

gestōdon him æt his līces hēafdum   *Rood* 63b

siððan hē hæfde his gāst onsended   *Rood* 49b

mid þȳ ic þē wolde cwealm āfyrran   *Chr. III* 1425b

gif hē nȁt hwā hine cwícne fēde *Gn. Ex.* 113b

Wȃ biȝ ȝonne ȝissum mȏdgum mȍnnum *Sol.* 318a

Six Syllables Resolved

hē ūsic wíle þāra lēana gemȍnian *Gn. Ex.* 6b

Seven Syllables [21]

nǣfre gē mèc of þissum wórdum onwȅndaȝ *Gu. I* 376a

Eight Syllables [21]

ȏȝer him ongan wyrcan ȝurh dȋerne crǣftas *Sol.* 443b

These examples show virtually all the possible variations of the weak opening. One is often uncertain which of a number of unimportant syllables to stress, and which of the openings with four or more syllables to read without initial rests; but these uncertainties are of small consequence. There is no weak opening that will not adjust itself to the 4/4 measure.

2. *Strong Openings*

Except in the gnomic poems, where antithetical formulas cause a marked departure from the usual practice, strong

[21] These are the only examples with seven and eight syllables. That with eight is probably incorrect, because it can scarcely be read in the allotted time. I have already suggested that *ongan wyrcan* has been wrongly substituted for *worhte*.

openings are almost entirely confined to the first half-line.[22] They are marked by alliteration and correspondingly prominent syllables. The number of syllables varies from two to eight, as does that of the weak opening, but the rhythmization of these syllables presents certain difficulties, which can best be understood by a systematic consideration of the syllabic patterns. These may be divided for convenience into the following categories: (a) those that begin with a long stressed syllable, (b) those that begin with a short stressed syllable, (c) those that begin with one or two unstressed syllables that can be treated as anacrusis, and (d) those that, beginning with unstressed and ending with stressed syllables, must be treated somewhat like weak openings. Under (a) and (b) are included about 81 per cent of the strong openings; under (c) about 16 per cent, and under (d) the remaining 3 per cent. Under a fifth heading (e) are presented the few verses of the preceding categories that can be regarded as pairs of normal rather than genuine hypermetric verses.

a. The Sequence $\acute{}$ × . . . . .

About sixty-eight per cent of the strong openings are of this pattern. The number of syllables varies from two to seven.[23] If there are only two syllables, the second must be potentially long: that is, either enclitic or, if proclitic, a

[22] They occur in the second half as follows: *Genesis A* once (2869b), *Daniel* once (449b; but this is almost certainly corrupt, because *se* alliterates), *Apostles* once (98b), *Rood* once (40b; but by omitting 39b–40a, which are suspect on other grounds, we obtain a weak opening with alliteration on *gealgan*, where it belongs, instead of on the mere finite verb *gestāh*), *Christ III* four times (1162b, 1514b, 1424b, and 1652b, the last two very doubtful), the *Meters of Boethius* once (7, 23b—a very dubious verse), *Solomon and Saturn* four times (304b, 427b, 303b, and 361b, the last two with crossed and transverse alliteration respectively). In contrast to these poems, containing thirteen examples at most, and to those containing none, stand the *Exeter Gnomes* with seventeen out of seventy-one and the *Cotton Gnomes* with six out of eight.

[23] A single syllable occurs in the opening of *Gen.* 2869a, *men mid sīðian*, but Holthausen rightly emends *men* to *mannan* (*monnan*).

10

separate word, not a mere prefix. In consequence of this restriction, the second syllable can always receive quarter-note quantity in the 4/4 measure. The minimal forms with enclitic and proclitic second syllables are thus illustrated by the following examples:

fēran folces rǣswan   *Jud.* 12a

blīðe, burga ealdor   *Jud.* 58a

frēoð hȳ fremde monnan   *Gn. Ex.* 102a

mon on middangearde   *Beow.* 2996a

sweord and swātigne helm   *Jud.* 338a

Ān is ælmihtig god   *Gu. I* 242a

More than a third of the openings of this pattern have only two syllables, but three, four, or five syllables are not uncommon, six openings have six syllables, and two have seven. The following are characteristic examples:

THREE SYLLABLES

landes ond locenra bēaga   *Beow.* 2995a

mǣl sceolon tīdum gongan   *Gn. Ex.* 124b

torht tō his trēowum gesīþe   *Gu. II* 1295a

Four Syllables

frēode, swā wit furðum sprǣcon   *Beow.* 1707a

wurpon hyra wǣpen ofdūne   *Jud.* 291a

Bǣron mē ðǣr beornas on eaxlum   *Rood* 32a

lāþað hine līþum wordum   *Gu. I* 363a

Five Syllables

mēðe æfter ðām miclan gewinne   *Rood* 65a

Lȳtel þūhte ic lēoda bearnum   *Chr. III* 1424a

or 𝄞 𝄞 *with elision*

Til biþ sē þe his trēowe gehealdeþ   *Wand.* 112a

Six Syllables

forht ic wæs for þǣre fægran gesyhðe   *Rood* 21a

ārode þē ofer ealle gesceafte   *Chr. III* 1382a

Seven Syllables

betre him wǣre þæt hē brōþor āhte   *Gn. Ex.* 174a

Ēadig bið sē þe in his ēþle geþihð   *Gn. Ex.* 37a

or 𝄞𝄞

It naturally happens that, when there is a large number of syllables in a strong opening, a syllable that takes secondary accent will be rather heavily stressed even when it is a relatively unimportant part of speech. We need not be surprised, therefore, to find that the secondary accent sometimes falls on a prominent word like *þūhte* in the example cited above, *Lȳtel þūhte ic lēoda bearnum,* or like *men* in *Glēawe men sceolon gieddum wrixlan* (*Gn. Ex.* 4a). The second members of compounds are freely admitted into openings with two or three syllables, and occasionally into those with four:

swiðmōd sinces brytta   *Jud.* 30a

ārfæst æt ecga gelācum   *Beow.* 1168a

winhātan wyrcean georne   *Jud.* 8a

lāðsearo lēoda cyninges   *Dan.* 435a

mundbyrd æt ðām mǣran þēodne   *Jud.* 3a

hyhtlīce in heofona rīce   *Rime* 83a

It has been stated above that the strong opening is characterized by alliteration and correspondingly prominent syllables. In the sequence now under discussion, there are thirty-one openings (about eleven per cent) in which the strongest syllable belongs to a finite verb, while the closes that follow all but one of these, *wealleð swīðe geneahhe* (*Sol.* 427b), contain words of the noun-adjective class.

There is also one opening in which the weak adverb *swā* takes precedence by alliteration of *ānra gehwæs* in the close: *Swā bīoð ānra gehwæs* (*Meters* 7, 23b). Whenever, as in the two examples just cited, the alliteration is confined to the opening, there can be no question of the proper reading. The alliterating syllable, however unimportant, must receive primary accent. There are altogether, however, only three instances of this phenomenon, the third being *læg ic on heardum stāne* (*Chr. III* 1424b). The twenty-nine other openings of this sort occur in the first half-line and are supplemented with alliteration in the close. It seems possible, therefore, that these openings should be treated as a compromise between weak and strong—that is, with initial rests and strong secondary accents on the alliterating syllables. In fifteen instances the initial rest would be out of place because of the structure of the sentence, but in the remaining fourteen it seems either distinctly desirable or possible. For example, no rest can be inserted before *sǣton* in the clause (*Beow.* 1163b-1164a),

þǣr þā gōdan twēgen

sǣton suhtergefæderan.

In fact a comma might very well be employed after *sǣton* to express its affinity with the preceding verse. On the other hand, an initial rest would be entirely in order before *healdað* in the following pair of clauses (*Gu. I* 89b-90a):

bēoþ hyra gēoca gemyndge,

healdað hāligra feorh.

No doubt it is impossible to be certain of the proper treatment of openings like this last, but a few openings to be considered under (b) and (d) below make it advisable to note the plausibility of readings with initial rests for what might be called semi-strong patterns of syllables.

b. The Sequence ◡◡× × . . . .

About thirteen per cent of the strong openings begin with short stressed syllables. Since we are accustomed to reckon a short stressed syllable and its successor as the equivalent of one long stressed syllable, we should expect to find that the minimum opening of this sort contained three syllables of the pattern ◡◡× ×. That is indeed the case,[24] but there is a further distinction to be made. In the opening of the hypermetric verse, the combination ◡◡× is not necessarily equivalent to ́, because it cannot always be extended, as can ́, to half-note quantity. This difference is reflected in the avoidance of certain combinations in the minimal sequence.

Thus, when the first syllable is long, the minimal sequence ́ × consists of a dissyllable 67 times, a compound (́ ́) 20 times, and a monosyllable plus a proclitic monosyllable 29 times. When, on the other hand, the first syllable is short, the minimal sequence consists of a trisyllable only twice, a compound (◡ × ́) 4 times, and a dissyllable plus a proclitic monosyllable 16 times. The reason for this striking difference in the proportions lies, presumably, in the fact that a simple trisyllable of the pattern ◡◡× × can fill only half of a 4/4 measure, whereas a compound (◡◡× ́) or a dissyllable plus a proclitic monosyllable (◡◡× + −) can fill at least three quarters of a measure. The limitation of the trisyllable arises from the circumstance that neither a short

---

[24] *The Lord's Prayer I* 3a reads *noma niþþa bearnum*, but this solitary exception could easily be emended to *noma mid niþþa bearnum*.

stressed syllable nor an unstressed medial syllable can take
more than eighth-note quantity. For example, the word
opene in *opene inwidhlemmas* (*Rood* 47a), if it is to receive
primary accent, must be read with the rhythm | ♫♩ ♩ ▬ |,
which leaves a disturbingly long rest before the close, and
contrasts itself unfavorably with the rhythm of the word
rōfe in *rōfe rondwiggende* (*Jud.* 20a), which can be read
with the rhythm | ♩ ♩ ˣ |. This difficulty does not arise with
the compound *egesful* in *egesful eorla dryhten* (*Jud.* 21a),
which, because of the enclitic nature of the second syllable,
can be read with the rhythm | ♪ ♩. ♩ |, nor with the words
mægen mid in *mægen mid mōdes snyttrum* (*Beow.* 1706a),
which can be read with the rhythm | ♪ ♩. ˣ ♩ |. It seems
proper to conclude, therefore, that simple trisyllables of the
form ⌣ ⌣ˣ ˣ were too short for the strong opening, and
should be regarded as not only rare but unorthodox.[25]

With this reservation, there is no essential difference
between the opening that begins with a short stressed syllable plus a complementary unstressed syllable and that which
begins with a long stressed syllable. Probably because the
short stressed syllable is less common, the openings that
contain it are fewer, and the maximum number of syllables
is only seven, the equivalent of six in the other sequence.
Examples are as follows:

[25] The two instances are *opene inwidhlemmas* (*Rood* 47a) and *trymede
tilmōdigne* (*Gen.* 2167a). The latter could be emended to *trymede hine,* or
excused as a semi-strong opening with initial rest (| ▬ ♫♩ ♩ |). The
former also would admit an initial rest, but the adjective ought to take primary
rather than secondary accent. I cannot avoid the suspicion that we should read
opne. Apparently this spelling has not been recorded, but there are two normal
verses in the *Elene* (791a and 1101a) in which the substitution of *geopnie* and
geopnigean for the MS. forms with *e* seems equally necessary. Cf. also, less
decisively, *Beow.* 3056b, *hord openian.*—A third opening, *Frige mec* in *Frige mec
frōdum wordum* (*Gn. Ex.* 1a), is probably acceptable, because *mec* may be
delayed long enough to take secondary accent (| ♪ ♩. ♩ ˣ |), or the whole may
be treated as a semi-strong opening and confined to the second half of the
measure after a rest (| ▬ ♫♩ ♩ |).

Three Syllables

mægen mid mōdes snyttrum   *Beow.* 1706a

egesful eorla dryhten   *Jud.* 21a

Four Syllables

boren æfter bencum gelōme   *Jud.* 18a

reced ofer rēadum golde   *Gen.* 2406a

roderas and rūme grundas   *Jud.* 349a

bealofull his beddes nēosan   *Jud.* 63a

Five Syllables

wunode under wolcna hrōfe   *Jud.* 67a

Gearo wæs sē him gēoce gefremede   *Dan.* 232a

Six Syllables

lifiað on ðisse lǣnan gesceafte   *Sol.* 319a

egeslīc of þǣre ealdan moldan   *Chr. III* 888a

(or like the preceding)

mete bygeþ, gif hē māran þearf   *Gn. Ex.* 110a

SᴇᴠᴇN Sʏʟʟᴀʙʟᴇs

Bifode ic þā mē se beorn ymbclypte *Rood* 42a

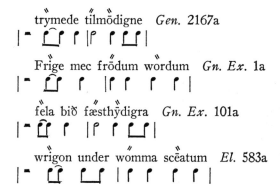

or

There are only four openings that, by the character of
their most prominent words and their readiness to admit
initial rests, might be classified as semi-strong:

trymede tilmōdigne *Gen.* 2167a

Frige mec frōdum wordum *Gn. Ex.* 1a

fela bið fæsthȳdigra *Gn. Ex.* 101a

wrigon under womma scēatum *El.* 583a

The first two have already been discussed. The third must
almost certainly be read in the suggested fashion, because
the *fela* is correlative with a second *fela* in the succeeding
half-line, where it cannot be allowed to count as an alliterating word. The third can easily be read as a full-fledged
strong opening.

One opening with seven syllables remains to be mentioned :

Scēomiande man sceal in sceāde hweorfan *Gn. Ex.* 66a

I believe that this is the correct reading, but the verse might
be treated like those mentioned below under (e), as a pair
of normal verses :

Scéomiande mán sceàl in sceáde hwéorfan.

The awkwardness of the rest is the chief argument against this otherwise plausible interpretation.

c. The Preceding Sequences with Anacrusis

It was affirmed by Sievers, and has been more exactly shown in this book, that the normal verse, with certain exceptions that need not concern us here, admits monosyllabic anacrusis freely, and dissyllabic sparingly. So likewise does the hypermetric verse, which follows the example of the normal and the dictates of the established rhythm in limiting this anacrusis, whether monosyllabic or dissyllabic, to such vocables as can be compressed within the time of an eighth-note. Some sixty-three strong openings appear to have monosyllabic anacrusis, some three dissyllabic. In all, these constitute about sixteen per cent of the strong openings. They have both long and short stressed syllables—about fifty-one long and fifteen short. In the following examples, a short stressed syllable and its successor are counted as one:

THREE SYLLABLES

beheáfdòd heáldend úre   *Jud.* 290a

gefriðode, frymða Wáldend   *Jud.* 5a [26]

[26] Without anacrusis, this would be unorthodox, as explained above under (b). There is one other verse in *Judith* (60a, *geðafian, þrymmes Hyrde*) that resembles this in syllabic sequence and syntax. In both these the modern editor has indicated by the insertion of a comma that the opening is more than usually distinct from the close. A third opening lacks the comma (*Judith* 32a, *āgotene gōda gehwylces*) and might be treated as semi-strong ( ), but is probably an acceptable companion to the others. No other poem employs this form.

beswyled mid swātes gange   *Rood* 23a

𝄐 | 𝅘𝅥 ᵡ 𝅘𝅥 | 𝅘𝅥 𝅘𝅥 𝅘𝅥 𝅘𝅥 |

Four Syllables

gebrōht on his būrgetelde   *Jud.* 57a

𝄐 | 𝅘𝅥 ᵡ 𝅘𝅥 𝅘𝅥 | 𝅘𝅥· 𝅘𝅥 𝅘𝅥 𝅘𝅥 |

āwyrged tō wīdan aldre   *Gen.* 1015a

𝄐 | 𝅘𝅥 𝅘𝅥 𝅘𝅥 | 𝅘𝅥 𝅘𝅥 𝅘𝅥 𝅘𝅥 |

gerēnode rēadum golde   *Jud.* 339a

𝄐 | 𝅘𝅥 𝅘𝅥 ᵡ | 𝅘𝅥 𝅘𝅥   𝅘𝅥 𝅘𝅥 |

æt fōtum sæt frēan Scyldinga   *Beow.* 1166a

𝄐 | 𝅘𝅥 𝅘𝅥 𝅘𝅥 ᵡ | 𝅘𝅥   𝅘𝅥 𝅘𝅥 𝅘𝅥 |

begoten of þæs guman sīdan   *Rood* 49a

𝄐 | 𝅘𝅥 𝅘𝅥· ᵡ 𝅘𝅥 𝅘𝅥 | 𝅘𝅥 𝅘𝅥· 𝅘𝅥 𝅘𝅥 |

Gefreoþa ūsic, frymþa scyppend   *Phoen.* 630a

𝄐 | 𝅘𝅥 𝅘𝅥· 𝅘𝅥 𝅘𝅥♪ | 𝅘𝅥 𝅘𝅥 𝅘𝅥 𝅘𝅥 |

Five Syllables

se rīca on his reste middan   *Jud.* 68a

𝄐 | 𝅘𝅥 𝅘𝅥 𝅘𝅥 𝅘𝅥 | 𝅘𝅥 𝅘𝅥 𝅘𝅥 𝅘𝅥 |

Bedealf ūs man on dēopan sēaþe   *Rood* 75a

𝄐 | 𝅘𝅥 𝅘𝅥 𝅘𝅥 𝅘𝅥· 𝄐 | 𝅘𝅥 𝅘𝅥 𝅘𝅥 𝅘𝅥 |

biwundenne mid wonnum clāþum   *Chr. III* 1423a

𝄐 | 𝅘𝅥 𝅘𝅥 𝅘𝅥 𝅘𝅥 | 𝅘𝅥 𝅘𝅥 𝅘𝅥 𝅘𝅥 |

þurhdrifan hī mē mid deorcan næglum   *Rood* 46a

𝄐 | 𝅘𝅥 𝅘𝅥 𝅘𝅥 𝅘𝅥· 𝄐 | 𝅘𝅥 𝅘𝅥 𝅘𝅥 𝅘𝅥 |

Six Syllables

geworhton him þǣr tō wǣfersȳne *Rood* 31a

gefǣstnodon mē þǣr fēondas genōge *Rood* 33a

Ongyrede hine þā geong hǣleð *Rood* 39a

Seven Syllables

āhōfon hine of ðām hefian wīte *Rood* 61a

Eight Syllables

āfielde hine ðā under foldan scēatas *Sol.* 449a

The only possible examples of dissyllabic anacrusis are the three that follow, all with the prefix *ofer-*:

oferdrencte his duguðe ealle *Jud.* 31a

oferwinnað þā āwyrgdan gǣstas *Gu. I* 25a

ofercumen biþ hē, ǣr hē ācwele *Gn. Ex.* 113a

These readings are by no means certain, however. The last verse is so irregular in alliteration that it is probably corrupt. The other two would run more smoothly if read as semi-strong, with initial rests:

oferdrencte his duguðe ealle

| ˣ 𝄐 𝄐 𝄐 𝄐 | 𝄐 𝄐 𝄐 𝄐 |

oferwinnað þā āwyrgdan gæstas

| ˣ 𝄐 𝄐 𝄐 𝄐 | 𝄐 𝄐 𝄐 𝄐 |

The semi-strong reading might also be preferable for some of the verses that have been credited with monosyllabic anacrusis. Among those most susceptible of this treatment are the following:

Geseah ðā swiðmōd cyning   *Dan.* 268a

| ˣ 𝄐 𝄐 𝄐 𝄐 | 𝄐 𝄐 𝄐 𝄐 |

Wearð fǣhþo fȳra cynne   *Gn. Ex.* 192a [27]

| ˣ 𝄐 𝄐 𝄐 𝄐 | 𝄐 𝄐 𝄐 𝄐 |

forlǣteð þās lǣnan drēamas   *Gu. I* 3a

| ˣ 𝄐 𝄐 𝄐 𝄐 | 𝄐 𝄐 𝄐 𝄐 |

Hwā dear ðonne dryhtne dēman   *Sol.* 329a

| ˣ 𝄐 𝄐 𝄐 𝄐 | 𝄐 𝄐 𝄐 𝄐 |

tōberað þec blōdgum lāstum   *Gu. I* 289a

| ˣ 𝄐 𝄐 𝄐 𝄐 | 𝄐 𝄐 𝄐 𝄐 |

d. Irregular Sequences

We must now consider thirteen openings which depart from the others in seemingly forbidden ways. Ten of these have the pattern × . ´ or × . ˘‿×. That is, the most prominent syllable, which should take primary accent, is final if long, penultimate if short, so that the problem of filling the 4/4 measure is acute. A fair example is the following:

---

[27] This verse is unlike the others in that *fǣhþo* should take primary accent, but the weight of *wearð* makes it unsuitable for anacrusis. Perhaps the two words should be transposed, *Fǣhþo wearð*; but see section (d) immediately below.

in fæðm fȳres līge　*Dan.* 233a

𝄐 |𝄐 ⁻|𝄐 𝄐 𝄐 𝄐|

The long rest between opening and close that this reading requires seems indefensible. On the other hand, all the verses in question can readily admit initial rests. It seems necessary, therefore, despite the prominence of the alliterating syllable, to treat them as semi-strong. Here is the complete list so treated:

in fæðm fȳres līge　*Dan.* 233a

|ˣ 𝄐 𝄐 　|𝄐 𝄐 𝄐 𝄐|

nē feax fȳre beswǣled　*Dan.* 437a

|ˣ 𝄐 𝄐 |𝄐 𝄐 𝄐 𝄐 𝄐|

on æht [28] ealdfēondum　*Dan.* 453a

|ˣ 𝄐 𝄐 |𝄐 𝄐 𝄐|

onwrēon [29] wyrda gerȳno　*El.* 589a

|ˣ � 𝄐 𝄐 　 |𝄐 𝄐 𝄐 𝄐 𝄐|

gesēoð [30] sorga mǣste　*Chr. III* 1208a

|ˣ , 𝄐 𝄐 　|𝄐 𝄐 𝄐 𝄐|

gemon morþa lisse　*Rime* 82a

|ˣ , 𝄐 𝄐 |𝄐 𝄐 𝄐 𝄐|

tō cwale cnihta fēorum　*Dan.* 225a

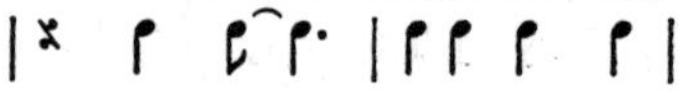

|ˣ 𝄐 𝄐 𝄐· |𝄐 𝄐 𝄐 𝄐|

onwrige worda gongum　*Gu. II* 1161a

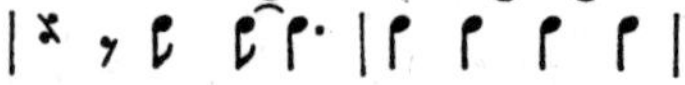

|ˣ , 𝄐 𝄐 𝄐· |𝄐 𝄐 𝄐 𝄐|

---

[28] MS. *ond nahte.*

[29] Or *onwrēon,* which would be entirely regular (♪| ♩ ♩ ˣ |).

[30] Or *gesēoð,* which would be regular. I have included this verse because it is certainly hypermetric as it stands, but it is isolated and almost certainly corrupt. (Instead of *On wērigum sefan / gesēoð sorga mǣste* the true reading might have been *Gesēoð on wērigum sefan* (type B, alliteration *w*) / *sorga mǣste.*)

ac þæt fȳr fȳr scȳde   *Dan.* 265a [81]

ne se brȳne bēotmæcgum   *Dan.* 264a [82]

Still another opening has the sequence ⌣ × × ⌣⌣×, where the full stress at the end carries the alliteration, yet the first syllable must receive primary accent if the words are to be adjusted to the 4/4 measure:

ealle him brimu blōdige þūhton Ex. 573a

A bare possibility is the reading,

ealle him brimu,

but this seems unlikely, for *ealle*, though it does not rank in importance with ordinary adjectives, generally receives more emphasis than this. Possibly the words should be reversed, *brimu ealle him* (|♪ ♩. ♩ ♫♩|), or possibly some deeper corruption has entered into the verse. There remains a chance, however, that the MS. is correct, and that this irregularity, which involves a real precedence of the secondary over the primary accent, is to be explained as a startling instance of a general tendency on the part of the long 4/4 measure to split into two 2/4 measures.

The two remaining openings, with the pattern × × ⌣ ×,

[81] The second half alliterates with *sc* instead of *f,* showing that something is wrong, but this half is acceptable in itself. (Substitute *firene* for *scylde* in the second half?)

[82] The last two verses could be differently divided, since the closes might be made to contain all the important words, leaving for the openings—weak, of course—only *ac þæt* and *ne se* (*nē sē*). This seems unlikely, however, in view of the other examples in this list from the same poem.

offer some confirmation of this tendency. The preliminary syllables are too prominent to be treated as anacrusis. Indeed, the openings are exactly equivalent to normal verses of the A3 type, in which the alliteration belongs to the second measure only:

þā wearð yrre ānmōd cyning   *Dan.* 224a

óft mon fēreð feor bi tūne   *Gn. Ex.* 145a

These two verses—especially the last—raise the question whether the hypermetric verse may not sometimes become indistinguishable from a pair of normal verses. This question is considered in the next section.

e. Openings that Resemble Normal Verses

It is clear that the hypermetric verse had a pattern of its own, one which can seldom be confused with that of a pair of normal verses. Whereas the second measure always resembles a normal verse, the first, despite its temporal equivalence, is ordinarily very different in syllabic pattern and consequently in rhythm. This applies even to the longer openings. For example, *Glēawe men sceolon gieddum wrixlan* (*Gn. Ex.* 4a), though it approximates a combination of types D and A, maintains its special hypermetric character by the proclitic nature of *sceolon,* which associates itself more readily with the close than with *Glēawe men.* Normal D, unlike C, very rarely runs on in this fashion.

Occasionally, however, we encounter hypermetric verses in the first half-line that could just as well be regarded as pairs of normal verses. An instance is *Beowulf* 1166a, *æt fōtum sæt / frēan Scyldinga,* which adjusts itself perfectly to the hypermetric scheme, yet cannot be distinguished from two normal verses of types B and D. In the gnomic poems

this phenomenon becomes not only conspicuous but troublesome. Seven times in the Exeter Gnomes and once in the
Cotton we encounter openings that are indistinguishable
from normal verses. Sometimes these openings have double
alliteration, which is otherwise unexampled, and sometimes
the hypermetric structure, which demands primary accent
at the beginning of the close, has to be abandoned altogether
if we are to give due recognition to the phrasing that an
analogous normal pair would require. In the following
examples, I have used dotted bars to indicate the additional
measures of the normal scheme wherever the hypermetric
reading would be substantially the same, and four full bars
in the two instances where it would be different:

widgongel wīf word gespringeð   *Gn. Ex.* 64a

Wīf sceal wiþ wer wǣre gehealdan   *Gn. Ex.* 100a

trymman ond tyhtan þæt hē teala cunne   *Gn. Ex.* 46a

Fela scēop meotud þæs þe fyrn gewearð   *Gn. Ex.* 164a

or

Hȳ twēgen sceolon tæfle ymbsittan   *Gn. Ex.* 181a [33]

Swā monige bēoþ men ofer eorþan   *Gn. Ex.* 167a [33]

oft mon fēreð feor bi tūne   *Gn. Ex.* 145a [33]

[33] The openings of these three verses resemble respectively normal B, B, and

11

Þēof sceal gàngan þȳstrum wēderum   *Gn. Cott.* 42a

|ſ· ſ |ſ ſ |ſ ſ |ʃ ſ|

Sievers may well have been correct in supposing that these gnomic forms were to be regarded as sporadic evidence of a strophic formation akin to the Old Norse, in which a normal long line of two verses is linked by alliteration to a hypermetric half-line.[34] Certainly such verses as these are rare or non-existent in other poems. Nevertheless, whether we are dealing with a consciously different form or an accidental variation of the hypermetric scheme, it is important to recognize the fact that the transition from the genuine hypermetric to the pair of normal verses is extremely easy. Consequently, these freakish verses provide a confirmation of the 4/4 reading of the others.

3. *The Alliterative Patterns*

Although the essentials of hypermetric alliteration have already been mentioned, a full description has been withheld until now, in order that all the details of hypermetric structure might be brought to bear on the problem. Let us begin by adopting a set of symbols to represent the four main accents of the hypermetric verse and the presence or absence of alliteration at these points. An x will serve for the primary or secondary accent of each measure: $x\, x \mid x\, x$. If any of these accents can be omitted by the substitution of a rest, we shall designate the fact by enclosing the x in parentheses: $x\, (x) \mid x\, x$ or $(x)\, x \mid x\, x$. Alliteration at one of these points will be designated by substituting an a for the

A3. The readings given are proper to these normal types or to the semistrong hypermetric type exemplified under (d) above.

[34] *Altgermanische Metrik*, p. 145, and *Beiträge* 12. 478.

x: a (x) | x x or (x) x | a x. The supplementary alliteration that occurs in crossed or transverse patterns will be indicated by b: a x | b x, etc.

In the second half-line, single alliteration is the invariable rule except in crossed or transverse patterns.[35] This alliteration must introduce the first of the two most prominent syllables, as in the normal verse, or the first of the three most prominent in the case of strong openings. With strong openings, it comes at the beginning of the first measure; with weak, at the beginning of the second. Since weak openings are almost exclusively employed in the majority of poems, the ordinary pattern for the second half-line is (x) x | a x, the occasional one a (x) | x x. There is no third possibility except with crossed or transverse alliteration, which will be considered presently.

In the first half-line, alliteration may be single, double, or triple, though in the overwhelming majority of verses it is double.[36] Out of 17 possible examples of single alliteration, 15 occur in conjunction with weak openings and have the pattern (x) x | a x.[37] The two others, which have the strong pattern a x | x x, are *girwan up swǣsendo* (*Jud.* 9a), where I suspect that we should read *girwan up gyteswǣsendo* (cf.

---

[35] Probably corrupt or careless is the solitary instance of double alliteration, *swā mīn gewyrhto wǣron* (*Resignation* 80b). Other instances are only apparent, as explained above, p. 127 f.

[36] Out of a total of 467 first half-lines (a figure which includes a few verses that are probably corrupt rather than hypermetric) I count 17 with single alliteration, 429 with double, 17 with triple, 3 with crossed, and 1 with transverse.

[37] Four of these might be said to have double alliteration, a x | a x or (x) a | a x, if one counted the alliteration on a weakly stressed syllable in the opening: *Ic þec ofer eorðan geworhte* (*Chr. II* 621a), *Ond ēac þā ealdan wunde* (*Chr. III* 1107a), *Swā cwæð snottor on mōde* (*Wand.* 111a), and *ǣr þæt ēadig geþenceð* (*Rime* 80a). One other verse, *gehēawan þysne morðres bryttan* (*Jud.* 90a), ought to rank as a strong opening, because *gehēawan* takes primary accent. That it does not alliterate with *morðres* is surprising and may indicate corruption. The fifteen are distributed as follows: *Judith* 90a, *Daniel* 447a, *Elene* 163a, 668a, *Christ II* 621a, *Christ III* 1107a, 1377a, 1488a, *Wanderer* 111a, *Order of the World* 98a, *Riming Poem* 80a, *Riddle 16*, 4a, *Lord's Prayer I* 4a, *Solomon and Saturn* 443a, *Meters of Boethius 25*, 45a. A few of these might be regarded as instances of crossed alliteration.

gytesālum in line 22b), and *Cyning sceal rīce healdan* (*Gn. Cott.* 1a), which may be correct, though one is tempted to substitute *cynedōm* for *rīce*.

Out of some 429 examples of double alliteration, 347 have the typical strong pattern, a (x) | a x, and 65 the typical weak pattern, (x) x | a a. Besides these, there are 16 with the semi-strong pattern (x) a | a x,[38] and one with the highly questionable pattern a x | x a.[39]

Out of 17 possible examples of triple alliteration, 9 have the pattern a x | a a,[40] 4 the pattern (x) a | a a,[41] and 4 the pattern a a | a x.[42]

Crossed alliteration occurs three times, twice with the whole-line pattern a x | b x || (x) x | a b, once with the whole-line pattern a x | b x || a x | b x. Transverse alliteration occurs once with the whole-line pattern b x | a x || a x | b x.[43]

These numerous patterns are summarized in the following table:

---

[38] Included here are the verses like *in fæðm fȳres līge* (*Dan.* 233a) listed as irregular sequences under strong openings (Section 2d above), and a few others that seem relatively certain. The number might be swelled by the addition of several verses that have been included under the regular strong type, a (x) | a x.

[39] This is the troublesome verse already mentioned, *ofercumen biþ hē ǣr hē ācwele* (*Gn. Ex.* 113a). Except that it occurs in an otherwise irregular poem, it would certainly be considered corrupt.

[40] *Judith* 2a (*gifena in ðȳs ginnan grunde,* where editors have placed *gifena* wrongly at the end of the preceding incomplete verse), *Daniel* 270a, 237a, 204a, and 266a (perhaps (x) a | a a), *Christ III* 1162a, *Seafarer* 106a, *Cotton Gnomes* 3a, *Runic Poem* 28a.

[41] *Christ III* 1487a, *Exeter Gnomes* 54 (no mate), *Solomon and Saturn,* 358a, 329a. All these could be regarded as instances of double alliteration of the form (x) x | a a, because the syllable that takes secondary accent in the first measure is relatively unimportant.

[42] All four belong to the *Exeter Gnomes*: 114a, 46a, 100a, and 64a. The secondary accent in the first measure may carry alliteration only by accident in the first of these, since the syllable concerned is the comparatively unemphatic indefinite pronoun *mon*. The last three verses are among those that should probably be considered as normal pairs rather than hypermetric.

[43] The crossed alliteration may be found in *Genesis* 2867 and *Solomon and Saturn* 303 and 320; the transverse in *Solomon and Saturn* 361. The latter poem has crossed alliteration in the following normal lines: 214, 226, 254, and 256. See also note 37 above.

	First Half-Line				Second Half-Line			
Single,	a (x)	x x	2	‖	(x) x	a x	427	
	(x) x	a x	15	‖	a (x)	x x	34	
Double,	a (x)	a x	347					
	(x) x	a a	65					
	(x) a	a x	16					
	a x	x a	1					
Triple,	a (x)	a a	9					
	(x) a	a a	4					
	a a	a x	4					

Crossed

a x	b x	‖	(x) x	a b	2
a x	b x	‖	a x	b x	1

Transverse

b x | a x ‖ a x | b x   1

A remarkable correspondence should be noticed between the hypermetric and the normal patterns. The normal verse, though only half as long, has the same quadruple structure. If we chart its alliteration in the same way, according to the primary and secondary accents of each measure, we shall find identical patterns for the second half-line and the first four variations of the first half-line. The forms with single alliteration are much more frequently represented in the first half of the normal line, but it is clear that the same principles are at work. The patterns characteristic of hypermetric verses with weak openings, (x) x | a x and (x) x | a a, are duplicated on a smaller scale by types A3, B, and C of the normal verse. Those characteristic of hypermetric verses with strong openings, a (x) | x x and a (x) | a x, are duplicated by the other normal types. Only the semistrong form (x) a | a x and the forms with triple alliteration (not to mention the erratic a x | x a) are peculiar to the hypermetric verse, and these are readily accounted for by its greater length.[44] The crossed and transverse patterns, though rare, have exact parallels in the normal line.

[44] It is tempting to suppose that the pattern (x) a | a x may be represented in the normal scheme by a few verses of the first half-line that have been classed with type D. These are verses that begin with finite verbs. Several of them could be read with initial rests and secondary rather than primary accent on the verbs. For example, *onband beadurūne* (*Beow.* 501a) could be read | ♩ ♪ ♩ | ♪ ♪ ♪ ♪ | instead of ♪ | ♩ | ♪ ♪ ♪ ♪ |. Cf. *gecēas ēcne rǣd* (*Beow.* 1201b), which has to be read | ♩ ♪ ♩ | ♩ ³♪ ♩ |, because *ēcne* alliterates, not *gecēas*.

CONCLUSION

Having now examined the manifold variations of the hypermetric form in Old English poetry, and seen how the present metrical theory could accommodate itself to them, we may properly take stock of our findings. It is clear that, with certain understandable exceptions, the hypermetric verses are distinct from the normal in syllabic pattern, and that they can most easily be read in the time of two 4/4 measures, the first of which is allotted to the opening, the second to the close. The close is immediately recognizable as the equivalent of a normal verse, or, in the case of types B and C, that portion of a normal verse which follows the preliminary syllables. The opening is either weak, lacking alliteration and the most emphatic class of syllables, or strong, with alliteration and a syllable of at least moderate importance. If the opening is weak, it must be read with an initial rest unless there are so many syllables that they demand the entire measure for their proper utterance. If the entire measure is thus filled, its accents will be weaker than those of the close. If the opening is strong, the most prominent syllable will ordinarily take the primary accent, leaving the secondary to be occupied by a less emphatic syllable or a rest. Exceptionally, and only in the first half-line, the strongest syllable may better be deferred to the secondary position after an initial rest. Monosyllabic anacrusis is freely admitted, dissyllabic sparingly, the only plausible instances being supplied by the short prefix *ofer-*. Rests may occur at the beginning of the verse, in the third quarter of the first measure, or in any weakly accented position. They may never be longer than half a measure. Alliteration follows the principles established by the normal line, with such added variations in the first half-line as the longer form makes possible. Indeed, in every important respect, the principles that have been established for the normal verse—not only the alliterative pattern, but also the treatment of accent, quantity, and rests—hold good for the hypermetric.

There remain unsolved, to be sure, and probably insoluble, a few troublesome problems. Thus, it seems impossible to decide whether a small number of verses are to be regarded as genuinely hypermetric or only corrupt. Again, suspicion must necessarily fall upon single hypermetric lines, still more upon single half-lines, in the midst of normal sequences, just as it must fall upon single normal lines or half-lines in the midst of hypermetric sequences. Nevertheless, although most of the hypermetric verses occur in sequences of at least two lines, there are enough exceptions to make any decisions concerning them extremely delicate. It seems very possible, at any rate, that sequences beginning or ending in the middle of a line should be considered legitimate. Despite these difficulties, however, which are inevitable concomitants of the uncertain MS. tradition of the poetry, the 4/4 reading makes the hypermetric form both intelligible in itself and thoroughly harmonious with the 4/8 reading of the normal lines.

We have strayed far from the eleven hypermetric lines of *Beowulf* which rendered necessary this elaborate discussion of the form in Old English poetry generally, but the excursion has shown clearly that these lines are representative of the class, and indeed that they are among the most orthodox members of it. Final judgment of their potential beauty and effectiveness cannot be gained without consecutive reading of normal and hypermetric passages in the order which they assume in the poetry. Accordingly, the section of illustrative notations that follows includes six of the hypermetric lines in *Beowulf* and several in *Judith* and *The Dream of the Rood*. When the vital sensory evidence of these passages is added to the argument and analysis of the present section, the case for the 4/4 reading will be complete.

INTRODUCTORY NOTE

The following passages have been selected with a view to representing as fully as possible the aesthetic effect of the new system. *Beowulf* has naturally been favored, but three other poems find places at the end. The first of these, Cædmon's Hymn, is included partly for the sake of comparison with Heusler's reading, partly because of the antiquity of its text, and not least because of its unpretentious charm. The selections from *Judith* and *The Dream of the Rood* are included primarily to exhibit the hypermetric form, which is illustrated from *Beowulf* only by six lines in the fifth selection.

Brief notes on the texts employed will be found at the appropriate places. A word of explanation may here be added. In the absence of any critical apparatus, which would have been out of place, I have nevertheless included the signs of emendation—square brackets for additions to the MS., round brackets for conjectural readings of damaged passages, italics for alterations of letters—in order to show at a glance the degree of editing in a given line. Only a few trivial omissions, largely normalizations of spelling, have thus passed unnoticed. For full information, however, the edition in question must be consulted, for the MS. reading is quoted only when I myself have made an emendation.

Musical notation has been preferred to numbers or arbitrary signs because so many people are already familiar with it that they will be spared the labor of learning a new system. For the sake of those who may be puzzled, however, I append the following table showing in numbers the quantities of the notes and rests that I have used:

Note		Rest	Numerical Value
Half-note	♩	▬	4
Dotted quarter	♩·	𝄽 ⸼	3
Quarter-note	♩	𝄽	2
Eighth-notes	♪ ♫	⸼	1
Sixteenth-notes	♬ ♬		1/2

Triplets

$$2/3 + 2/3 + 2/3 = 2$$

$$1 + 1/3 + 2/3 = 2 \quad *$$

$$4/3 + 2/3 = 2$$

The notation is devoid of all the special signs that are used elsewhere in this book. Thus, no accents are marked, for the musical bars prescribe primary accent at the start of each measure and secondary at its center, and it seemed best to leave the reader free to govern the degree of strength within this specified scheme in accordance with his response to the words. Again, the ligature with which I have sometimes called attention to a short syllable of eighth-note quantity is omitted, for it is only of use in the analysis of different types of verses.

Extrametric pauses have been inserted very sparingly, and the reader should feel entirely at liberty to pause at other points if he so desires. On the other hand, I would urge him to make it a general practice to proceed without intermission from line to line. The frequent rests—some of them too short to be specified—and the half-line phrasing supplied jointly by meaning and rhythm will ordinarily be sufficient to bring out the structure of the verse. Pauses after every half-line or line will greatly injure the effect.

I have indulged in one purely conventional device, which is illustrated by the notation of *Beowulf* 46 f. in the first

---

* Used where the middle syllable is nearly elided. Extrametric pauses are marked with the hold (⌢).

selection. Line 46 ends with an incomplete measure of three eighth-notes, and the first syllable of line 47 completes this measure with the fourth eighth-note. The first line, however, ends a sentence, and a pause is necessary after it, so that the measure is recorded as | ♪ ♪ ♪ ⌒ ♪ |. Now this notation is really a fiction, because a pause destroys the exactness of the quantity that precedes it. One could just as well mark the measure at the end of line 46 complete, | ♪ ♪ ♪ |, and start afresh with line 47. Indeed, the effect of anacrusis at the start of a sentence, as opposed to that which occurs in the midst of a closely united sequence, is very similar to that of an unaccented grace-note, and it does not need to be measured too exactly. I have adopted the fiction, | ♪ ♪ ♪ ⌒ ♪ |, merely to preserve the logic of the notation. It may be taken to indicate the quantities that would obtain if there were no pause.

It is my earnest hope that the reader will not be discouraged by the difficulty of the notation, for unless he can read the poetry in accordance with it he will miss the enjoyment toward which this book has been directed. Most people will find it easy to acquire the fundamentals if they will begin by beating time, or even tapping the rhythms of particular verses with their fingers. Once they have acquired a feeling for the characteristic movement of the lines, they will be able to anticipate most of the details of the notation and concentrate their attention on the meaning of the words. Then they will achieve without effort the expressive yet metrical reading that poetry requires.

No one need be alarmed if his interpretation of a passage causes him to disagree here and there with the details of my notation. I have often been in doubt about the treatment of minor syllables and the choice between two equally metrical alternatives. The important thing is to attain harmony between metre and meaning.

SELECTIONS FROM *BEOWULF*[1]

1. THE PROLOGUE

Hwæt, wē Gār-Dena   in gēardagum,[2]

$\frac{4}{8}$

þēodcyninga   þrym gefrūnon,

hū ðā æþelingas   ellen fremedon!

Oft Scyld Scēfing   sceaþena þrēatum,

5   monegum mǣgþum   meodosetla oftēah,

egsode eorl[as],   syððan ǣrest wearð

fēasceaft funden;   hē þæs frōfre gebād,

wēox under wolcnum   weorðmyndum þāh,

oð þæt him ǣghwylc   ymbsittendra

or

---

[1] The text is that of Klaeber's third edition (Heath & Co. 1936), except for a few lines in the tenth selection, as there noted. A point beneath a vowel indicates its suppression, a circumflex above prescribes the substitution of a dissyllabic form. Italics indicate altered letters, square brackets editorial additions, round brackets doubtful readings.

[2] See above, p. 90 f.

10   ofer hronrāde   hȳran scolde,

gomban gyldan;   þæt wæs gōd cyning!

Ðǣm eafera wæs   æfter cenned

geong in geardum,   þone God sende

folce tō frōfre;   fyrenðearfe ongeat,

15   þē hīe ǣr drugon   aldor(lē)ase

lange hwīle;   him þæs Līffrêa,

wuldres Wealdend   woroldāre forgeaf,

Bēowulf wæs brēme   — blǣd wīde sprang —

Scyldes eafera   Scedelandum in.

20   Swā sceal (geong g)uma   gōde gewyrcean,

fromum feohgiftum   on fæder (bea)rme,

þæt hine on ylde   eft gewunigen

wilgesīþas,   þonne wīg cume,

lēode gelǣsten;   lofdǣdum sceal

25   in mǣgþa gehwǣre   man geþeôn.

Him ðā Scyld gewāt   tō gescæphwīle

felahrōr fēran   on Frēan wǣre;

hī hyne þā ætbǣron   tō brimes faroðe,

swǣse gesīþas,   swā hē selfa bæd,

30   þenden wordum wēold   wine Scyldinga—

lēof landfruma   lange āhte.

þǣr æt hȳðe stōd   hringedstefna

īsig ond ūtfūs,   æþelinges fær;

ālēdon þā   lēofne þēoden,

35   bēaga bryttan   on bearm scipes,

mǣrne be mǣste.   Þǣr wæs mādma fela

of feorwegum   frætwa gelǣded;

ne hȳrde ic cȳmlīcor   cēol gegyrwan

hildewǣpnum   ond heaðowǣdum,

40   billum ond byrnum;   him on bearme læg

mādma mænigo,   þā him mid scoldon

on flōdes ǣht   feor gewītan.

Nalæs hī hine lǣssan   lācum tēodan,

þēodgestrēonum,   þon þā dydon,

45   þē hine æt frumsceafte   forð onsendon

ǣnne ofer ȳðe   umborwesende.

þā gȳt hīe him āsetton   segen g(yl)denne

hēah ofer hēafod,   lēton holm beran,

gēafon on gārsecg;   him wæs geōmor sefa,

50   murnende mōd.   Men ne cunnon

secgan tō sōðe,   selerǣden*de*,

12

hæleð under heofenum,   hwā þǣm hlæste onfēng.

| ℭ ℭ ℭ ℭ | ℭ ℭ ℾ | ˣ ℭ ℭ | ℭ ⌣ ℾ ‖

2. Beowulf's Voyage

Þæt fram hām gefrægn   Higelāces þegn

| ˣ ℭ ℭ | ℾ ³ ℭ ℾ | ℭ ℭ ℭ ℭ | ℾ ˣ |

195   gōd mid Gēatum,   Grendles dǣda;

| ℾ· ℭ | ℾ ℾ | ℾ ℾ | ℾ ℾ |

sē wæs moncynnes   mægenes strengest

| ˣ ℭ ℭ | ℾ ℭ ℭ | ℭ ℭ ℾ | ℾ ℾ |

on þǣm dæge   þysses līfes,

| ˣ ℾ | ℾ ℭ ℭ | ℾ ℾ | ℾℭ ? |

æþele ond ēacen.   Hēt him ȳðlidan

| ℭ ℭ ℭ ℭ | ℾℾ | ˣ ℭ ℭ | ℾℭ ℭ |

gōdne gegyrwan;   cwæð, hē gūðcyning

| ℾ ℭ ℭ| ℾ ℾ | ˣ ℾ ³ ℭ | ℾ ℭ ℭ |

200   ofer swanrāde   sēcean wolde,

| ˣ ℭ ℭ | ℾ ℭ ℭ | ℾ ℾ | ℾ ℭ ? |

mǣrne þēoden,   þā him wæs manna þearf.

| ℾ ℾ | ℾ ℾ | ? ℭ ℭ ℭ | ℾ³ℭ ℾ |

Ðone sīðfæt him   snotere ceorlas

| ˣ ℭ ℭ| ℭ ℭ ℾ | ℭ ℭℾ | ℾ ℾ |

lȳthwōn lōgon,   þēah hē him lēof wǣre;

| ℾ ℾ | ℾ ℾ | ˣ ℾ ℾ ℾ | ℾ ℭ ℭ |
       ₃

hwetton hige(r)ōfne,   hǣl scēawedon.

| ℾ ℾ | ℭℭ ℭ ℭ | ℾ | ℾ ℭ ℭ | ⌒

205   Hæfde se gōda   Gēata lēoda

| ℾ ℭ ℭ | ℾℭ ? | ℾ ℾ | ℾ ℾ |

cempan gecorone   þāra þe hē cēnoste

| ♩ ♪ ♪ | ♪♪♪ ⸽ | ♪♪ ♪ ♪ | ♩♪♪ |

findan mihte;   fīftȳna sum

| ♩ ♩ | ♩ ♪ ⸽ | ♩♪♪ | ♩ |

sundwudu sōhte,   secg wīsade,

| ♩ ♪♪ | ♩ ♪ ⸽ | ♩ | ♩♪♪ |

lagucræftig mon   landgemyrcu.

| ♪♪♪♪ | ♩ ⸸ | ♩· ♪ | ♩ ♪ ⸽ |

210   Fyrst forð gewāt;   flota wæs on ȳðum,

| ♩ | ♩³♪ ♩ |♪♪ ♪ ♪ | ♩ ♪ ⸽ |

bāt under beorge.   Beornas gearwe

| ♩ ♪ ♪ | ♩ ♪ ⸽ | ♩ ♩ | ♩ ♪ |

on stefn stigon,—   strēamas wundon,

♪ | ♩ | ♪♪ ⸸ | ♩ ♩ | ♩ ♩ |

sund wið sande;   secgas bǣron

| ♩· ♪ | ♩ ♪ ⸽ | ♩ ♩ | ♩ ♪ |

on bearm nacan   beorhte frætwe,

♪ | ♩ | ♪ ♩· | ♩ ♩ | ♩ ♪ ⸽ |

215   gūðsearo geatolīc;   guman ūt scufon,

| ♩ ♪ ♪ | ♪♪♪ ⸽ | ♪ ♩·| ♩ ♪ ♪ |

weras on wilsīð   wudu bundenne.

| ♪ ♩ ♪ | ♩♩ | ♪ ♩·| ♩ ♪ ♭⌢ |

Gewāt þā ofer wǣgholm   winde gefȳsed

♭ | ♪ ♪ ♪ ♪ | ♩ ♩ | ♩ ♪ ♪ | ♩♩ |

flota fāmīheals   fugle gelīcost,

| ♪♩·| ♪ ♪ ♩ | ♩ ♪ ♪ | ♩ ♪ ⸽ |

oð þæt ymb āntīd   ōþres dōgores

| ♩ ♪ ♪ | ♩♩ | ♩ ♩ | ♩ ♩ |

220　　wundenstefna　　gewaden hæfde,

þæt ðā līðende　　land gesāwon,

brimclifu blīcan,　　beorgas stēape,

sīde sænæssas;　　þā wæs sund liden,

eoletes æt ende.　　Þanon up hraðe

225　　Wedera lēode　　on wang stigon,

sǣwudu sǣldon,—　　syrcan hrysedon,

gūðgewǣdo;　　Gode þancedon

þæs þe him ȳþlāde　　ēaðe wurdon.

þā of wealle geseah　　weard Scildinga,

230　　sē þe holmclifu　　healdan scolde,

beran ofer bolcan　　beorhte randas,

fyrdsearu fūslicu;　　hine fyrwyt bræc

mōdgehygdum,　　hwæt þā men wǣron.

Gewāt him þā tō waroðe   wicge rīdan

235 þegn Hrōðgāres,   þrymmum cwehte

mægenwudu mundum,   meþelwordum frægn:

'Hwæt syndon gē   searohæbbendra,

byrnum werede,   þē þus brontne cēol

ofer lagustrǣte   lǣdan cwōmon,

240 hider ofer holmas?   [Hwæt, ic hwī]le wæs

endesǣta,   ǣgwearde hēold,

þē on land Dena   lāðra nǣnig

mid scipherge   sceðþan ne meahte.

Nō hēr cūðlīcor   cuman ongunnon

245 lindhæbbende,   nē gē lēafnesword

gūðfremmendra   gearwe ne wisson,

māga gemēdu.   Nǣfre ic māran geseah

eorla ofer eorþan,   ðonne is ēower sum,

secg on searwum;   nis þæt seldguma,

250   wǣpnum geweorðad,   næfne him his wlite lēoge,

ǣnlīc ansȳn.   Nū ic ēower sceal

frumcyn witan,   ǣr gē fyr heonan

lēasscēaweras   on land Dena

furþur fēran.   Nū gē feorbūend,

255   mereliðende,   mīn[n]e gehȳrað

ānfealdne geþōht: ofost is sēlest

tō gecȳðanne,   hwanan ēowre cyme syndon.'

Him se yldesta   andswarode,

werodes wīsa,   wordhord onlēac:

260   'Wē synt gumcynnes   Gēata lēode

ond Higelāces   heorðgenēatas.

Wæs mīn fæder   folcum gecȳþed,

æþele ordfruma,   Ecgþēow hāten;

gebād wintra worn,   ǣr hē on weg hwurfe,

265   gamol of geardum;   hine gearwe geman

witena wēlhwylc   wīde geond eorþan.

Wē þurh holdne hige   hlāford þīnne,

sunu Healfdenes   sēcean cwōmon,

lēodgebyrgean;   wes þū ūs lārena gōd!

270   Habbað wē tō þǣm mǣran   micel ǣrende

Deniga freân;   ne sceal þǣr dyrne sum

wesan, þæs ic wēne.   Þū wāst, gif hit is

swā wē sōþlīce   secgan hȳrdon,

þæt mid Scyldingum   sceaðona ic nāt hwylc,

275   dēogol dǣdhata   deorcum nihtum

ēaweð þurh egsan   uncūðne nīð,

hȳnðu ond hrāfyl.   Ic þæs Hrōðgār mæg

þurh rūmne sefan   rǣd gelǣran,

hū hē frōd ond gōd   fēond oferswȳðeþ—

280   gyf him edwenden   ǣfre scolde

bealuwa bisigu   bōt eft cuman—,

ond þā cearwylmas cōlran wurðaþ;

oððe ā syþðan   earfoðþrāge,

þrēanȳd þolað,   þenden þǣr wunað

285   on hēahstede   hūsa sēlest.'

Weard maþelode,   ðǣr on wicge sæt,

ombeht unforht: 'Ǣghwæþres sceal

scearp scyldwiga   gescād witan,

worda ond worca,   sē þe wēl þenceð.

290 Ic þæt gehȳre, þæt þis is hold weorod

frēan Scyldinga. Gewītaþ forð beran

wǣpen ond gewǣdu, ic ēow wīsige;

swylce ic maguþegnas mīne hāte

wið fēonda gehwone flotan ēowerne,

295 nīwtyrwydne nacan on sande

ārum healdan, oþ ðæt eft byreð

ofer lagustrēamas lēofne mannan

wudu wundenhals tō Wedermearce,

gōdfremmendra swylcum gifeþe bið,

300 þæt þone hilderǣs hāl gedīgeð.'

3. The Swimming Match

Unferð maþelode, Ecglāfes bearn,

500 þē æt fōtum sæt frēan Scyldinga,

onband beadurūne—   wæs him Bēowulfes sīð,

mōdges merefaran,   micel æfþunca,

forþon þe hē ne ūþe,   þæt ænig ōðer man

æfre mærða þon mā   middangeardes

505   gehēde under heofenum   þonne hē sylfa—:

'Eart þū sē Bēowulf,   sē þe wið Brecan wunne,

on sīdne sæ   ymb sund flite,

ðær git for wlence   wada cunnedon

ond for dolgilpe   on dēop wæter

510   aldrum nēþdon?   Nē inc ænig mon,

nē lēof nē lāð,   belēan mihte

sorhfullne sīð,   þā git on sund rēon;

þær git ēagorstrēam   earmum þehton,

mæton merestrǣta,   mundum brugdon,

515   glidon ofer gārsecg;   geofon ȳþum wēol,

wintrys wylm[um].   Git on wæteres ǣht

seofon niht swuncon;   hē þē æt sunde oferflāt,

hæfde māre mægen.   Þā hine on morgentīd

on Heaþo-Rǣmes   holm up ætbær;

520   ðonon hē gesōhte   swǣsne ēþel,

lēof his lēodum,   lond Brondinga,

freoðoburh fægere,   þǣr hē folc āhte,

burh ond bēagas.   Bēot eal wið þē

sunu Bēanstānes   sōðe gelǣste.

525   Ðonne wēne ic tō þē   wyrsan geþingea,

ðēah þū heaðorǣsa   gehwǣr dohte,

grimre gūðe,   gif þū Grendles dearst

nihtlongne fyrst   nēan bīdan.'

178   SPECIMEN NOTATIONS

Bēowulf maþelode,   bearn Ecgþēowes:

530   'Hwæt, þū worn fela,   wine mīn *Unferð*,

bēore druncen   ymb Brecan sprǣce,

sægdest from his sīðe!   Sōð ic talige,

þæt ic merestrengo   māran āhte,

earfeþo on ȳþum,   ðonne ǣnig ōþer man.

535   Wit þæt gecwǣdon   cnihtwesende

ond gebēotedon   —wǣron bēgen þā gīt

on geogoðfēore—   þæt wit on gārsecg ūt

aldrum nēðdon,   ond þæt geæfndon swā.

Hæfdon swurd nacod,   þā wit on sund reôn,

540   heard on handa;   wit unc wið hronfixas

werian þōhton.   Nō hē wiht fram mē

flōdȳþum feor   flēotan meahte,

hraþor on holme,   nō ic fram him wolde.

Ðā wit ætsomne   on sǣ wǣron

545 fīf nihta fyrst,   oþ þæt unc flōd tōdrāf,

wado weallende,   wedera cealdost,

nīpende niht,   ond norþanwind

heaðogrim ondhwearf;   hrēo wǣron ȳþa.

Wæs merefixa   mōd onhrēred;

550 þǣr mē wið lāðum   līcsyrce mīn

heard hondlocen   helpe gefremede,

beadohrægl brōden,   on brēostum læg

golde gegyrwed.   Mē tō grunde tēah

fāh fēondscaða,   fæste hæfde

555 grim on grāpe;   hwæþre mē gyfeþe wearð,

þæt ic āglǣcan   orde gerǣhte,

hildebille;   heaþorǣs fornam

| ſſ |ſℂ   ﭳ | ℂ ℂ ſ³ℂ | ſ |

mihtig meredēor   þurh mīne hand.

| ſſ | ℂ ℂ ſ | ˣ ſ | ſ³ℂ ſ | ⌒

Swā mec gelōme   lāðgetēonan

| ſ   ℂ   ℂ | ſ ℂ ﭳ | ſ·ℂ | ſ ſ |

560   þrēatedon þearle.   Ic him þēnode

| ſℂ ℂ | ſ ſ | ˣ ℂ ℂ | ſ ℂℂ |

dēoran sweorde,   swā hit gedēfe wæs.

| ſ ſ | ſ ℂ ﭳ | ˣ   ℂ ℂ ſ | ſ³ℂ ſ |
                                    3

Næs hīe ðǣre fylle   gefēan hæfdon,

| ℂ ℂ   ℂℂ |ſℂ   ℂ | ſ | ſ ℂ ﭳ |

mānfordǣdlan,   þæt hīe mē þēgon,

| ſ· ℂ | ſ ſ | ˣ ℂ   ℂ | ſ ℂℂ |

symbel ymbsǣton   sǣgrunde nēah;

| ſ ℂ   ℂ | ſ ſ | ſ ſ³ ℂ | ſ |

565   ac on mergenne   mēcum wunde

| ˣ ℂ ℂ | ſ ℂ ℂ | ſ ſ | ſ ℂ ﭳ |

bē³ ȳðlāfe   uppe lǣgon,

| ˣ ſ | ſ ℂ ℂ | ſ ſ | ſ ſ |

sweo[r]dum āswefede,   þæt syðþan nā

| ſ   ℂ ℂ | ℂℂℂ ﭳ | ˣ ſ | ℂ ℂ ſ |

ymb brontne ford   brimlīðende

| ˣ ſ | ſ³ ℂ ſ | ſ | ſ ℂℂ |

lāde ne letton.   Lēoht ēastan cōm,

| ſℂ ℂ | ſ ℂ   ﭳ | ſ | ℂ ℂ ſ |

³ I have supplied the macron because the more emphatic form of the preposition (normally spelled *bī*) is required after an initial rest. It would be
possible, of course, to retain *be* and treat it as anacrusis.

570 beorht bēacęn Godes, brimu swaþredon,

or

 þæt ic sǣnæssas gesēon mihte,

 windige weallas. Wyrd oft nereð

or

 unfǣgne eorl, þonne his ellen dēah!

 Hwæþere mē gesǣlde, þæt ic mid sweorde ofslōh

575 niceras nigene. Nō ic on niht gefrægn

 under heofones hwealf heardran feohtan,

 nē on ēgstrēamum earmran mannon;

 hwæþere ic fāra feng fēore gedīgde

or

 sīþes wērig. Ðā mec sǣ oþbær,

580 flōd æfter faroðe on Finna land,

 wadu weallendu. Nō ic wiht fram þē

 swylcra searonīða secgan hȳrde,

billa brōgan.   Breca nǣfre gīt

æt heaðolāce,   nē gehwæþer incer,

585   swā dēorlīce dǣd gefremede

fāgum sweordum   —nō ic þæs [fela] gylpe— ,

þēah ðū þīnum brōðrum   tō banan wurde,

hēafodmǣgum;   þæs þū in helle scealt

werhðo drēogan,   þēah þīn wit duge.

590   Secge ic þē tō sōðe,   sunu Ecglāfes,

þæt nǣfre Gre[n]del swā fela   gryra gefremede,

atol ǣglǣca   ealdre þīnum,

hȳnðo on Heorote,   gif þīn hige wǣre,

sefa swā searogrim,   swā þū self talast;

595   ac hē hafað onfunden,   þæt hē þā fǣhðe ne þearf,

atole ecgþræce   ēower lēode

swīðe onsittan,   Sige-Scyldinga;

nymeð nŷdbāde,   nænegum ārað

or

lēode Deniga,   ac hē lust wigeð,

600   swefeð ond s*nē*deþ,   secce ne wēneþ

tō Gār-Denum.   Ac ic him Gēata sceal

eafoð ond ellen   ungeāra nū,

gūþe gebēodan.   Gæþ eft sē þe mōt

tō medo mōdig,   siþþan morgenlēoht

605   ofer ylda bearn   ōþres dōgores,

sunne sweglwered   sūþan scīneð!'

4. The Fight with Grendel

Ðā him Hrōþgār gewāt   mid his hæleþa gedryht,

eodur Scyldinga   ūt of healle;

wolde wīgfruma   Wealhþēo sēcan,

13

665   cwēn tō gebeddan.   Hæfde Kyningwuldor

Grendle tōgēanes,   swā guman gefrungon,

seleweard āseted;   sundornytte behēold

ymb aldor Dena,   eotonweard' ābēad.

Hūru Gēata lēod   georne truwode

670   mōdgan mægnes,   Metodes hyldo.—

Ðā hē him of dyde   īsernbyrnan,

helm of hafelan,   sealde his hyrsted sweord,

īrena cyst   ombihtþegne,

ond gehealdan hēt   hildegeatwe.

675   Gespræc þā se gōda   gylpworda sum,

Bēowulf Gēata,   ær hē on bed stige:

'Nō ic mē an herewæsmun   hnāgran talige

gūþgeweorca,   þonne Grendel hine;

forþan ic hine sweorde   swebban nelle,

680   aldre benēotan,   þēah ic eal mæge;

nāt hē þāra gōda,   þæt hē mē ongēan sleâ,

rand gehēawe,   þēah ðe hē rōf sîe

nīþgeweorca;   ac wit on niht sculon

secge ofersittan,   gif hē gesēcean dear

685   wīg ofer wǣpen,   ond siþðan wītig Goð

on swā hwæþere hond   hālig Dryhten

mǣrðo dēme,   swā him gemet þince.'

Hylde hine þā heaþodēor,   hlēorbolster onfēng

eorles andwlitan,   ond hine ymb monig

690   snellīc sǣrinc   selereste gebēah.

Nǣnig heora þōhte,   þæt hē þanon scolde

eft eardlufan   ǣfre gesēcean,

folc oþðe frēoburh,   þǣr hē āfēded wæs;

|ſ C C |ſ ſ | ᵡ ᴄ__ſſ|C C ſ|⌒

ac hīe hæfdon gefrūnen,   þæt hīe ǣr tō fela micles

|C C C ᴄ_ſ|ſ C ᵧ |C C C C |CC C C|

695   in þǣm wīnsele wældēað fornam,

| ᵡ C C |ſ CC |ſ ſ ³C |ſ ᵡ |

Denigea lēode.   Ac him Dryhten forgeaf

|C Cſ |ſ C ᵧ |ᵡ C C |C ᴄ_ſ ſ |

wīgspēda gewiofu,   Wedera lēodum,

|ſ C ᴄ_ſ |CC ᵡ |C Cſ |ſ C ᵧ|

frōfor ond fultum,   þæt hīe fēond heora

|ſ C C |ſ ſ | ᵡ C C |ſ   C C|

ðurh ānes cræft   ealle ofercōmon,

| ᵡ ſ |CC ſ |ſ³C CC|ſ C ᵧ|

700   selfes mihtum.   Sōð is gecȳþed,

|ſſ |ſ C ᵧ |ſ C C|ſ ſ |

þæt mihtig God   manna cynnes

| ᵡ ſ |CC ſ |ſ ſ |ſ ſ |

wēold wīdeferhð.

| ſ |ſ³C ſ |

Cōm on wanre niht

| ᵡ C   C |ſ³C ſ |

scrīðan sceadugenga.   Scēotend swǣfon,

|ſ ſ |C C C C |ſ ſ |ſ ſ|

þā þæt hornreced   healdan scoldon,

| ᵡ C C |ſ C C |ſ ſ |ſ C ᵧ|

705   ealle būton ānum.   Þæt wæs yldum cūþ,

|ſ³C C C|ſ ſ | ᵡ C   C |C C ſ|

þæt hīe ne mōste,   þā Metod nolde,

sē [4] s[c]ynscaþa   under sceadu bregdan;—

ac hē wæccende   wrāþum on andan

bād bolgenmōd   beadwa geþinges.

710   Ðā cōm of mōre   under misthleoþum

Grendel gongan,   Godes yrre bær;

mynte se mānscaða   manna cynnes

sumne besyrwan   in sele þām hēan.

Wōd under wolcnum   tō þæs þe hē wīnreced,

715   goldsele gumena   gearwost wisse

fǣttum fāhne.   Ne wæs þæt forma sīð,

þæt hē Hrōþgāres   hām gesōhte;

nǣfre hē on aldordagum   ǣr nē siþðan

---

[4] Klaeber omits the macron, which is indispensable to the reading here
suggested. Perhaps, however, we ought to allow both *se* and *under* to be counted
as anacrusis in an unbroken line, with the rhythm.

heardran hǣle, healðegnas fand!

720 Cōm þā tō recede rinc sīðian

drēamum bedǣled. Duru sōna onarn

fȳrbendum fǣst, syþðan hē hire folmum (æthr)ān;

onbrǣd þā bealohȳdig, ðā (hē ge)bolgen wæs,

recedes mūþan. Raþe æfter þon

725 on fāgne flōr fēond treddode,

ēode yrremōd; him of ēagum stōd

ligge gelīcost lēoht unfǣger.

Geseah hē in recede rinca manige,

swefan sibbegedriht samod ætgædere,

730 magorinca hēap. þā his mōd āhlōg;

mynte þæt hē gedǣlde, ǣr þon dæg cwōme,

atol āglǣca ānra gehwylces

líf wið líce,   þā him ālumpen wæs

wistfylle wēn.   Ne wæs þæt wyrd þā gēn,

735   þæt hē mā mōste   manna cynnes

ðicgean ofer þā niht.   Þrȳðswȳð behēold

mǣg Higelāces,   hū se mānscaða

under fǣrgripum   gefaran wolde.

Nē þæt se āglǣca   yldan þōhte,

740   ac hē gefēng hraðe   forman sīðe

slǣpendne rinc,   slāt unwearnum,

bāt bānlocan,   blōd ēdrum dranc,

synsnǣdum swealh;   sōna hæfde

unlyfigendes   eal gefeormod,

745   fēt ond folma.   Forð nēar ætstōp,

nam þā mid handa   higeþīhtigne

rinc on ræste,   ræhte ongēan

fēond mid folme;   hē onfēng hraþe

inwitþancum   ond wið earm gesæt.

750   Sōna þæt onfunde   fyrena hyrde,

þæt hē ne mētte   middangeardes,

eorþan scēata   on elran men

mundgripe māran;   hē on mōde wearð

forht on ferhðe;   nō þȳ ær fram meahte.

755   Hyge wæs him hinfūs,   wolde on heolster flēon,

sēcan dēofla gedræg;   ne wæs his drohtoð þær

swylce hē on ealderdagum   ær gemētte.

Gemunde þā se gōda,   mæg Higelāces,

æfensprǣce,   uplang āstōd

760   ond him fæste wiðfēng;   fingras burston;

eoten wæs ūtweard,   eorl furþur stōp.

Mynte se mæra,   (þ)ær hē meahte swā,

wīdre gewindan   ond on weg þanon

flēon on fenhopu;   wiste his fingra geweald

765   on grames grāpum.   þæt wæs gēocor sīð,

þæt se hearmscaþa   tō Heorute ātēah!

Dryhtsele dynede;   Denum eallum wearð,

ceasterbūendum,   cēnra gehwylcum,

eorlum ealuscerwen.   Yrre wæron bēgen,

770   rēþe renweardas.   Reced hlynsode.

Þā wæs wundor micel,   þæt se wīnsele

wiðhæfde heaþodēorum,   þæt hē on hrūsan ne fēol,

fæger foldbold;   ac hē þæs fæste wæs

innan ond ūtan   īrenbendum

775 searoþoncum besmiþod.   Þær fram sylle ābēag

medubenc monig   mīne gefrǣge

golde geregnad,   þær þā graman wunnon.

Þæs ne wēndon ǣr   witan Scyldinga,

þæt hit ā mid gemete   manna ǣnig

780 betlīc ond bānfāg   tōbrecan meahte,

listum tōlūcan,   nymþe līges fæþm

swulge on swaþule.   Swēg up āstāg

nīwe geneahhe: Norð-Denum stōd

atelīc egesa,   ānra gehwylcum

785 þāra þe of wealle   wōp gehȳrdon,

gryrelēoð galan   Godes andsacan,

sigelēasne sang,   sār wānigean

helle hæfton.   Hēold hine fæste

sē þe manna wæs mægene strengest

790 on þǣm dæge þysses līfes.

Nolde eorla hlēo ænige þinga

or

þone cwealmcuman cwicne forlǣtan,

nē his līfdagas lēoda ænigum

i. e. hh

nytte tealde. Þǣr genehost brægd

795 eorl Bēowulfes ealde lāfe,

wolde frēadrihtnes feorh ealgian,

mǣres þēodnes, ðǣr hīe meahton swā.

Hīe þæt ne wiston, þā hīe gewin drugon,

heardhicgende hildemecgas,

800 ond on healfa gehwone hēawan þōhton,

sāwle sēcan: þone synscaðan

ænig ofer eorþan   īrenna cyst,

gūðbilla nān   grētan nolde;

ac hē sigewǣpnum   forsworen hæfde,

805   ecga gehwylcre.   Scolde his aldorgedāl

on ðǣm dæge   þysses līfes

earmlīc wurðan,   ond se ellorgāst

on fēonda geweald   feor sīðian.—

Ðā þæt onfunde   sē þe fela ǣror

810   mōdes myrðe   manna cynne,

fyrene gefremede   —hē [wæs] fāg wið God—,

þæt him se līchoma   lǣstan nolde,

ac hine se mōdega   mǣg Hygelāces

hæfde be honda;   wæs gehwæþer ōðrum

815   lifigende lāð.   Līcsār gebād

atol ǣglǣca;   him on eaxle wearð

syndolh sweotol,   seonowe onsprungon,

burston bānlocan.   Bēowulfe wearð

gūðhrēð gyfeþe;   scolde Grendel þonan

820   feorhsēoc flēon   under fenhleoðu,

sēcean wynlēas wīc;   wiste þē geornor,

þæt his aldres wæs   ende gegongen,

dōgera dægrīm.   Denum eallum wearð

or

æfter þām wælrǣse   willa gelumpen.

825   Hæfde þā gefǣlsod   sē þe ǣr feorran cōm,

snotor ond swȳðferhð,   sele Hrōðgāres,

genered wið nīðe.   Nihtweorce gefeh,

ellenmǣrþum.   Hæfde Ēast-Denum

Gēatmecga lēod   gilp gelǣsted,

| ſ   ℂ   ℂ | ſ | ſ·   ℂ | ſ ſ |

830   swylce oncȳþðe   ealle gebētte,

| ˣ   ℂ ℂ | ſ ℂ ℂ | ſ ℂ   ℂ | ſ ℂ ꜚ |

inwidsorge,   þē hīe ǣr drugon

| ſ ſ | ſ ℂ ꜚ | ˣ ℂ ℂ | ſ   ℂ ℂ |

ond for þrēanȳdum   þolian scoldon,

| ˣ ℂ   ℂ | ſ ℂ ℂ | ℂ ℂ ſ | ſ   ℂ ꜚ |

torn unlȳtel.   Þæt wæs tācen sweotol,

| ſ | ſ ℂ ℂ | ˣ   ℂ   ℂ | ℂ ℂ   ℂ ℂ |

syþðan hildedēor   hond ālegde,

| ˣ ℂ   ℂ | ſ³ ℂ ſ | ſ·   ℂ | ſ ℂ ꜚ |

835   earm ond eaxle   —þǣr wæs eal geador

| ſ·   ℂ | ſ ℂ ꜚ | ˣ   ℂ   ℂ | ſ   ℂ   ℂ |

Grendles grāpe —   under gēapne hr(ōf).

| ſ ſ | ſ ℂ ꜚ | ˣ ℂ ℂ | ſ³ ℂ   ſ ‖

5. Rejoicing in Heorot: Wealhþeow's Speech

Lēoð wæs āsungen,

| ſ   ℂ ℂ | ſ ſ |

1160   glēomannes gyd.   Gamen eft āstāh,

| ſ ℂ ℂ | ſ ˣ | ℂ ſ· | ſ³ ℂ ſ |

beorhtode bencswēg,   byrelas sealdon

| ſ ℂ ℂ | ſ   ſ | ℂ ℂ ſ | ſ ſ |

wīn of wunderfatum.   Þā cwōm Wealhþēo forð

| ſ· ℂ | ſ   ℂ ℂ | ˣ   ℂ   ℂ | ℂ   ℂ   ſ |

$\frac{4}{4}$ gān under gyldnum bēage   þǣr þā gōdan twēgen

| ſ ˣ ℂ ſ | ſ ſ   ſ ſ | ˉ ſ   ſ | ſ ſ   ſ ſ |

sǣton suhtergefǣderan;　　þā gȳt wæs hiera sib ætgædere,

ǣghwylc ōðrum trȳwe.　　Swylce þǣr *Unferþ* þyle

æt fōtum sæt frēan Scyldinga;　　gehwylc hiora his ferhþe

trēowde,

þæt hē hæfde mōd micel,　　þēah þe hē his māgum nǣre

ārfæst æt ecga gelācum.　　Sprǣc ðā ides Scyldinga:

4/8　'Onfōh þissum fulle,　　frēodrihten mīn,

1170　sinces brytta!　　Þū on sǣlum wes,

goldwine gumena,　　ond tō Gēatum sprǣc

mildum wordum,　　swā sceal man dôn!

Bēo wið Gēatas glæd,　　geofena gemyndig,

nēan ond feorran　　þū nū hafast.

1175　Mē man sægde,　　þæt þū ðē for sunu wolde

hereri[n]c habban.　　Heorot is gefǣlsod,

bēahsele beorhta;　　brūc þenden þū mōte

manigra mēdo,　　ond þīnum māgum lǣf

folc ond rīce,　　þonne ðū forð scyle,

1180　metodsceaft seôn.　Ic mīnne can

glædne Hrōþulf,　　þæt hē þā geogoðe wile

ārum healdan,　　gyf þū ǣr þonne hē,

wine Scildinga,　　worold oflǣtest;

wēne ic þæt hē mid gōde　　gyldan wille

1185　uncran eaferan,　　gif hē þæt eal gemon,

hwæt wit tō willan　　ond tō worðmyndum

umborwesendum ǣr　　ārna gefremedon.'

Hwearf þā bī bence,　　þǣr hyre byre wǣron,

Hrēðrīc ond Hrōðmund,　　ond hæleþa bearn,

1190　giogoð ætgædere;　þǣr se gōda sæt,

Bēowulf Gēata　　be þǣm gebrōðrum twǣm.

6. Hroðgar's Description of Grendel's Home

1345   'Ic þæt londbūend,   lēode mīne,

selerǣdende   secgan hȳrde,

þæt hīe gesāwon   swylce twēgen

micle mearcstapan   mōras healdan,

ellorgǣstas.   Ðǣra ōðer wæs,

1350   þæs þe hīe gewislīcost   gewitan meahton,

idese onlīcnes;   ōðer earmsceapen

on weres wæstmum ·   wrǣclāstas træd,

næfne hē wæs māra   þonne ǣnig man ōðer;

þone on gēardagum   Grendel nemdon

1355   foldbūende;   nō hīe fæder cunnon,

hwæþer him ǣnig wæs   ǣr ācenned

dyrnra gāsta.   Hīe dȳgel lond

14

warigeað wulfhleoþu,   windige næssas,

or

frēcne fengelād,   ðær fyrgenstrēam

1360   under næssa genipu   niþer gewīteð,

flōd under foldan.   Nis þæt feor heonon

mīlgemearces,   þæt se mere standeð;

ofer þǣm hongiað   hrinde bearwas,

or

wudu wyrtum fæst   wæter oferhelmað.

1365   þær mæg nihta gehwǣm   nīðwundor sēon,

fȳr on flōde.   Nō þæs frōd leofað

gumena bearna,   þæt þone grund wite.

Đēah þe hæðstapa   hundum geswenced,

heorot hornum trum   holtwudu sēce,

1370   feorran geflȳmed,   ær hē feorh seleð,

aldor on ōfre,   ǣr hē in wille,

hafelan [beorgan];   nis þæt hēoru stōw!

þonon ȳðgeblond   up āstīgeð

won tō wolcnum,   þonne wind styreþ

1375   lāð gewidru,   oð þæt lyft drysmaþ,

roderas rēotað.   Nū is se rǣd gelang

eft æt þē ānum.   Eard gīt ne const,

frēcne stōwe,   ðǣr þū findan miht

sinnigne secg;   sēc gif þū dyrre!

1380   Ic þē þā fǣhðe   fēo lēanige,

ealdgestrēonum,   swā ic ǣr dyde,

wund*num* golde,   gyf þū on weg cymest.'

7. Beowulf's Return

Cwōm þā tō flōde   felamōdigra,

hægstealdra [hēap];   hringnet bǣron,

1890   locene leoðosyrcan.   Landweard onfand

eftsīð eorla,   swā hē ǣr dyde;

nō hē mid hearme   of hlīðes nosan

gæs(tas) grētte,   ac him tōgēanes rād,

cwæð þæt wilcuman   Wedera lēodum

1895   scaþan scīrhame   tō scipe fōron.

þā wæs on sande   sǣgēap naca

hladen herewǣdum   hringedstefna,

mēarum ond māðmum;   mǣst hlīfade

ofer Hrōðgāres   hordgestrēonum.

1900   Hē þǣm bātwearde   bunden golde

swurd gesealde,   þæt hē syðþan wæs

on meodubence   māþme þȳ weorþra,

yrfelāfe.　Gewāt him on naca

drēfan dēop wæter,　Dena land ofgeaf.

1905　þā wæs be mæste　merehrægla sum,

segl sāle fæst;　sundwudu þunede;

nō þǣr wēgflotan　wind ofer ȳðum

sīðes getwǣfde;　sǣgenga fōr,

flēat fāmigheals　forð ofer ȳðe,

1910　bundenstefna　ofer brimstrēamas,

þæt hīe Gēata clifu　ongitan meahton,

cūþe næssas;　cēol up geþrang

lyftgeswenced,　on lande stōd.

8. The Burial of the Hoard

þǣr wæs swylcra fela

in ðām eorð(hū)se　ǣrgestrēona,

swā hȳ on gēardagum   gumena nāthwylc,

eormenlāfe   æðelan cynnes,

2235   þanchycgende   þǣr gehȳdde,

dēore māðmas.   Ealle hīe dēað fornam

ǣrran mǣlum,   ond sē ān ðā gēn

lēoda duguðe,   sē ðǣr lengest hwearf,

weard winegeōmor   wēnde þæs ylcan,

2240   þæt hē lȳtel fæc   longgestrēona

brūcan mōste.   Beorh eallgearo

wunode on wonge   wæterȳðum nēah,

nīwe be næsse,   nearocræftum fæst;

þǣr on innan bær   eorlgestrēona

2245   hringa hyrde   hordwyrðne dǣl,

fǣttan goldes,   fēa worda cwæð:

‘ Heald þū nū, hrūse,   nū hæleð ne mōstan,

eorla æhte!   Hwæt, hyt ǣr on ðē

gōde begēaton;   gūðdēað fornam,

2250   feorhbealo frēcne   fȳra gehwylcne

lēoda mīnra   þāra ðe þis [līf] ofgeaf,

gesāwon seledrēam.   Nāh, hwā sweord wege

oððe fe(o)r(mie)   fǣted wǣge,

dryncfæt dēore;   dug(uð) ellor s[c]eōc.

2255   Sceal se hearda helm   (hyr)stedgolde,

fǣtum befeallen;   feormynd swefað,

þā ðe beadogrīman   bȳwan sceoldon;

gē swylce sēo herepād,   sīo æt hilde gebād

ofer borda gebræc   bite īrena,

2260   brosnað æfter beorne.   Ne mæg byrnan hring

æfter wīgfruman   wīde fēran,

hæleðum be healfe.   Næs hearpan wyn,

gomen glēobēames,   nē gōd hafoc

geond sæl swingeð,   nē se swifta mearh

2265   burhstede bēateð.   Bealocwealm hafað

fela feorhcynna   forð onsended!'

9. THE SORROW OF HREÐEL

2425   Bīowulf maþelade,   bearn Ecgðēowes:

'Fela ic on giogoðe   gūðrǣsa genæs,

orleghwīla;   ic þæt eall gemon.

Ic wæs syfanwintre,   þā mec sinca baldor,

frēawine folca   æt mīnum fæder genam;

2430   hēold mec ond hæfde   Hrēðel cyning,

geaf mē sinc ond symbel,   sibbe gemunde;

næs ic him tō līfe   lāðra ōwihte,

beorn in burgum,   þonne his bearna hwylc,

Herebeald ond Hæðcyn   oððe Hygelāc mīn.

2435   Wæs þām yldestan   ungedēfelīce

mæges dædum   morþorbed strêd,

or

syððan hyne Hæðcyn   of hornbogan,

his frēawine   flāne geswencte,

miste mercelses   ond his mæg ofscēt,

2440   brōðor ōðerne   blōdigan gāre.

or

Þæt wæs feohlēas gefeoht,   fyrenum gesyngad,

hreðre hygemēðe;   sceolde hwæðre swā þeah

æðeling unwrecen   ealdres linnan.

Swā bið geōmorlīc   gomelum ceorle

2445 tō gebīdanne, þæt his byre rīde

giong on galgan; þonne hē gyd wrece,

sārigne sang, þonne his sunu hangað

hrefne tō hrōðre, ond hē him helpe ne mæg

eald ond infrōd ænige gefremman.

    or

2450 Symble bið gemyndgad morna gehwylce

eaforan ellorsīð; ōðres ne gȳmeð

tō gebīdanne burgum in innan

yrfeweardas, þonne se ān hafað

þurh dēaðes nȳd dæda gefondad.

2455 Gesyhð sorhcearig on his suna būre

wīnsele wēstne, windge reste

rēote berofene,— rīdend swefað,

hæleð in hoðman;   nis þær hearpan swēg,

gomen in geardum,   swylce ðær iū wæron.

2460   Gewīteð þonne on sealman,   sorhlēoð gæleð

ān æfter ānum;   þūhte him eall tō rūm,

wongas ond wīcstede.

Swā Wedra helm

æfter Herebealde   heortan sorge

weallinde wæg;   wihte ne meahte

2465   on ðām feorhbonan   fæghðe gebētan;

nō ðȳ ær hē þone heaðorinc   hatian ne meahte

lāðum dǣdum,   þēah him lēof ne wæs.
       or

Hē ðā mid þære sorhge,   þē him tō sār belamp,

or

gumdrēam ofgeaf,   Godes lēoht gecēas;

2470   eaferum lǣfde,   swā dēð ēadig mon,

lond ond lēodbyrig,   þā hē of līfe gewāt.'

10. Beowulf's Funeral

Him ðā gegiredan   Gēata lēode

ād on eorðan   unwāclīcne,

helm[um] behongen,   hildebordum,

3140   beorhtum byrnum,   swā hē bēna wæs;

ālegdon ðā tōmiddes   mǣrne þēoden

hæleð hīofende,   hlāford lēofne.

Ongunnon þā on beorge   bǣlfȳra mǣst

wīgend weccan;   wud(u)rēc āstāh

3145   sweart ofer swioðole,   swōgende lēg

wōpe bewunden   — windblond gelæg —,

oð þæt hē ðā bānhūs   gebrocen hæfde

hāt on hreðre.   Higum unrōte

| r· c | r c , | c r· | r c c |

mōdceare mǣndon,   mondryhtnes cw(e)alm;

| r c c | r c , | r c   c | r ˣ |

3150   swylce giōmorgyd   (G)ēat(isc) mēowle [5]

| ˣ   c c | c c r | r r | r c , |

(æfter Bīowulfe   b)undenheorde

| ˣ c c | r c c | r r| r c , |

(song) sorgcearig,   sǣde geneahhe,

| r | r c c | rc c| r c , |

þæt hīo hyre (hēofun)g(da)gas   hearde ond(rē)de,

| c c c c | c c   c c | r c c | r c , |

wælfylla worn,   werudes egesan,

| r c c | r ˣ | c c r| cc c , |

3155   hȳ[n]ðo (ond) h(æ)f(t)nȳd.   Heofon rēce swe(a)lg.

| r c c | r   c , | c r·| c c c·   ⌒

Geworhton ðā   Wedra lēode

c| r r | r | r r| r c , |

hl(ǣw) on hōe,   sē wæs hēah ond brād,

| r· c | rc ,|ˣ c c | r ³ c   r |

(wǣ)glīðendum   wīde g(e)sȳne,

| r | r c c | r c c | r c , |

ond betimbredon   on tȳn dagum

| ˣ c c| r c c |ˣ r| r c c|
        or | r ³ c r

3160   beadurōfes bēcn,   bronda lāfe

| c c c c | r ˣ | r r| rr |

[5] For the text of lines 3150-57 see Appendix, p. 232 ff.

wealle beworhton,   swā hyt weorðlīcost

foresnotre men   findan mihton.

Hī on beorg dydon   bēg ond siglu,

eall swylce hyrsta,   swylce on horde ǣr

3165   nīðhēdige men   genumen hæfdon;

forlēton eorla gestrēon   eorðan healdan,

gold on grēote,   þǣr hit nū gēn lifað

eldum swā unnyt,   swā hi(t ǣro)r wæs.

þā ymbe hlǣw riodan   hildedēore,

3170   æþelinga bearn,   ealra twelf*e*,

woldon (care) cwīðan,   [ond] kyning mǣnan,

wordgyd wrecan,   ond ymb w(er) sprecan;

eahtodan eorlscipe   ond his ellenweorc

duguðum dēmdon, —   swā hit gedē(fe) bið,

3175 þæt mon his winedryhten   wordum herge,

ferhðum frēoge,   þonne hē forð scile

of līchaman   (læded) weorðan.

Swā begnornodon   Gēata lēode

hlāfordes (hry)re,   heorðgenēatas;

3180 cwædon þæt hē wære   wyruldcyning[a]

manna mildust   ond mon(ðw)ærust,

lēodum līðost   ond lofgeornost.

CÆDMON'S HYMN [6]

Nū scylun hergan   hefaenrīcaes uard,

metudæs maecti   end his mōdgithanc,

uerc uuldurfadur,   suē hē uundra gihuaes,

ēci dryctin,   ōr āstelidæ.

5   Hē ǣrist scōp   ælda barnum

heben til hrōfe,   hāleg sceppend;

thā middungeard   moncynnæs uard,

ēci dryctin,   æfter tīadæ,

fīrum foldu,   frēa allmectig.

---

[6] The text is the consensus of the two best Northumbrian MSS. as presented by E. V. K. Dobbie, *The MSS. of Cædmon's Hymn and Bede's Death Song* (Columbia University Press 1937), p. 44, with the addition of long marks over the vowels and punctuation. The metrical differences from Heusler's West Saxon text (above, p. 23) are so trivial that they will not interfere with a comparison of the two notations.

JUDITH

The Slaying of Holofernes [7]

Swā hēt se gumena [b]aldor

$\frac{4}{4}$

fyl*l*an fletsittendum,   oðþæt fīra bearnum

nēa (1) æhte niht sēo þystre.   Hēt ðā nīða geblonden

35   þā ēadgan mægð   ofstum fetigan

$\frac{4}{8}$

tō his bedreste   bēagum gehlæste,

hringum gehrodene.   Hīe hraðe fremedon,

anbyhtscealcas,   swā him heora ealdor bebēad,

byrnwigena brego: bearhtme stōpon

40   tō ðām gysterne,   þær hīe Iūdithe

fundon ferhðglēawe,   and ðā fromlīce

---

[7] The text is that of A. S. Cook's edition (Heath & Co. 1904), unless otherwise noted. I have substituted Klaeber's editorial signs for Cook's: italics for alterations of words, square brackets for additions, and round brackets for readings by Thwaites of passages no longer legible in the MS.

15

lindwiggende   lǣdan ongunnon

þā torhtan mægð   tō træfe þām hēan,

þǣr se rīca hyne   reste on symb(el),

45   nihtes inne,   Nergende lāð

Ōlofernus.[8]   þǣr wæs eallgylden

flēohnet fæger   ymbe þæs folctogan

bed āhongen,   þæt se bealofulla

mihte wlītan þurh,   wigena baldor,

50   on ǣghwylcne   þe ðǣrinne cōm

hæleða bearna,   and on hyne nǣnig

monna cynnes,   nymðe se mōdga hwæne

nīðe rōfra   him þē nēar hēte

rinca tō rūne gegangan.   Hīe ðā on reste gebrōhton

[8] Cook follows the MS. spelling *Holofernus*, but the name always alliterates with a vowel. Long *o* is metrically necessary.

55 (sn)ūde ðā snoteran idese; ēodon ðā

ste(rcedf)erhðe [9]

hæleð heora hearran cȳðan þæt wæs sēo hālge mēowle

gebrōht on his būrgetelde. þā wearð se brēma on mōde

blīðe, burga ealdor, þōhte ðā beorhtan idese

mid wīdle and mid womme besmītan; ne wolde þæt

wuldres Dēma

60 geðafian, þrymmes Hyrde, ac hē him þæs ðinges gestȳrde,

Dryhten, dugeða Waldend. Gewāt ðā se dēofulcunda,

gālferhð [10] gumena ðrēate

bealofull his beddes nēosan, þǣr hē sceolde his

blǣd forlēosa(n)

ǣdre binnan ānre nihte; hæfde ðā his ende gebidenne

[9] The alliteration of *s* and *st* is improper.

[10] Cook supplies *gangan*, making a normal line out of this lone hypermetric half. There is surely something missing, but it seems unwise to insert a single normal line into this series.

65   on eorðan unswǣslīcne,   swylcne hē ǣr æfter worhte,

þearlmōd ðēoden gumena,   þenden hē on ðysse worulde

wunode under wolcna hrōfe.   Gefēol ðā wīne swā druncen

se rīca on his reste middan,   swā hē nyste rǣda nānne

$\frac{4}{8}$ on gewitlocan;   wiggend stōpon

70   ūt of ðām inne   ofstum miclum,

wer(as) wīnsade,   þe ðone wǣrlogan,

lāðne lēodhatan,   lǣddon tō bedde

nēhstan sīðe.   Þā wæs Nergendes

þēowen þrymful   þearle gemyndig

75   hū hēo þone atolan   ēaðost mihte

ealdre benǣman   ǣr se unsȳfra,

womfull, onwōce.   Genam ðā wundenlocc

Scyppendes mægð   scearpne mēce,

scūrum heardne,   and of scēaðe ābrǣd

80 swīðran folme;   ongan ðā swegles Weard

be naman nemnan,   Nergend ealra

woruldbūendra,   and þæt word ācwæð:

'Ic ðē frymða God,   and frōfre Gǣst,

Bearn Alwaldan,   biddan wylle

85 miltsc þīnre   mē þearfendre,

ðrȳnesse ðrym.   þearle ys mē nū ðā

heorte onhǣted   and hige geōmor,

$\frac{4}{4}$ swȳðe mid sorgum gedrēfed;   forgif mē, swegles Ealdor,

sigor and sōðne gelēafan,   þæt ic mid þȳs sweorde mōte

90 gehēawan [11] þysne morðres bryttan;   geunne mē

mīnra ge(sy)nta,

---

[11] This word ought to alliterate. See above, p. 129 n. 15 and p. 153 n. 37.

þearlmōd þēoden gumena: nāht(e) ic þīnre nǣfre

miltse þon māran þearf(e):   gewrec nū, mihtig Dryhten,

torhtmōd tīres Brytta,   þæt mē ys þus torne on mōde,

hāte on hreðre mīnum.'   Hī ðā se hēhsta Dēma

95   ǣdre mid elne onbryrde,   swā hē dēð ānra gehwylcne

[hēanra] [12] hērbūendra   þe hyne him tō helpe sēceð

mid rǣde and mid rihte gelēafan.   þā wearð hyre

rūme on mōde,

hāligre hyht genīwod;   genam ðā þone hǣðnan mannan

fæste be feaxe sīnum,   tēah hyne folmum wið hyre weard

100   bysmerlīce,   and þone bealofullan

listum ālēde,   lāðne mannan,

swā hēo ðæs unlǣdan   ēaðost mihte

[12] I have added this word in an effort to make an isolated normal half-line hypermetric.

wel gewealdan.   Slōh ðā wundenlocc

þone fēondsceaðan   fāgum mēce

105   heteþoncolne,   þæt hēo healfne forcearf

þone swēoran him,   þæt hē on swīman læg,

druncen and dolhwund.   Næs ðā dēad þā gȳt,

ealles orsāwle: slōh ðā eornoste

ides ellenrōf   (ōþ)re sīðe

110   þone hǣðnan hund,   þæt him þæt hēafod wand

forð on ðā flōre;   læg se fūla lēap

gēsne beæftan,   gǣst ellor hwearf

under neowelne næs,   and ðǣr genyðerad wæs,

sūsle gesǣled   syððan ǣfre,

115   wyrmum bewunden,   wītum gebunden,

hearde gehæfted   in hellebryne

æfter hinsīðe.   Ne ðearf hē hopian nō,

$|^{\times}\ \complement\complement\ |\ \Gamma\ \complement\complement\ |\ _{\gamma}\ \complement\ \ \complement\ \ \ \complement\ |\ \underset{3}{\Gamma\Gamma}\ \Gamma\ \complement\ _{\gamma}\ |$

þȳst(rum) forðylmed,   þæt hē ðonan mōte

$|\ \Gamma\ \ \complement\ \ \ \complement\ |\ \Gamma\ \Gamma\ |\ ^{\times}\ \complement\ \ \complement\ |\ \complement\ \complement\ \ \complement\ \complement\ |$

of ðām wyrmsele,   ac ðǣr wunian sceal

$|^{\times}\ \complement\ \ \complement\ \ |\ \Gamma\ \ \complement\complement\ |\ _{\gamma}\ \complement\ \ \Gamma\ \ |\ \underset{3}{\Gamma\Gamma}\ \ \Gamma\ |$

120   āwa tō aldre   būtan ende forð

$|\ \Gamma\ \complement\ \ \complement\ |\ \Gamma\ \ \complement\ _{\gamma}\ |^{\times}\ \complement\ \ \complement\ |\ \complement\ \complement\ \ \Gamma\ |$

in ðām heolstran hām   hyhtwynna lēas.

$|^{\times}\ \complement\ \ \complement\ \ |\ \complement\ \ \ \complement\ \ \ \Gamma\ \ \ |\ \Gamma\ \ \complement\ \ \complement\ \ |\ \Gamma\ \ \|$

THE DREAM OF THE ROOD

Lines 1-56 [13]

Hwæt, ic swefna cyst   secgan wylle,

h[w]æt mē gemǣtte   tō midre nihte,

syðþan reordberend   reste wunedon.

þūhte mē þæt ic gesāwe   syllicre trēow

5 on lyft lǣdan   lēohte bewunden,

bēama beorhtost.   Eall þæt bēacen wæs

begoten mid golde;   gimmas stōdon

fægere æt foldan scēatum,   swylce þær fīfe wǣron

uppe on þām eaxlgespanne.   Behēoldon þær

engeldryhta *feala*,[14]

---

[13] The text is that of A. S. Cook's edition (Oxford 1905) unless otherwise noted. Also cited is that of the latest editors, Bruce Dickins and Alan S. C. Ross (Methuen's Old English Library, 1934), which differs materially only at line 9. The editorial signs are changed to accord with Klaeber's—square brackets for additions to the MS., italics for alterations of letters.

[14] MS. *engel dryhtnes ealle*, Cook *englas Dryhtnes ealle*, Dickins and Ross *engeldryhte* (which makes good sense and good metre, but does not account for MS. *ealle*). See above p. 111 n.

10   fægere þurh forðgesceaft: ne wæs ðæt hūrū

fracoðes gealga,

$\frac{4}{8}$ ac hine þær behēoldon   hālige gāstas,

or |ΓΓ

men ofer moldan,   and eall þēos mære gesceaft.

Syllic wæs se sigebēam,   and ic synnum fāh,

forwundod mid wommum.   Geseah ic wuldres trēow

15   wǣdum geweorðod   wynnum scīnan,

gegyred mid golde;   gimmas hæfdon

bewrigen weorðlice   Weald[end]es trēow;

hwæðre ic þurh þæt gold   ongytan meahte

earmra ǣrgewin,   þæt hit ǣrest ongan

20   $\frac{4}{4}$ swǣtan on þā swīðran healfe.   Eall ic wæs mid

sorgum gedrēfed;

forht ic wæs for þǣre fǣgran gesyhðe.   Geseah

ic þæt fūse bēacen

wendan wǣdum and bleôm: hwīlum hit wæs mid

wǣtan bestēmed,

besyled mid swātes gange,   hwīlum mid since gegyrwed.

Hwæðre ic þǣr licgende   lange hwīle

25 behēold hrēowcearig   Hǣlendes trēow,

oððæt ic gehȳrde   þæt hit hlēoðrode;

ongan þā word sprecan   wudu sēlesta:

' Þæt wæs gēara iū   — ic þæt gȳta geman —

þæt ic wæs āhēawen   holtes on ende,

30 āstyred of stefne mīnum.   Genāman mē ðǣr strange fēondas,

geworhton him þǣr tō wǣfersȳne,   hēton mē heora

wergas hebban;

bǣron mē ðǣr beornas on eaxlum,   oððæt hīe mē on

beorg āsetton,

gefæstnodon mē þǣr fēondas genōge.

'Geseah ic þā Frēan mancynnes

efstan elne mycle   þæt hē mē wolde on gestīgan.

35    $\frac{4}{8}$ þǣr ic þā ne dorste   ofer Dryhtnes word

būgan oððe berstan,   þā ic bifian geseah

eorðan scēatas;   ealle ic mihte

fēondas gefyllan,   hwæðre ic fæste stōd.

$\frac{4}{4}$ 'Ongyrede hine þā geong Hæleð $\frac{4}{8}$ —þæt wæs God ælmihtig—

40   strang and stīðmōd;   gestāh hē on gealgan hēanne [15]
     $\frac{4}{4}$

but properly

---

[15] By omitting 39b (which is hypermetric in form but has to be read as if it were normal D with anacrusis) and 40a (which is normal), we obtain a sound hypermetric line with proper alliteration. This has been noticed by Dickins and Ross, who think that the Ruthwell Cross may represent the original. It reads . . *geredæ hinæ god almehttig / þa he walde on galgu gistiga,* but as this sound line embodies parts of four half-lines in the poem, its value as evidence is uncertain. See above, p. 135 n. 22.

mōdig on manigra gesyhðe,   þā hē wolde mancyn lȳsan.

Bifode ic þā mē se Beorn ymbclypte;   ne dorste ic hwæðre

būgan tō eorðan,

feallan tō foldan scēatum,   ac ic sceolde fæste standan.

'Rōd wæs ic ārǣred;   āhōf ic rīcne Cyning,

45   heofona Hlāford;   hyldan mē ne dorste.

'Þurhdrifan hī mē mid deorcan næglum;   on mē syndon þā

dolg gesīene,

opene [16] inwidhlemmas;   ne dorste ic hira ǣnigum sceððan.

or

or

Bysmeredon hīe unc būtū ætgædere.   Eall ic wæs mid

blōde bestēmed,

begoten of þæs Guman sīdan,   siððan hē hæfde his gāst

onsended.

50   'Feala ic on þām beorge   gebiden hæbbe

[16] See above, p. 141 n.

wrāðra wyrda: geseah ic weruda God

þearle þenian;   þȳstro hæfdon

bewrigen mid wolcnum   Wealdendes hrǣw,

scīrne scīman;   sceadu forðēode,

55   wann under wolcnum.   Wēop eal gesceaft,

cwīðdon Cyninges fyll;   Crīst wæs on rōde.'

APPENDIX

CATALOGUE OF RHYTHMIC VARIATIONS IN THE NORMAL VERSES OF *BEOWULF*

INTRODUCTORY NOTES

The following catalogue not only supplies the evidence upon which the new theory is based, but indicates the proper or at any rate possible rhythm of every normal half-line in *Beowulf*. Excluded are the twenty-two hypermetric verses (1163-8, 1705-7, 2995-6), eight verses that have been supplied conjecturally by modern editors (62, 389b-390a, 403b, 1803a, 2792b, 3151a), and the ten illegible verses extending from 2226b to 2231a. Several others in the poem are doubtful, of course, but I have preferred to include every verse of whose authenticity there was a reasonable chance. All the verses are registered by line-number except a few of the commonest sort about which no mistake could possibly be made (for example, the 831 verses like *gomban gyldan* in type A). For these I have merely given examples with the sign *etc.*, though even here I have tried to specify all verses that had achieved their form by conjectural reading or emendation. For the less common variations, and all those for which my theory provides new rhythms, I have given the complete record, including copious citations of the verses as well as their line-numbers. If I have erred on the side of inclusion, it is because I hope that the catalogue will serve as a kind of rhythmic concordance, to which textual critics as well as students of versification may turn. The similar lists of Sievers have been invaluable for many years, and it seemed proper to renew and perhaps increase their usefulness by showing how they adjusted themselves to the rhythmic principles set forth in this book.

The arrangement of the catalogue and the rhythms proposed for the verses will be clear enough in the main, but certain details require special mention.

16

THE TEXT

The basis of the catalogue is the text of Klaeber's third edition of *Beowulf* (Heath and Co. 1936),[1] with the omissions indicated above and the following modifications:

1. Five verses have been changed by new readings of the last page of the MS. from the photographs published by A. H. Smith, " The Photography of MSS.," *London Mediaeval Studies* 1 (1938). 200 ff., Plates III-VI), of which the clearest was made with the use of ultraviolet light:

	Klaeber		New Reading
(a)	(s)īo g(eō)mēowle	3150b	(Gē)at(isc) mēowle
(b)	sǣde geneahhe	3151b	s(w)īðe geneahhe
(c)	þæt hīo hyre		þæt hīo hyre
	(hearmda)gas	3152a	(hēofun)g(da)gas
(d)	(wīgend)es egesan	3154b	werudes egesan
(e)	hl(ǣw) on [h]līðe	3157a	hl(ǣw) on hōe

Dr. Smith himself has pointed out that the true reading of 3154b is *werudes egesan*,[2] and believes that 3157a should be *hlēo on hōe*, but the photographs do not convince me that *hlēo* should be preferred to the almost inevitable *hlǣw* (cf.

---

[1] Klaeber's *Supplement to the Third Edition* (Heath and Co., 1940) came to hand too late to be of service in establishing the text. The only changes affecting the metre are at line 457, where Klaeber recommends Grundtvig's emendation *for werefyhtum* in place of *for gewyrhtum* where the MS. has *fere fyhtum* (but *for werefyhtum þū* gives the unlikely type E with anacrusis instead of type B), and at line 2212, where Sedgefield's reading *hofe* for *hæþe* gives type B instead of type C, at the same time rendering the contraction of *hēaum* unnecessary. In his note on 3150 ff. Klaeber refers to the article by A. H. Smith that I have cited immediately below. He accepts *werudes* 3154 and suggests *hefige dagas* 3153 where I have conjectured *hēofungdagas*. He expresses some doubt of *hōe* 3157.

[2] It is a vindication of Sievers' analysis of syllabic patterns (which my own analysis confirms) that I had conjectured *werudes* for the metrically improbable *wīgendes* before Professor Menner called my attention to the photographs. *Wīgendes* would give Sievers' expanded A (A*), which was avoided in the second half-line.

2802 and 3169). Of *Gēatisc mēowle* I am much more
certain than the parentheses would suggest, because I can
see traces of every letter—the tail of the *g,* a very black *i*
which could once have been *e, at* unmistakable, *i,* high *s,* and
c very faint but not hard to identify in the vestiges that
remain.[3] This, of course, is the most interesting discovery,
because it effectually disposes of Beowulf's mysterious wife.
Of *swīðe* for what has heretofore been read as *sǣlðe* and
emended to *sǣde* I can see all but the *w,* which would have
occurred where the page is torn. *Swīðe geneahhe* occurs
nine times in Old English poetry, according to Grein-
Köhler's *Sprachschatz,* so that a tenth instance is not at all
unlikely. I have substituted *hēofungdagas,* an extant compound, for the otherwise unrecorded *hearmdagas* because
Dr. Smith has detected the crucial *g,* which can barely be
made out in the clearest of his plates. With the changes
thus made, and a few confirmations of letters already
conjectured, lines 3150 ff. become:

> swylce giōmorgyd   (Gē)at(isc) mēowle
> . . . .   (b)undenheorde,
> (song) sorgcearig   s(w)īðe geneahhe
> þæt hīo hyre (hēofun)g(da)gas   hearde on(drē)de,
> hȳ[n]ðo (ond) h(æ)f(t)n(ȳ)d.

I regret that I can supply nothing satisfactory for the half-
line that is missing.[4] Feeling that a traditional error is

---

[3] Dr. Smith doubts *geōmēowle* and says (p. 204) that he can see after the
t " traces of two letters, the first like *s* or *i* or a much distorted *g,* the second
e, c, or *o.*" I select *s* and *c,* with room for *i* before *s.* Cf. *Afrisc mēowle* in
Exodus 580b, often unwisely emended to *Afrisc nēowle.*

[4] It should have contained a verb parallel to *song* and *b* for alliteration (Dr.
Smith confirms the *bunden-* though I still have faint doubts). If it contained a
verb it could not have belonged to type B or C, because a rest would be improper
between the verb and its antecedent object. The appearance of *æ*(?) and a very
clear *d* shortly after *mēowle,* but raised above the line by the tear in the MS.
that has completely obliterated everything else, made me conjecture something
like *sǣde ymb Bēowulf,* but even type A3 is out of place in the midst of a
grammatical sequence. The only other verb that would fit the traces and alliterate seems to be the past tense of *bregdan, brǣd,* which is used absolutely of vocal

better than a fresh one, I have retained Klaeber's reading, and consequently *sǣde* in the next line, for the notation of the passage on p. 211 above; but I am almost certain that *swīðe* is right.

2. Words or lines are differently divided in the following instances:

(a) For Klaeber's *an wīg gearwe* 1247b I have adopted Sievers' reading (*Beiträge* 10.222), *anwīggearwe*, which is rendered necessary by the alliteration. The first half-line reads, *þæt hīe oft wǣron*, where *oft* is unmistakably the bearer of the heaviest stress and must alliterate. It is true that *anwīggearwe* (= *andwīggearwe*, " ready for combat ") does not appear elsewhere, but the meaning is clear, and the first member of the compound is supported by *Guthlac* 176 (Krapp-Dobbie), *ēadig ōretta, ondwīges heard.* The MS. has *anwig gearwe.*

(b) For Klaeber's *þēah ðe ōðer his / ealdre gebohte* 2481 I have substituted *þēah ðe ōðer / his ealdre gebohte,* of which he himself admits the possibility. This division gives us an unusually light specimen of type A3 in the first half-line and the rare type A1 with anacrusis in the second, but the proclitic *his* can hardly be allowed to take the strong secondary accent and the quantitative separation from its noun that Klaeber's division necessitates. We must either keep the reading of the MS. and divide as I have done, or follow Heyne, Schücking, and Sedgefield—as I am half inclined to do—in changing *his* to *hit* and retaining Klaeber's division.

(c) For Klaeber's *Līgȳðum forborn / bord wið rond* 2672b-73a I have substituted *līgȳðum fōr./ Born bord wið*

activity in the phrase *hlēoðrum brugdon, Guthlac* 906 (Krapp-Dobbie), and similarly *Meters of Boethius* 13, line 47, but I am not sure that it can take a direct object in this sense. If so, we might perhaps read *brǣd on bearhtme,* " chanted clamorously," or perhaps *brǣd ond bodode.*

rond, as the MS. itself suggests. My reasons for the change, which removes *bord wið rond* from the dwindling list of trisyllabic verses, are given under I F 2 below.

3. Two minor emendations involve the substitution of parallel forms for metrically excessive ones:

(a) For *sē wæs betera ðonne ic* 469b I have substituted *sē wæs betera ðon ic.* As I have shown in the detailed discussion of this verse on page 71 above, mere elision is ruled out by the occurrence of the same formula where *ðonne* is followed by *nū* or *þū.*

(b) Similarly, I have corrected *heals ealne ymbefēng* 2691b to *heals ealne ymbfēng.*

4. Klaeber's quantities have been altered in the following cases: (a) short *a* for long in *-getawe,* for which see below under I F b; (b) long *e* (or *i*) for short in *be* 566a and 1284b, for which see I C 1 and II B 1; and (c) long *e* for short in *se* 707a, for which see I C 21.[5]

5. I have doubled the consonants in *het[t]ende* 1828a, *geneh[h]ost* 794b, and *īren[n]a* 673a, 1697a, 2259b, in order to normalize their metrical treatment. Klaeber preserves the single consonants largely as an illustration of an orthographic convention. See his *Introduction,* lxxxiv.

6. I have not only preserved all the dots underneath vowels by which Klaeber indicates that they are to be dropped, but have added others in order to make the treat-ment of such words as *mistige, dōgera* consistent. Failure to underdot consistently in such cases (even when the verse in question is readable) results in a host of otherwise un-

---

[5] I think we should return to the long *o* in *nosan,* 2803b and 1892b, for which see II C 39. It should be understood, of course, that the quantities of vowels in unimportant words must have varied with the amount of stress they received. Hence, though I have retained Klaeber's marks of quantity everywhere except in the places just specified, these marks are not always to be taken seriously.

duplicated rhythms. I have not added to the list of under-dotted vowels before vocalic or semi-vocalic consonants (r, l, m, n), and have doubted the wisdom of these dots in some cases (see I E 17), but recognize their necessity in most. I have further extended the dot to the genitive plural -*ẹna* after long stems, but have been too timid to apply it here consistently, as strict metre really requires. Consequently many such words (*lārena, Ēotena*, etc.) will be found under the rhythm to which their longer form would assign them, though in each case reference is made to the desirability of the syncopated form (*lārna, Ēotna,* etc.).[6] This applies likewise to the form *Ēotenum* in 1145a and 902b. Syncope is particularly desirable here because the proper form is *Ēotum*. Finally, I have used the dot under various forms of *lifigan* and under *herige* 1833b, because the *i* of weak verbs in Classes I and III must have been pronounced *j*. (The spellings *herian, styrian*, etc. are to be understood as *herjan, styrjan*.)

7. Elision can seldom be detected with certainty. Hence I have rarely marked it. In a few places, however, it seems obligatory, and there I have used a ligature to indicate it. The instances are, *Hȳrde ic* 2172a, *wēne ic* 525a and 1184a, *hwæþere ic* 578a (*hwæþre ic* would do) and *sunde oferflāt* 517b.

Such changes as those indicated in the last two paragraphs cannot of course be introduced with perfect consistency, for we often have to deal with parallel forms that were used by the poet at his discretion. A thorough-going

[6] The real reason for applying syncope rigorously is that a vowel subject to it was probably not stressed even when not completely dropped. The verse *sẽ was wreccena* has been classified by Sievers and by me as type C, but the accentuation *wreccena* appears improbable. More likely we should read *wrecna*, type A3. *Wreccena* with retention of the medial vowel seems possible, but does not exactly fit any type, the final stress being too weak for B.

normalization would therefore be impossible, and I have attempted only to avoid unnecessary variations, such as can be laid entirely to the charge of late scribes.

Besides the changes that I have thus adopted, several others seem to me to be necessary, but I have preferred to keep Klaeber's readings in the analysis, if only to show their faults more strikingly. The changes that I have suggested, together with the places in the catalogue where they are discussed, are as follows:

1. I think we should return to the readings of Klaeber's second edition in several instances:

Verse	MS. and	Klaeber 3	Klaeber 2	Catalogue
473a, 1724b		secganne	secgan	I & II D 32
2562a		sēceanne	sēcean	I D 31
1941a		efnanne	efnan	I D 32
2093a		reccenne	reccan	I D 38
2252a		gesāwon	secga	I A 50
3027a		wulf	wulfe	I F 4
414a		hādor	haðor	I F 5
2297a		ūtanweardne	ūtanweard	I F 6
2435b		ungedēfelice	ungedēfe	II F 7
402b		þā secg	secg	II D 13

2. For Klaeber's *stīðra nægla gehwylc* 985a I think we should substitute the MS. *steda nægla gehwylc*. See I D 53.

3. Two readings that Klaeber marks as emendations may be supported by the MS. For the possibility that the MS. reads *ond cyning* for Klaeber's [*ond*] *kyning* 3171b, see II C 10. For *bea(dwe) weorces* instead of Klaeber's *bea(du)* [*we*] *weorces* 2299a, see I F a.

4. There may be MS. authority for reading *him sw(ā) rǣhte ongēan* instead of Klaeber's *rǣhte ongēan* 747b. See II F 3.

5. I have suggested the following emendations:

Verse	Klaeber	Emendation	Catalogue
1766b	oððe ēagena bearhtm	ēagna bearhtm	II B 33
2488a	hrēas [heoro] blāc	hrēa*w*blāc [gehrēas]	I D 14
947a, 1759a	secg betsta	secg bet[e]sta	I F 1
1871b	þegn betstan	þegn bet[e]stan	II F 1

6. The alliterative scheme should almost certainly be normalized by transposing *hē is manna gehyld* 3056a to *hē is gehyld manna,* as in Sedgefield's edition (see I B 50), *manna ǣnig* 779b to *ǣnig manna,* as in Holthausen's edition (see I B 51), and *hringde byrnan* 2615b to *byrnan hringde,* again as in Holthausen's edition (see I E 1d).

THE CLASSIFICATION

Enough has been said in the preceding sections of this book to show that Sievers' types are not to be taken as so many different and mutually exclusive rhythmic forms, but as convenient groupings of the manifold variations of a single basic pattern. As such they are perhaps no better than other groupings, but they are so well known to scholars of the present day that I have thought it wise to adhere to them as far as possible. Here and there I have thought it best to transfer verses from one type to another, and here and there to change the subtypes. The following list will explain the relation of my classification to that of Sievers, as the latter is given in *Altgermanische Metrik,* pp. 33-5:

1. Type A has been subdivided as in Sievers into A1, A2, and A3, according to the number and position of strong accents (A1 = ⸍ ⸜ ⸍ ⸜ , A2a = ⸍ ⸜ ⸍ ⸜ , A2b = ⸍ ⸜ ⸍ ⸜ , A2ab = ⸍ ⸜ ⸍ ⸜ , A3 = ⸍ ⸜ ⸍ ⸜ or ⸍ ⸜ ⸍ ⸜). I have removed from these categories, however, the short form which Sievers called A2ak (*gūðrinc monig*), and combined it with the rare instances of short endings for A1 and A3 to make

a fourth category A4. Thus the second measure in A1, A2, and A3 is limited to the two forms | ♩ ♩ | and | ♪ ♪ ♩ |, while the second measure of A4 has the shortened form | ♪ ♩. |, which is found also in E and a small part of B and C. In the interest of avoiding any further variation of the second measure, I have put such verses as *fyrdsearu fūslicu* (second measure | ♩ ♪ ♪ |) under type D2, where indeed Sievers admitted that they might belong (*Altgermanische Metrik* p. 36; but Sievers thought that a real rhythmic distinction was involved in the choice between the two types, whereas in my system the rhythm is the same regardless of the classification). The very rare " expanded " A, which Sievers labelled A* (*Bēowulf wæs brēme*), has the accentual scheme of A2, either ´ ` ´ ` or ´ ` ´ ` , and differs from it only in the addition of an unstressed syllable at the end of the first measure (which makes this measure resemble type E). I have placed A*, therefore, immediately after A2 in the catalogue.

2. Type B is subdivided as in Sievers into B1, B2, and B3. B1 ends with the sequence ´ × ´ , B2 with ´ × × ´ , while B3 (like A3) defers the alliteration to the second stress. (I do not believe in the legitimacy of B3, but have listed the two verses which are supposed to illustrate it.) In addition to Sievers' classification, I have introduced a distinction between Ba (Ba1, Ba2, Ba3) and Bb, depending on whether the verse is read with a light first measure and both the stressed syllables in the second measure, or with anacrusis and one stressed syllable in each measure.

3. In type C I have combined Sievers' C1 and C2 into C1 (the ending ´ ´ × or its resolutions) and have changed C3 to C2 (the ending ´ ` × or its resolution—the latter being rare or non-existent). As in type B, I have distinguished likewise between Ca and Cb.

4. In type D I have preserved the full series of sub-types enumerated by Sievers: D1 with ending like C1, D2 with ending like C2, D3 with ending ´ ` × (but see my comment on this accentual scheme at the head of I D3 below), D4 with ending like B1 or B2, and D*1, D*2, D*4 with the same endings and an " expanded " first measure. (D1, D2, and D3 are usually grouped as Da against D4 as Db, but if my notion of the rhythm of D3 is correct, it stands closer to D4 than to D1 or D2.)

5. In type E there are no distinctions except for the admission of the somewhat doubtful variation E* with the sequence ´ × ` × in the first measure.

6. Under F I have placed the recalcitrant verses that, as they stand in Klaeber's text, will not fit any of the other categories. There are many fewer than in Sievers' time, largely because of his influence.

Since the chief value of the types lies in their convenience as a rough system of classification, and the subtypes are often of little importance, I have numbered the many rhythmic variations consecutively within each of the five main types. Thus I A 50 means first half-line, type A, number 50, which happens to be a variation of A2b.

In order to show, during the description of the first half-line, whether or not a particular variation is represented in the second (and vice versa), I have listed all variations under each half, and have placed a dagger opposite the number if there are no examples of it in the other half.

Those who are familiar with Sievers will have little difficulty in using the more complicated analysis here provided. So far as I am aware, the only verses that may be hard to find in the catalogue are those that may belong to either D4 or E, or short A2 (A4) or D2, the choice depending on one's opinion of the proper gradation of accents and grouping of syllables. I have differed from Sievers in several instances here. There are also the verses containing *ungemete*, which I have perhaps unwisely chosen to stress *ùngeméte*. These will be found under II A 47 instead of under type D.

The summary tables at the end bring together the rather alarming array of statistics, and may prove helpful as an index to the catalogue.

THE DETERMINATION OF QUANTITY

The main principles of quantity in Old English poetry have been set forth in the earlier part of this work,[7] but it seems wise to bring together in one place the rules that have been established, in order that the details of the notation in the catalogue may be clearly understood.

No syllable has a definite quantity until it is placed in a rhythmic series. Its quantity is then the interval of time that elapses between its moment of greatest intensity (normally the onset of the vowel) and that of the next syllable, the intervals being measured relatively to other intervals in the series. It is therefore impossible to speak of the quantity of a syllable that is removed from its context. Certain ranges of quantity, however, are inherent in language, and were further limited by the conventions of Old English poetry. It is necessary, therefore, to distinguish between long and short syllables, especially when they are stressed, and to note carefully the position of a syllable within the word or phrase, especially when it is unstressed.

A syllable is considered long if it contains a long vowel or is closed by a consonant. Long, therefore, are all stressed monosyllables or monosyllabic members of compounds, and

---

[7] See especially p. 9, and for additional details concerning final rests, minimum quantities, proclitic and enclitic syllables, etc., see pp. 18, 24, 28, 40, 67, and 74.

also the first syllables of such words as *beal-de, bid-dan*. A syllable is considered short if it contains a short vowel not closed by a consonant. Short, therefore, is the first syllable in *o-pen*.

Long stressed syllables have a normal value of a quarter-note, but are capable of compression to an eighth-note or extension to a half-note. The eighth-note limit is fixed by the impossibility of uttering a long syllable clearly in a shorter time (granted the tempo established by the verses collectively, which for me is in the neighborhood of 120 quarter-notes to the minute).[8] The half-note limit is less definite, for the characteristic of a long syllable is that it is capable of extension by the holding of its vowel or terminal consonant, or by a slight pause at its close. Indeed, the limit is surpassed by long stressed monosyllables in the hypermetric verses, if we count the rests which often follow them as part of their quantity. Within the normal form, however, the limit of a long syllable is necessarily the limit of a measure—that is, a half-note.

Short stressed syllables are much more rigidly controlled, because it is their primary characteristic to be incapable of extension. The word *o-pen*, for example, cannot be split into component syllables by such a pause as the hyphen suggests, for the *p* really belongs to both vowels at once, and the division is only a grammatical convenience. Holding the vowel would make it long and therefore unrecognizable, or at least unpleasantly distorted. Pausing before or after the *p* would be ludicrous. Hence the normal quantity of the short stressed syllable, the eighth-note, is also its maximum quantity. It can be compressed, however,

---

[8] If not very heavily stressed nor cluttered with consonants, a long syllable can sometimes take a slightly shorter quantity—that of an eighth-note in a triplet, which is two-thirds of the normal eighth-note. I have so marked a good many long syllables that take light primary or secondary accent in the first measures of types B, C, and A3. This is not really necessary, but it seems probable.

to the value of a sixteenth-note. Any quantity shorter than this can be assigned only to a syllable that is virtually elided.[9]

Unstressed syllables can without exception be reduced to sixteenth-note quantity, because their lack of stress permits them to be slurred. Their upper limit, on the other hand, varies in accordance with their position. We must distinguish, therefore, between proclitic, medial, and enclitic syllables.

Proclitic syllables — those that immediately precede stressed syllables and are more closely united to them than to preceding syllables—may never, with one exception, be longer than an eighth-note. The exception is a proclitic monosyllable (hence grammatically long) that is preceded by a rest. Its grammatical length makes it capable of extension to quarter-note quantity, and the rest preserves its proclitic character even when it is extended. By the extension, of course, it ceases to be a completely unstressed syllable, because it starts at the middle of a measure and receives light secondary accent.

Unstressed medial syllables—those that follow short stressed syllables, and probably also those that undergo syncope—are strictly limited to eighth-note quantity whether they are long or short. (This statement assumes that my interpretation of the stressing of the medial syllable of *cyninges* is correct. See I D3 below.)

Enclitic syllables, whether they are long or short, are capable of indefinite extension, because they can either be held or supplemented by rests. The metre fixes as a practical limit three quarters of a measure, the value of a dotted quarter-note.

One final restriction was presumably as valid for Old English as for modern languages. The concluding syllable of

[9] This range of quantities is determined by my analysis of the verse, but it corresponds almost exactly to the range postulated by William Thomson for speech in general. (Cf. *The Rhythm of Speech,* p. 190.)

a phrase, and to a slighter degree of a word, exercises a backward pressure, as it were, upon the stressed syllable that precedes it. Its accentual moment, the onset of the vowel, tends to be at least as close to that of its predecessor as to that of the stressed syllable at the start of the next measure. Consequently, one reads the last measure of *gomban gyldan,* and probably the first also (since the pace is too slow for the burden of the long syllable to counteract phrasing), with the rhythm | ♩ ♩ |, not | ♩. ♪ |.

Within the limits imposed by the rules of long and short stressed syllables, which are a special Old English conventionalization of the manifold differences in burden between syllables, and by those of position within the phrase, which belong to speech generally, the quantities are determined by the adjustment that is effected between the metre and the syllables. The most prominent syllables take possession of the most strongly accented places available to them, and the other syllables accommodate themselves to the remainder of the measures.

THE TREATMENT OF ANACRUSIS

Since the verses in the catalogue are presented out of their context, the quantities assigned to anacrusis (as well as to the final syllables of the verses that precede it in the poem) are not exact. For monosyllabic anacrusis, the eighth-note is used throughout, though its real value in the context might be as little as a sixteenth. For dissyllabic anacrusis, which is very rare, two sixteenth-notes are employed whenever it begins a new phrase, as it does only in Types A and D in the first half-line. This is presumably its real value, because, although its relation to the preceding measure can be neglected in view of the pause in the sense, it would counteract the " falling " effect of the rhythm if it extended to half a measure. Dissyllabic anacrusis within a longer phrase is recorded only for a few verses of Type C in the first half-line. It is assigned the value of two eighth-notes, because it is only the vacancy of the last half of the preceding measure and the continuity of the phrase that makes the reading with anacrusis plausible. For further remarks on my treatment of anacrusis in its context, see the introductory note to Part III (p. 162 f.), and for practical illustrations, the notations there presented.

THE NOTATION

In addition to the conventional symbols of music, which are described in the introductory note to Part III (p. 162), I have used two kinds of special signs for analytical purposes:

1. A ligature between an eighth-note and its successor indicates that the syllable corresponding to the eighth-note is grammatically short. Thus ♪♪, ♪♩, ♪♩., and ♫♩ have the same quantity as ♪♪, ♪♩, ♪♩., and ♫♩, but by an arbitrary convention the first syllable of each group joined by ligature is stated to be grammatically short, whereas the first syllable of the unjoined groups is either long or indeterminate. Since the distinction between long and short syllables is of importance only when the syllables are heavily accented, I have used the indeterminate notation for all sequences of lightly accented syllables. It is a question whether one can say that there is any rhythmic difference between ♪♪ and ♪♪ . If the notation is entirely accurate, there is no distinction except in burden—that is, it requires more effort to utter a long syllable in the time of an eighth-note than a short, so that one feels a greater fulness in the combination with a long syllable. It is not always possible, however, to be entirely accurate when one is generalizing about the rhythm of a verse. There is often

a tendency to convert ♪ ♪ into ♪₃♩ , especially when the second syllable is grammatically long; and there is the opposite tendency to convert ♪ ♪ into ♩₃♪ , especially when the second syllable is grammatically short. Hence there is a rhythmic as well as grammatical reason for employing the ligature. In addition, it serves as a convenient substitute for the ligature with which Sievers denoted "resolution." Owing, however, to the fact that at the close of a measure a short stressed syllable may replace a long without the compensatory addition of another syllable, the ligature appears in some places where Sievers would not have been able to use the term resolution. The ligature is valid in the two schemes | ♩ | ♩ ♪ ♪ | and | ♩ ♩ | ♪ ♪ ♩ |, but one can speak of resolution only in the second.

2. Instead of the conventional musical symbols for accent I have used here as formerly the grammatical ones, acute ´ for primary, grave ` for secondary accent, double acute ˝ for strong primary, double grave ˵ for strong secondary. This decision was made because the accents could be applied indifferently to notes or words, and because there was a peculiar need for the quadruple gradation thus obtained. The accents of speech vary greatly in strength, but a useful if mechanical distinction can be made between the relatively strong and weak accents by these double and single marks. Thus we can distinguish between *sȋdra sȍrga* and *ȍmbeht ȕnforht*, between *wēox under wolcnum* and *þā wæs on sande*, between the legitimate *weorðmyndum þāh* and the illegitimate or at least unusual *lȋssa gelȍng*. Many of the subtypes of A are distinguishable only by the strength of their accents, yet the analysis below corroborates that of Sievers in showing that for the Anglo-Saxons this was a very noteworthy difference.

I. FIRST HALF-LINE

TYPE A

A1

1. |♪ ♩|♪ ♩|, with double, crossed, or single alliteration. Altogether, 371 examples:

a. Double alliteration, 93 examples:

gomban gyldan 11	beorhtre bōte 158
wuldres Wealdend 17	furþur fēran 254, etc.

Here are included *heân hūses* 116, *gyddum geōmore* 151, *mistige mōras* 162, *windige weallas* 572, *mōdiges mannes* 2698, and *Ēotena trēowe* 1072, besides the emended verses *wintrys wylm[um]* 516, *secge (sealde)* 2019, and *fēondes fæð(mum)* 2128. The only compounds are *hildehlæmmum* 2201 and *hildehlemma* 2351, 2544.

b. Crossed alliteration (i. e. chief alliteration on first stress and supplementary on second), 11 examples:

hildewǣpnum 39	mǣrne þēoden 201

and similarly 589, 1131, 1475, 1849, 1910, 2170, 2721, 2723, and 3026.

c. Alliteration on first stress alone, 267 examples:

lange hwīle 16	ēadiglīce 100
georne hȳrdon 66	ylda bearnum 150, etc.

Here are included *endedōgores* 2896, *werian þōhton* 541, *hǣþene sāwle* 852, *mihtigan Drihtne* 1398, *sāwele hyrde* 1742, and the emended verses *d[r]ēore fāhne* 447, *eorþan scēata* 752, *fǣtte bēagas* 1750, *āge[n]dfrēan* 1883, *(ærnes) þearfa* 2225, *mǣrðu fremman* 2514, and *hilderinc[a]* 3124.

2. | ♩. ♪ | ♩ ♩ |, with double, crossed, or single alliteration. Altogether, 144 examples:

a. Double alliteration, 94 examples:

geong in geardum 13
fen ond fæsten 104

torht getǣhte 313
bearngebyrdo 946, etc.

Here are included *hēa[h on] healle* 1926, *(ho)r(d on) hrūsan* 2276, *hēold on hrūsa*n 2279, *gold on grund(e)* 2765, *hl(ǣw) on hōe* 3157, and *māþmgestrēona* 1931. The last could be included under no. 5 below. For 3157 see introductory note on text.

b. Crossed alliteration, 1 example:

bēodgenēatas 343

c. Alliteration on first stress alone, 49 examples:

wilgesīþas 23
rand gehēawe 682

nēan ond feorran 1174
folc ond rīce 1179, etc.

Here are included *þēo[d]gestrēona* 1218, *hondgemōt[a]* 2355, and *wrǣc ādrēoga*n 3078.

3. | ♪ ♪ ♩ | ♩ ♩ |, no. 1 with resolution of the first stress, with double, crossed, or single alliteration. Altogether, 60 examples:

a. Double alliteration, 19 examples:

monegum mǣgþum 5
fyrene fre(m)man 101

worolde wilna 950
æþeling, ēadig 1225

Uton nū efstan 3101, etc.

Perhaps the last example should be assigned to A3, since the alliteration of *Uton* may be accidental.

b. Crossed alliteration, 4 examples:

gumena dryhten 1824
manigra sumne 2091

winia bealdor 2567
sigora Waldend 2875

c. Alliteration on first stress alone, 37 examples:

Wedera lēode 225
recedes mūþan 724

fæderenmǣge 1263
cyninge mīnum 3093, etc.

1263 is the only compound. Here are included *Deniga frêan* 271 and 359, *hafelan* [*beorgan*] 1372, *bea*(*du*)[*we*] *weorces* 2299 (but see below under group Fa), *egesan ðeòn* 2736, and *Deniga lēodum* 389, of which the alliterative scheme can only be conjectured in the absence of a second half-line.

4. |♪̗̗ ♩ ♪|♩ ♩|, no. 2 with resolution of the first stress, with double or (once) single alliteration. Altogether, 29 examples:

a. Double alliteration, 28 examples:

leomum ond lēafum 97	waca wið wrāþum 660
sigon ætsomne 307	hyse, mid hæle 1217, etc.

Here are included *swefeð ond snēdeþ* 600, *eafoð ond ellen* 902, (*micel*) *gemēting* 2001, and *gomel on giohðe* 2793.

b. Alliteration on first stress alone, 1 example:

dæges ond nihtes 2269

5. |♩ ♪ ♪|♩ ♩|, the second syllable being either short or long (more frequently short), with double, crossed, or single alliteration. Altogether, 275 examples:

a. Double alliteration, 252 examples:

wēox under wolcnum 8	hēah ofer hēafod 48
folce tō frōfre 14	wæpnum geweorðad 250, etc.

Here is included *mōdige on meþle* 1876. — Three other verses, *symbel ymbsǣton* 564, *frōfor ond fultum* 698, and *ādl nē yldo* 1736, could be included under no. 2a by treating the first two syllables as one. Indeed, I have treated *ādl* as monosyllabic in *ādl opðe īren* 1848, and so included it here, but the ensuing vowel renders a monosyllabic reading easier in this verse than in 1736.—The first measure contains three monosyllables (or sometimes two monosyllables and a prefix) in *Ād wæs geæfned* 1107, *cen þec mid cræfte* 1219, *Heht þā se hearda* 1807, *wearð on ðām wange* 2003, *Eft þæt gelode* 2200, *Heald þū nū, hrūse* 2247, *hēold mec ond hæfde* 2430, *wēoll of gewitte* 2882, *mon mid his (mā)gum* 3065, and *Ic wæs þǣr inne* 3087. The last of these, and less probably 1807, 2003, and 2200 might be included under A3 if the alliteration of the first stress were considered accidental. I have so considered the alliteration of *oð* in *oð þæt him ǣghwylc* 9 and *oð þæt ymb āntīd* 219, which will therefore be found under A3 below.—Emended verses here included, other than those already mentioned, are *ēame on eaxle* 1117, *fylle gefægnod* 1333, *wordum ond weorcum* 1833, *f(ācne) bifongen* 2009, *m(ǣrða)gemunde* 2678, *wrǣte giondwlītan* 2771, *lēana (mid) lēodum* 2990, *bēagas (geboh)te* 3014, and *helm[um] behongen* 3139.

b. Crossed alliteration, 2 examples:

cynna gehwylcum 98   sǣla ond mǣla 1611

c. Alliteration on first stress alone, 21 examples:

geongum ond ealdum 72   gūþe gebēodan 603, etc.

Here are included *eaxlgestealla, -an* 1326 and 1714, which could be included under no. 2c by treating the first two syllables as one. (I have put the similar verse *māþmgestrēona* 1931 under no. 2c because the monosyllabic reading seemed a little easier than in the other two.) — Two monosyllables and a prefix occupy the first measure in *cwēn tō gebeddan* 665.—There is one conjectural verse, *(swīðe ondrǣ)da(ð)* 2275.

6. |♩♪ ♩|♩ ♩|, a minor variant of the preceding, occurs in one verse with double alliteration:

eft æt þē ānum 1377

Here also would belong, presumably, such verses as *mistige mōras* 162 (see no. 1) if they were read without syncope of the medial vowel.

7. |♪ ♪ ♪ ♪|♩ ♩|, with the first and third syllables either long or short, and double or single alliteration. When the first syllable is short, this form may be regarded as no. 5 with resolution. Altogether, 84 examples:

a. Double alliteration, 82 examples:

ǣnne ofer ȳðe 46	Metod for þȳ māne 110
Hwīlum hīe gehēton 175	eotenas ond ylfe 112
wǣpen ond gewǣdu 292	beran ofer bolcan 231, etc.

The "resolved" form illustrated in the second column occurs 44 times.—In *Hyne þā mid handa* 2720 and perhaps *Hraðe wæs gerȳmed* 1975 the alliteration of the first stress may be accidental, so that we could assign these verses to A3. (I have so assigned *oð þæt him on innan* 1740 and *oð ðæt hī oðēodon* 2934.)—Emended verses here included are *seomode on sāle* 302, *hæleðum tō handa* 1983, *(ǣnig) ofer eorðan* 2007, *[o]reðes ond attres* 2523, *wrǣte under wealle* 3060, and *syfone (tō) somne* 3122.—Attention may be called to *Wēn' ic þæt hē wille* 442 and *meltan mid þām mōdigan* 3011.—The verses *wunder æfter wundre* 931, *wundur under wealle* 3103, and *māððum tō gemyndum* 3016 could be included under no. 5 by reading the first two syllables as one.

b. Alliteration on first stress alone, 2 examples:

gumena gehwylcum 2859   Iofore ond Wulfe 2993

(8. |𝅘𝅥 𝅘𝅥𝅮𝅘𝅥𝅮𝅘𝅥𝅮|𝅘𝅥 𝅘𝅥|, only in second half-line.)

9. |𝅘𝅥𝅮 𝅘𝅥𝅮 𝅘𝅥𝅮𝅘𝅥𝅮𝅘𝅥𝅮|𝅘𝅥 𝅘𝅥 |, with double alliteration, 3 examples:

siðþan hē under segne 1204   þegnas syndon geþwǣre 1230
wesan, þenden ic wealde 1859

†10. |𝅘𝅥𝅮𝅘𝅥𝅮𝅘𝅥𝅮 𝅘𝅥𝅮 𝅘𝅥𝅮|𝅘𝅥 𝅘𝅥|, with double alliteration, 4 examples:

Wēn' ic þæt gē for wlenco 338	rǣsde on ðone rōfan 2690
Secge ic þē tō sōðe 590	bitere ond gebolgne 1431

All but the first of these would be reduced to the pattern of no. 7 by elision. Here as elsewhere I have used a triplet for simplicity. In 590 and 2690, with only partial elision, the first three syllables might really be 𝅘𝅥𝅭 𝅘𝅥𝅮 𝅘𝅥.

11. | ♩ ♩ | ♪♪ ♩ |, no. 1 with resolution of the second stress, with double, crossed, or single alliteration. Altogether, 27 examples:

a. Double alliteration, 10 examples:

mādma mænigo 41   uncran eaferan 1185
feohtan fremedon 959   feorran feredon 3113

and similarly 488, 1265, 1547, 1965, 2143, and 3083.

b. Crossed alliteration, 2 examples:

Scyldes eafera 19   drihten We*de*ra 2186

c. Alliteration on first stress alone, 15 examples:

byrnum werede 238   Wælses eafera 897
lēode Deniga 599   feorran cumene 1819

and similarly 1235, 1582, 2134, 2238, 2358, 2658, 2920, 2945, and 2992. Two other verses are doubtful:

æppelfealuwe 2165   Wuldurcyninge 2795

The first could as well have been spelled *-fealwe*, and would then have been included under no. 1c. The second, if *Wuldur-* were treated as a monosyllable, would fall together with *þēodcyninga* 2 under type D.

12. | ♩.♪ | ♪♪ ♩ |, no. 2 with resolution of the second stress, with double or single alliteration. Altogether, 11 examples:

a. Double alliteration, 9 examples:

helm of hafelan 672   forð gefremede 1718
stōd on stapole 926   fūs æt faroðe 1916

and similarly 1581, 1588, 2141, and 3043. One other verse,

fēond on frætewum 962

might better be included under 2a by reading *frætwum*.

b. Alliteration on first stress alone, 2 examples:

forðgewitenum 1479   handgewriþene 1937

13. |♪̷ ♪ ♩|♪̷ ♪ ♩|, no. 1 with resolution of both stresses, with double or single alliteration. Altogether, 4 examples:

a. Double alliteration, 2 examples:

bealuwa bisigu 281   niceras nigene 575

The reading *bealwa* would place the first under 11a.

b. Alliteration on first stress alone, 2 examples:

hafelan weredon 1327   eoferas cnysedan 1328

14. |♪̷ ♩̷ ♪|♪̷ ♪ ♩|, no. 2 with resolution of both stresses, with double alliteration, 2 examples:

gumum ætgædere 321   · giogoð ætgædere 1190

15. |♩̷ ♪ ♪|♪̷ ♪ ♩|, no. 5 with resolution of the second stress, with double or (once) single alliteration. Altogether, 30 examples:

a. Double alliteration, 29 examples:

þrāge geþolode 87   cempan gecorone 206
fǣhðe ond fyrene 137   flōd æfter faroðe 580, etc.

Here are included *ōmige þurhetone* 3049 and the two emended verses, *sweo[r]dum āswefede* 567 and *fūse tō farenne* 1805. The latter is perhaps dubious because it is the only one in this group with a long penultimate syllable. —The verse *māþðum for Metode* 169 could be included under no. 12a by treating the first two syllables as one.

b. Alliteration on first stress alone, 1 example:

[fuglum] tō gamene 2941

The singularity of this emended verse need not arouse suspicion. Compare no. 16b.

16. |♪̷ ♪ ♩ ♪|♪̷ ♪ ♩|, no. 7 with resolution of the second stress, with double or single alliteration. Altogether, 6 examples:

a. Double alliteration, 4 examples:

hæleð under heofenum 52   fyrene gefremede 811
seomade ond syrede 161   wigge under wætere 1656

The last example could be reduced to conformity with no. 15a by elision. The three others could be likened to no. 5 with resolution of both stresses.

b. Alliteration on first stress alone, 2 examples:

duguþe ond geogoþe 621 and 1674 (iogoþe)

†17. | ♩ ♩ ♩ ♪ ♪ | ♪ ♪ ♩ | , no. 10 with resolution of the second stress (or no. 7 with resolution of both stresses), occurs once, with double alliteration:

receda under roderum 310

18. ♪ | ♩. ♪ | ♩ ♩ | , no. 2 with monosyllabic anacrusis and double alliteration, 3 examples:

gewāc æt wīge 2629   geswāc æt sæcce 2681
gesæt on sesse 2717

19. ♪ | ♪ ♩ ♪ | ♩ ♩ | , no. 4 with monosyllabic anacrusis and double alliteration, 3 examples:

genered wið nīðe 827   āhæfen of horde 1108
ætgifan æt gūðe 2878

20. ♪ | ♩ ♪ ♪ | ♩ ♩ | , no. 5 with monosyllabic anacrusis and either double or single alliteration. Altogether, 16 examples:

a. Double alliteration, 14 examples:

in Cāines cynne 107   Onfōh þissum fulle 1169
Ārās þā se rīca 399   wið ord ond wið ecge 1549

and similarly 1151, 1304, 1518, 1557, 1977, 1987, 2538, 2659, 2703, and 3121.

b. Alliteration on first stress alone, 2 examples:

in mǣgþa gehwǣre 25   Gefēng þā be eaxle 1537

†21. ♪♪ | ♩ ♪ ♪ | ♩ ♩ |, no. 5 with dissyllabic anacrusis and double alliteration, 1 example:

gē æt hām gē on herge 1248

Partial elision makes the recommended reading very easy.

†22. ♪ | ♪ ♪ ♪ ♪ | ♩ ♩ |, no. 7 with monosyllabic anacrusis and either double or single alliteration. Altogether, 6 examples:

a. Double alliteration, 5 examples:

Gewiton him ðā wīgend 1125   forsiteð ond forsworceð 1767
forgyteð and forgȳmeð 1751   Gebīde gē on beorge 2529
onmunde ūsic mǣrða 2640

b. Alliteration on first stress alone, 1 example:
Gemunde þā se gōda 758

†23. ♪♪ | ♪ ♪ ♪ ♪ | ♩ ♩ |, no. 7 with dissyllabic anacrusis and double alliteration, 2 examples:

ne gefeah hē þǣre fǣhðe 109
ne gewēox hē him tō willan 1711

†24. ♪ | ♩♩♩ ♪ ♪ | ♩ ♩ |, no. 10 with monosyllabic anacrusis and double alliteration, 1 example:

Ofslōh ðā æt þǣre sæcce 1665

With elision, this would fall under the preceding.

†25. ♪ | ♩ ♩ | ♪ ♪ ♩ |, no. 11 with monosyllabic anacrusis and the alliteration on the first stress alone, 1 doubtful example:

[be] Finnes eaferum 1068

†26. ♪ | ♩ ♪ ♪ | ♪ ♪ ♩ |, no. 15 with monosyllabic anacrusis and double alliteration, 1 example:

ongunnen on geogoþe 409

†27. ♪|♪ ♪ ♪ ♪|♪ ♪ ♩|, no. 16 with monosyllabic anacrusis and double alliteration, 3 examples:

Gewāt him þā tō waroðe 234   gehēde under heofenum 505
Ne hēdde hē þæs heafolan 2697

A2a

28. |♩ ♩|♩ ♩| (cf. 1), with double, crossed, or single alliteration. Altogether, 53 examples:

a. Double alliteration, 39 examples:

fēasceaft funden 7   lȳthwōn lōgon 203
frumsceaft fīra 91   heard swyrd hilted 2987, etc.

Dissyllabic compounds in the first measure are the rule. Two monosyllables occur only in 2987, cited above (but this is in part a modern distinction; cf. *heardecg habban* 1490). A tetrasyllabic compound occurs once, *geōsceaft-gāsta* 1266.—Somewhat lighter secondary stress may be admitted in *eorlīc ellen* 637 and *Hæðcen Hrēþling* 2925, because these compounds would have been less distinctly felt as such (cf. Sievers, *Altgermanische Metrik,* p. 125).— The substitution of an uncontracted form is required in *feorhsēoc fleôn* 820, and of monosyllabic *māþm* in *sinc-māðþum sēlra* 2193 and *māðþumfæt mēre* 2405.—Emended verses here included are *gūðmōd grimmon* 306, *geōsceaft grimme* 1234, *āðsweord eorla* 2064, *b(ig)folc beorna* 2220.

b. Crossed alliteration, 1 example:

Wīglāf lēofa 2745

c. Alliteration on first stress alone, 13 examples:

Bēowulf nemnað 364, *also with proper names* 676, 1191, 1483.
earmlīc wurðan 807, *also with* -līc 842, 892, 1809.
inwidsorge 831, *also with* inwit- 1858, 1947.
orleghwīla, -e 2427, 2911

In all these examples under b and c the secondary stress may be comparatively light, hardly distinguishable from that of type A1.

29. | ♪̷ ♪ ♩| ♩ ♩ | (cf. 3), with double alliteration only, 21 examples:

    felahrōr fēran 27   sigehrēð secgum 490

and similarly 381, 401, 517 (*seofon niht swuncon*), 552, 1176 (*hereri[n]c habban*), 1180 (*metodsceaft sêon*), 1435, 1519, 1553, 1590, 2016, 2017, 2404, 2474, 2553, 2757.— The secondary stress may be weaker in the following verses:

    geatolīc gende 1401   Higelāc sēcan 1820
            Higelāc Hrēþling 1923

30. | ♩ ♪ ♪| ♩ ♩ | (cf. 5), with double alliteration only, 51 examples:

    folcstede frætwan 76   morðbeala māre 136

and similarly 41 others, including one verse with two words in the first measure, *beorht hofu bærnan* 2313.—In three other verses the first two syllables must be treated as one:

    morþorbealo māga 1079, 2742   aldorbealu eorlum 1676

In five others the secondary stress may be weaker:

    egsode eorl[as] 6   geōmrode giddum 1118
    þrēatedon þearle 560   weorðode weorcum 2096
         sw eðrian syððan 2702

†31. | ♪̷ ♪ ♪ ♪| ♩ ♩ | (cf. 7), with double alliteration only, 4 examples:

    mægenwudu mundum 236   hreþerbealo hearde 1343
    gomenwudu grēted 1065   gomenwudu grētte 2108

†32. | ♩ ♩| ♪̷ ♪ ♩ | (cf. 11), with double alliteration only, 15 examples:

    hordburh hæleþa 467   blīðheort bodode 1802
    ealdsweord eotenisc 1558, 2616 (eton-), 2979 (eoton-)

and similarly 819, 1047, 1205, 1607, 1670, 1852, 2043, 2072, 3006. One other verse requires monosyllabic *māðm*:

    hordmāðum hæleþa 1198

†33. |♪♪ ♩|♪♪ ♩| (cf. 13), with double alliteration only, 2 examples:

> freoðoburh fægere 522   atelīc egesa 784

The secondary stress may be weaker in the second example.

34. |♩ ♪♪|♪♪ ♩| (cf. 15), with double alliteration only, 10 examples:

> gūðsearo gumena 328   gestsele gyredon 994
>   wīcstede weligne 2607

and similarly 715, 767, 1171, 1239, 1476, 1534, 1602.

A2b

35. |♩ ♩|♩ ♩| (cf. 1), with double or (in four verses with proper names) single alliteration. Altogether, 18 examples:

a. Double alliteration, 14 examples:

> wīges weorðmynd 65   īren ǣrgōd 989, 2586

and similarly 127, 773, 1000, 1522, 1527, 2214, 2215 (*nið[ð]a nāthwylc*), 2289, 2564 (*ecgum unslāw*), 2953, and 823 (*dōgera dægrīm*).

b. Alliteration on first stress alone, 4 examples:

> þēoden Hrōðgār 417   glædne Hrōþulf 1181
> glædne Hrōðgār 863   Lēofa Bīowulf 2663

These are hardly to be distinguished from type A1.

†36. |♩.♪|♩ ♩| (cf. 2), with double alliteration only, 23 examples:

> hēah ond horngēap 82   Eft wæs anrǣd 1529
> Strǣt wæs stānfāh 320   frōd on forðweg 2625

and similarly 305, 336, 350, 357 (*eald ond* a*nhār*), 912, 1533, 1546 (*brād [ond] brūnecg*), 1785, 1800, 2037, 2292,

2296, 2449, 2509 (*hond ond heard sweord*).—In five other verses the secondary stress may be weaker:

lāð ond longsum 134, 192   sīd ond syllīc 2086
Bold wæs betlīc 1925   sōð ond sārlīc 2109

37. | ♪ ♪ ♩ | ♩ ♩ | (cf. 3), with double alliteration only, 7 examples:

æþeling ǣrgōd 130, [1329], 2342   þolode ðrȳðswȳð 131
witena wēlhwylc 266   wigena weorðmynd 1559
                  æðeling unfrom 2188

†38. | ♪ ♩ ♪ | ♩ ♩ | (cf. 4), with double alliteration only, 7 examples:

gamol ond gūðrēouw 58, similarly 826, 2682, 3021
weras on wilsīð 216   eoten wæs ūtweard 761

and with somewhat weaker secondary stress,

wlitan on Wīlāf 2852

†39. | ♩ ♪ ♪ | ♩ ♩ | (cf. 5), with double alliteration only, 24 examples:

hȳnðu ond hrāfyl 277   eald under eorðweall 2957
folc oþðe frēoburh 693   scōc ofer scildweall 3118

and similarly 413, 1087 (*healle ond hēahsetl*), 1127, 1200, 1277, 1430, 1506 (*Bǣr þā sēo brimwyl*[*f*]), 1575, 1921, 2420, 2638 (*helmas ond heard sweord*), 3105 (*bēagas ond brād gold*), 2739, 2893, 2991, 3090, 3132, 3155 (*hȳ*[*n*]*ðo* (*ond*) *h*(*æftnȳ*)*d*), 3168; and with weaker secondary stress,

hwīle wið Hrōþgār 152

40. | ♪ ♪ ♪ ♪ | ♩ ♩ | (cf. 7), with double alliteration only, 4 examples:

ðicgean ofer þā niht 736   Hyrte hyne hordweard 2593
Hyge wæs him hinfūs 755   brecan ofer bordweal 2980

†41. |♪ ♪ ♪♪♪ | ♪ ♪ | (cf. 9), with double alliteration only, 2 examples:

Wōd þā þurh þone wælrēc 2661   Reste hine þā rūmheort 1799

> Probably accidental is the supplementary alliteration of *h* in the latter. The second half-line is *reced hlīuade*.

(42. |♪♪♪ ♪ ♪|♪ ♪| (cf. 10), only in second half-line.)

†43. |♪♪♪ ♪♪♪ | ♪ ♪ |, with double alliteration, 1 example:

> Hȳrde ic þæt hē ðone healsbēah 2172
> Elision is imperative. Cf. *wēn' ic* in line 338.

44. |♪ ♪|♪♪ ♪| (cf. 11), with double alliteration, 3 examples:

> manna mægencræft 380   mihtig meredēor 558
> ferhðes foreþanc 1060

†45. |♪.♪|♪♪ ♪| (cf. 12), with double alliteration, 7 examples:

> mǣg ond magoðegn 408
> and similarly 1444, 1564, 2196, 2691; and with somewhat lighter secondary stress,
> gōd ond geatolīc 1562   eald ond egesfull 2929

†46. |♪ ♪ ♪|♪ ♪ ♪| (cf. 14), with double alliteration, 2 examples:

> sefa swā searogrim 594   biter ond beaduscearp 2704

47. |♪ ♪ ♪|♪ ♪ ♪| (cf. 15), with double alliteration, 6 examples:

symbel ond seleful 619   bēagas ond bregostōl 2370
sōna him seleþegn 1794   byrne ond beaduscrūd 2660
swancor ond sadolbeorht 2175 Heht ðā þæt heaðoweorc 2892

†48. |♪ ♪ ♪♪♪|♪ ♪ ♪|, with double alliteration, 1 example:

> Hylde hine þā heaþodēor 688

†49. ♪|♪ ♪ ♪ ♪|♪ ♪| (cf. 22), with double alliteration, 1 example:

> Gewāt þā ofer wægholm 217

†50. ♪|♪ ♪|♪♪ ♪| (cf. 25), with double alliteration, 1 example:

> gesāwon seledrēam 2252

But this verse is almost certainly corrupt (see Klaeber). Probably Klaeber's earlier reading, *secga seledrēam,* was right.

†51. ♫|♪ ♪|♪♪ ♪| (cf. preceding), with double alliteration, 1 example:

> Hē gcfēng þā fetelhilt 1563

It would be possible, of course, to delete *hē.*

†52. ♪|♪ ♪ ♪ ♪|♪♪ ♪| (cf. 27), with double alliteration, 2 examples:

> Ofsæt þā þone selegyst 1545
> Bebeorh þē ðone bealoniŏ 1758

A2ab

53. |♪ ♪|♪ ♪| (cf. 1), with double or (once) crossed alliteration. Altogether, 11 examples:

a. Double alliteration, 10 examples:

> ombeht unforht 287   brēosthord blōdrēow 1719
>   gūðrinc goldwlanc 1881

and with somewhat weaker secondary stress in one measure,

ǣnlīc ansȳn 251	wrǣtlīc wǣgsweord 1489
snellīc sǣrinc 690	ǣghwæs unrīm 2624, 3135
fūslīc f(yrd)lēoð 1424	wīgbord wrǣtlīc 2339

b. Crossed alliteration, 1 example with two proper names:
Hrōðgār Bēowulf 653

†54. | ♪ ♪ ♩ | ♩ ♩ | (cf. 3), with double alliteration, 1 example:

wliteséon wrǣtlīc 1650

†55. | ♩ ♪ ♪ | ♩ ♩ | (cf. 5), with double alliteration, 10 examples:

nȳdwracu nīþgrim 193   drihtsele drēorfāh 485

and with somewhat weaker secondary stress in one measure,

frēolicu folccwēn 641	healsode hrēohmōd 2132
tryddode tīrfæst 922	þrecwudu þrymlīc 1246
beorhtode bencswēg 1161	fyrdsearo fūslīc 2618
sīðode sorhfull 2119	lēodbealo longsum 1722

†56. | ♩ ♩ | ♪ ♪ ♩ | (cf. 11), with double alliteration, 3 examples:

æscholt ufan grǣg 330

and with weaker secondary stress in one measure,

gūðsweord geatolīc 2154   grimlīc gry(refāh) 3041

†57. | ♪ ♪ ♩ | ♪ ♪ ♩ | (cf. 13), with double alliteration, 1 example:

heorowearh hetelīc 1267

†58. | ♩ ♪ ♪ | ♪ ♪ ♩ | (cf. 15), with double alliteration, 2 examples:

gūðsearo geatolīc 215   grāpode gearofolm 2085

A*

†59. |♩ ♩₃♪|♩ ♩| (cf. 5), with double or single alliteration, 2 examples:

    a. Double alliteration, 1 example:

        Bēowulf wæs brēme 18

    b. Alliteration on first stress alone, 1 example:

        Wīglāf wæs hāten 2602

60. |♩ ♩₃♪|♩ ♩| (cf. 59), with double alliteration, 3 examples:

        þetlīc ond bānfāg 780   Hrōðgār ond Hrōþulf 1017
              Hrēðrīc ond Hrōðmund 1189

†61. |♪ ♪ ♩₃♪|♩ ♩| (59 with resolution of the first stress, cf. 7), with double alliteration, 2 examples:

        geolorand tō gūþe 438   egeslīc for eorlum 1649

†62. |♪ ♪ ♩ ♪|♩ ♩| (cf. 61), with double alliteration, 5 examples:

    gamolfeax ond gūðrōf 608   Heorogār ond Hrōðgār 61
    wreoþenhilt ond wyrmfāh 1698   Herebeald ond Hæðcyn 2434
              geatolīc ond goldfāh 308

    By refusing to consider -līc and the second members of proper names as syllables requiring heavy stress, we could reduce this entire category called A* to three examples, 438, 608, and 1698.

A3

†63. |♩ ♩|♩ ♪| (cf. 1), with alliteration on second stress alone, 2 examples:

        Ēow hēt secgan 391   Mē man sægde 1175

18

†64. | ♩ ♪ ♪ | ♩ ♩ |, with alliteration on second stress alone, 4 examples:

ðē wē ealle 941   Lēt se hearda 2977
þæt se mǣra 2587   þēah ðe ōðer 2481

Klaeber divides 2481 differently, *þēah ðe ōðer his / ealdre gebohte*, which would make the first half-line a normal B, but the effect of this is to destroy the meaning of *his*, which is naturally proclitic. We could escape the difficulty by substituting *hit* for *his* and retaining Klaeber's division, but I think there is enough precedent for my division to render the emendation unnecessary. For Klaeber's doubts about the division and the opinions of others see his note on the line.—It would be more accurate to record the rhythm of the last three examples as | ♩ ♪₃ ♪ | ♩ ♩ |.—Perhaps also *Sē wæs wrecna* (MS. *wreccena*) 898, which has been included under type C no. 22c.

†65. | ♪ ♪ ♩ | ♩ ♩ | (cf. 3), with alliteration on second stress alone, 4 examples:

Æfter þǣm wordum 1492   Þæt is undyrne 2000
Æfter ðām wordum 2669   Þæt ys sīo fǣhðo 2999

This reading gives a prominence that seems to me desirable to the demonstratives and *un-*. Otherwise, these verses could be included under the ensuing category.

†66. | ♩ ♪ ♪ | ♩ ♩ | (cf. 5), with transverse or single alliteration. Altogether, 58 examples:

a. Transverse alliteration (i. e. chief alliteration on second stress and supplementary, whether intentional or not, on first stress), 7 examples:

hwearf þā be wealle 1573   nǣnig þæt dorste 1933
nō hē mid hearme 1892   cwæð þæt hyt hæfde 2158

eall swylce hyrsta 3164

Wit þæt gecwǣdon 535   Þā wæs gesȳne 3058

The supplementary alliteration of the last two is almost
certainly accidental.

b. Alliteration on second stress alone, 51 examples:

Đā wæs on burgum 53, *similarly* 126, 607, 710 (Đa cōm
of mōre), 837, 847 (Đǣr wæs on blōde), 1288, 1647,
1884, 1896, 1905, 2821.

Fand þā ðǣr inne 118, *similarly* 746, 1188, 1623, 1782,
1888, 2550, 3110, 3126 (Næs ðā on hlytme).

ðǣr git for wlence 508, Đā wit ætsomne 544, Swā mec
gelōme 559, *similarly* 550, 809, 1130 (þēah þe *ne*
meahte), 1508, 2075, 2115, 2573, 2797.

Ic þæt gehȳre 290, Ic hine cūðe 372, *similarly* 798, 1292,
1700 and 2864 (Þæt, lā, mæg secgan), 2135, 2490,
2611, 2779, 2794.

siþðan him Scyppend 106, Hæfde se gōda 205, efne swā
swīðe 1092, *similarly* 470, 1223, 1283, 2305 (wolde *se*
lāða), 3120.

†67. | 𝅘𝅥 𝅘𝅥𝅮 𝅘𝅥𝅮| 𝅘𝅥 𝅘𝅥 | (no. 66 with heavy secondary stress at
end, cf. 39), with alliteration on second stress alone, 3
examples:

Mē þone wælrǣs 2101   oð þæt him ǣghwylc 9
oð þæt ymb āntīd 219

I have placed the two *oð þæt* verses here instead of under
no. 39 because I think the double alliteration is accidental.

†68. | 𝄾 𝅘𝅥𝅮 𝅘𝅥 𝅘𝅥𝅮| 𝅘𝅥 𝅘𝅥 | (cf. 66), with alliteration on second
stress alone, 26 examples:

ond þǣr on innan 71   Ic þē þā fǣhðe 1380
þæt hīe ne mōste 706   gif ic æt þearfe 1477
hwæt wit tō willan 1186   wæs ðā gebolgen 2304

and similarly 393, 751, 1082, 1347, 1661 (*ac mē geūðe*),
1777, 1834, 1846, 1878, 1972, 2104, 2195, 2494, 2714, 2716,
2966, 3081, 3104, beside 355 (*ðē mē se gōda*) and 2385
(*hē þǣr [f]or feorme*), where it could be argued that the
initial syllables were intended to carry supplementary

alliteration and ought therefore to receive primary accent.
I think that these, however, like *ond* and *ac* in 71 and 1661,
are really too weak to be counted in the alliterative scheme
even if one honors them with primary accent.—The distinction between this form and no. 66 is that here the second
syllable seems to deserve a little more emphasis than the
first. There is often room for doubt about this, however,
and I have probably been inconsistent.

†69. | ♪ ♪ ♪ ♪ | ♪ ♪ | (no. 68 with heavy secondary stress
at end), with alliteration on second stress alone, 2
examples:

Eart þū sē Bēowulf 506   Forþan bið andgit 1059

†70. | ♪ ♪ ♪ ♪ | ♪ ♪ | (cf. 7), with transverse or single
alliteration. Altogether, 90 examples:

a. Transverse alliteration, 6 examples:

Heht him þā gewyrcean 2337   Sē wæs on ðām ðrēate 2406
cwǣdon þæt hē wǣre 3180

þæt hē þæs gewinnes 1721   Gif ic þæt gefricge 1826
ac hē him on hēafde 2973

The supplementary alliteration of the last three is almost
certainly accidental.

b. Alliteration on second stress alone, 84 examples:

þā wæs æfter wiste 128	Þanon hē gesōhte 463
Mǣl is mē tō fēran 316	Hafast þū gefēred 1221
syðþan hīe þæs lāðan 132	Setton him tō hēafdon 1242
Nǣnig heora þōhte 691	oð ðæt hīe forlǣddan 2039, etc.

Here are included two verses in which the first syllable
echoes the alliteration, but I think merely by accident, *oð
þæt him on innan* 1740 and *oð ðæt hī oðēodon* 2934.—In
two others the second syllable might take precedence of the
first, in which case the latter would form anacrusis, *Ful oft
ic for lǣssan* 951 and *forþan hē tō lange* 1336.—Emended
verses are *(h)afað þæs geworden* 2026, *sceolde [ofer]
willan* 2589, and *Þā wæs æt ðām geong*an 2860.

†71. |♪ ♪ ♪ ♪|♩ ♩| (no. 70 with heavy secondary stress at end, cf. 40), with alliteration on second stress alone, 11 examples:

nō hē þone gifstōl 168	þæt hē þone nīðgæst 2699
ǣr hē þone grundwong 1496	þæt hē þone grundwong 2770
þæt hēo þone fyrdhom 1504	Hwæt, wē þē þās sǣlāc 1652
þæt hē þone brēostwylm 1877	Gif him þonne Hrēþrīc 1836
	syððan hyne Hæðcyn 2437

þæt ðū þone wælgǣst 1995   oð þæt hē ðā bānhūs 3147

In the last two examples the final syllable has supplementary alliteration, perhaps by accident.

†72. |♩ ♫♩|♩ ♩| (a minor variant of 70), with alliteration on second stress alone, 2 examples:

Swā hē ne forwyrnde 1142   þæs wǣron mid Ēotenum 1145

Syncope of the *e* in *Ēotenum* seems especially desirable because the proper form of the name is *Ēotum,* the *n* having crept in either from the genitive *Ēot(e)na* or more probably from a scribe's confusion of the name with the common noun *eoten.*

†73. |♫♩ ♩|♩ ♩| (the opposite variant of 70), with alliteration on second stress alone, 1 example:

efne swā hwylc mægþa 943

†74. |♪ ♫♩|♩ ♩| (another variant of 70), with alliteration on second stress alone, 8 examples:

þæt hine on ylde 22	ðā hyne gesōhtan 2204
ac hine se mōdega 813	ond þone gebringan 3009
ic hine ne mihte 967	ond þonne geferian 3107
þæt hire wið halse 1566	þæt ðū ne ālǣte 2665

†75. |♪ ♫♩|♩ ♩| (no. 74 with heavy secondary stress at end), with alliteration on second stress alone, 1 example:

þæt hine sēo brimwylf 1599

†76. |♪ ♪ ♪♪♪|♪ ♪| (cf. 9), with alliteration on second stress alone, 11 examples:

Nalæs hī hine lǣssan 43   Mæg þæs þonne ofþyncan 2032
þæt ðū mē ne forwyrne 429   þæt wē hine swā gōdne 347
ic þæt þonne forhicge 435   ac hē hafað onfunden 595
ac hīe hæfdon gefrūnen 694   ond hī hyne þā bēgen 2707
Gif ic þonne on eorþan 1822   ac hē hyne gewyrpte 2976
        sealde hiora gehwæðrum 2994

†77. |♪♪♪ ♪ ♪♪|♪ ♪| (cf. 10), with transverse or single alliteration. Altogether, 17 examples:

a. Transverse alliteration, 1 example:

     wēne‿ic þæt hē mid gōde 1184 (cf. 338)

b. Alliteration on second stress alone, 16 examples:

hī hyne þā ætbǣron 28   syþðan hē æfter dēaðe 1589
Habbað wē tō þǣm mǣran 270   Ēodon him þā tōgēanes 1626
Hæbbe ic ēac geāhsod 433   hēt [h]ine mid þǣm lācum 1868
Hwæþere mē gesǣlde 574   þæs ðe ic ðē gesundne 1998
mynte þæt hē gedǣlde 731   þone þe ðū mid rihte 2056
þāra þe ic on foldan 1196   Hȳrde ic þæt þām frætwum 2163
ðāra þe hē geworhte 1578   Hē ðā mid þǣre sorhge 2468
symle ic him on fēðan 2497   efne swā hwylcum manna 3057

†78. |♪♪♪ ♪♪♪|♪ ♪| (cf. 43), with transverse or single alliteration. Altogether, 6 examples:

a. Transverse alliteration, 1 very doubtful example:

     hwæðre hē hine on folce 2377

b. Alliteration on second stress alone, 5 examples:

     Nǣnigne ic under swegle 1197
     syðþan hē hine tō gūðe 1472
     þæs þe hī hyne gesundne 1628
     Ic hit þē þonne gehāte 1671
     Nōðer hȳ hine ne mōston 2124

†79. | ♩ ♪ ♪ | ♩ ♪ ♩ | (cf. 11 and 64), with alliteration on second stress alone, 2 examples:

> Ic þæt hogode 632   on him gladiað 2036

†80. | ♩ ♪ ♪ | ♩ ♪ ♩ | (cf. 15), with transverse or single alliteration. Altogether, 10 examples:

   a. Transverse alliteration, 1 example:

   > Hwīlum for (d)uguðe 2020

   b. Alliteration on second stress alone, 9 examples:

Bēo ðū on ofeste 386	Wearð him on Heorote 1330
Cōm þā tō recede 720	Bīo nū on ofoste 2747
Đā hīe getruwedon 1095	Þæt wæs þām gomelan 2817
Cōm þā tō Heorote 1279	Đā wæron monige 2982
	Him ðā gegiredan 3137

†81. | ♩ ♪ ♪ | ♩ ♪ ♩ | (no. 80 with heavy secondary stress at end, cf. 47), with alliteration on second stress alone, 1 example:

> lēt ðone bregostōl 2389

†82. | ♩ ♪ ♪ ♪ | ♩ ♪ ♩ | (cf. 15 and 68), with alliteration on second stress alone, 1 example:

> sē ðone gomelan 2421

†83. | ♪ ♪ ♪ ♪ | ♩ ♪ ♩ | (cf. 16), with transverse or single alliteration. Altogether, 8 examples:

   a. Transverse alliteration, 1 example:

   > Nū hēr þāra banena 2053

   b. Alliteration on second stress alone, 7 examples:

nē þǣr nǣnig witena 157	būton þone hafelan 1614
Đonne wæs þēos medoheal 484	þonne bīoð (āb)rocene 2063
efne swā of hefene 1571	Fela ic on giogoðe 2426
	syððan ic for dugeðum 2501

†84. | ♪ ♪ ♪ ♪ | ♪ ♪ ♩ | (no. 83 with heavy secondary stress at end), with alliteration on second stress alone, 1 example:

> oððe þone cynedōm 2376

†85. | ♩ ♩♩♩ | ♪ ♪ ♩ | (a minor variant of 83), with alliteration on second stress alone, 1 example:

> Hēr syndon geferede 361

†86. | ⁊ ♪ ♩♩♩ | ♪ ♪ ♩ | (another variant of 83, cf. 74), with alliteration on second stress alone, 1 example:

> þæt hire on hafelan 1521

†87. | ♩♩♩ ♪ ♪ | ♪ ♪ ♩ | (cf. 17), with alliteration on second stress alone, 1 example:

> þone þe him on sweofote 2295

†88. | ♩♩♩ ♩♩♩ | ♪ ♪ ♩ |, with alliteration on second stress alone, 1 example:

> nō ðȳ ǣr hē þone heaðorinc 2466

†89. ♪ | ♩ ♪ ♪ | ♩ ♩ | (cf. 20), with alliteration on second stress alone, 5 examples:

> Gespræc þā se gōda 675   Gesæt ðā on næsse 2417
> Geþenc nū, se mǣra 1474   Geseah ðā be wealle 2542
> Ne meahte se snella 2971

†90. ♪ | ♪ ♪ ♪ ♪ | ♩ ♩ | (cf. 22), with transverse or single alliteration. Altogether, 18 examples:

a. Transverse alliteration, 2 examples:

> þā gȳt hīe him āsetton 47
> gedēð him swā gewealdene 1732

b. Alliteration on second stress alone, 16 examples:

Gewiton him þā fēran 301

Gewāt him ðā se hearda 1963

Gewāt him ðā se gōda 2949

Gemunde ðā ðā āre 2606

Ne frīn þū æfter sǣlum 1322

Ne nōm hē in þǣm wīcum 1612

Ne meahte ic æt hilde 1659

ne mihte ðā forhabban 2609

Ne meahte hē on eorðan 2855

Ne meahton wē gelǣran 3079

Ne þynceð mē gerysne 2653

þæt mē is micle lēofre 2651

forþon þe hē ne ūþe 503

forþan ic hine sweorde 679

ālegdon ðā tōmiddes 3141

Ongunnon þā on beorge 3143

†91. ♩♩ | ♪ ♪ ♪ ♪ | ♩ ♩ | (cf. 23), with alliteration on second stress alone, 1 example:

Ne gefrægen ic þā mægþe 1011

†92. ♪ | ♩♩♩ | ♩ | ♩ ♩ | (cf. 73), with alliteration on second stress alone, 1 example:

gesaga him ēac wordum 388

†93. ♪ | ♪ ♪ ♩♩♩ | ♩ ♩ | (cf. 9), with alliteration on second stress alone, 1 example:

Gewīteð þonne on sealman 2460

†94. ♪ | ♩ ♪ ♪ | ♩ ♪ ♩ | (cf. 26), with alliteration on second stress alone, 2 examples:

Geseah hē in recede 728   Āhlēop ðā se gomela 1397

†95. ♪ | ♩ ♪ ♪ | ♩ ♪ ♩ | (94 with heavy secondary stress at end), with alliteration on second stress alone, 1 example:

gē swylce sēo herepād 2258

This might be read with initial rest, like no. 86.

†96. ♪|♪ ♪ ♪ ♪|♪ ♪ ♩| (cf. 27), with alliteration on second stress alone, 1 example:

þæt ic on þone hafelan 1780

†97. ♪|♪ ♪ ♪♪♪|♪ ♪ ♩| (cf. 48), with alliteration on second stress alone, 1 example:

Gesāwon ðā æfter wætere 1425

A4(= A1, A2, A3 with short ending)

Short A1

(98. |♩ ♩|♪ ♩.|, only in second half-line.)

(99. |♪ ♪ ♩|♪ ♩.|, only in second half-line.)

†100. |♩ ♪ ♪|♪ ♩.|, with alliteration on first stress alone, 2 examples:

êam his nefan 881   dædum gefremed 954

These differ from type E merely in having a light secondary stress.—Perhaps *Meaht ðū, mīn wine* 2047 should be included here, but I have placed it under expanded D by the dubious expedient of stressing *mīn*.

†101. |♪ ♪ ♪ ♪|♪ ♩.|, with alliteration on first stress alone, 1 example:

nīða ofercumen 845

Short A2a

102. |♩ ♩|♪ ♩.|, with double or single alliteration. Altogether, 17 examples:

a. Double alliteration, 12 examples:

wonsceaft wera 120	sorhlēas swefan 1672
þrēanȳd þolað 284	gromheort guma 1682
wælrēow wiga 629	dryhtbearn Dena 2035
syndolh sweotol 817	wælrǣs weora 2947
wīdcūþ werum 1256	wælnīð wera 3000
gūðhorn galan 1432	wordgyd wrecan 3172

b. Alliteration on first stress alone, 5 examples:

frumcyn witan 252	ðrȳþærn Dena 657
þrȳðword sprecen 643	fēasceaft guma 973
	grundwong þone 2588

The supplementary alliteration of -*wong* in the last example is probably accidental.

103. | ♪ ♪ ♩ | ♪ ♩. |, with double or single alliteration. Altogether, 8 examples:

a. Double alliteration, 6 examples:

magodriht micel 67	medubenc monig 776
medoærn micel 69	gryrelēoð galan 786
searonet seowed 406	medoful manig 1015

b. Alliteration on first stress alone, 2 examples:

heaðorōf cyning 2191	freoðowong þone 2959

Short A3

†104. | ♩ ♩ | ♪ ♩. | or | 𝄽 ♪ ♪ | ♪ ♩. |, with alliteration on second stress alone, 1 example:

Wæs mīn fæder 262

Cf. nos. 63 and 64.

†105. | ♪ ♪ ♩ | ♪ ♩. | or less probably | 𝄽 ♪♪♩ | ♪ ♩. |, with alliteration on second stress alone, 1 example:

þone þīn fæder 2048

Cf. no. 65.—Klaeber (p. 278, n. 3) calls attention to the suggestion of F. Schwartz (*Cynewulfs Anteil am Christ,*

Königsberg Diss., 1905, p. 31) and Trautmann (*Kynewulf*, Bonn. B. i, 1898, p. 77) that a parallel form *fædder* might have existed. Such a form would normalize nos. 104, 105, and 107.

†106. | ♪ ♪ ♪ ♪ | ♪ ♩. |, once with transverse alliteration, once with single, 2 examples:

   a. Transverse alliteration, 1 example:

     Hwīlum hē on lufan 1728

   b. Alliteration on second stress alone, 1 example:

     þǣr him nǣnig wæter 1514

     Cf. *nē þǣr nǣnig witena* 157, no. 83b above.

†107. ♪ | ♩ ♩ | ♪ ♩. | or less probably | 𝄾 ♪ ♪ ♪ | ♪ ♩. | (no. 104 with anacrusis), with alliteration on second stress alone, 1 example:

     Geslōh þīn fæder 459

The alliteration prevents us from reckoning this as type B.

TYPE B

a. FIRST MEASURE LIGHT, SECOND HEAVY

B1

1. | 𝄾 ♩ | ♪ ♪ ♪ | (sometimes | 𝄾 ♩ | ♩ ₃ ♪ ♪ |, but the penultimate syllable is enclitic; cf. no. 9 ff., where it is proclitic), with double, crossed, or single alliteration. Altogether, 18 examples:

   a. Double alliteration, 2 examples:

     þes hearda hēap 432   on sīdne sǣ 507

   b. Crossed alliteration, 2 examples:

     ðurh ānes cræft 699   Swā giōmormōd 2267

c. Alliteration on first stress alone, 14 examples:

on flōdes ǣht 42

Dǣm fēower bearn 59

þurh slīðne nīð 184

Hwæt syndon gē 237

mīn yldra mǣg 468

ymb brontne ford 568

þæt mihtig God 701

þurh Drihtnes miht 940

hē fēara sum 1412

hū mihtig God 1725

hwylc (orleg)hwīl 2002

þurh dēaðes nȳd 2454

þǣr Ongenþēow 2486

þis ellenweorc 2643

2. $|\overset{u}{\underset{x}{}} \ ♪ \ ♪|\overset{\prime\prime}{♪} \ ♪ \ \overset{\prime}{♪}|$, with double, crossed, or single alliteration. Altogether, 98 examples:

a. Double alliteration, 23 examples:

þenden wordum wēold 30

wæs se grimma gǣst 102

ond gehealdan hēt 674

Đā wæs swīgra secg 980

and similarly 983, 997, 1030, 1057, 1173, 1300, 1393 (*nē on foldan fæþm*), 1405, 1448, 1551, 1764, 2255, 2316, 2989 (*Hē ð(ām) frætwum fēng*), 3117, and 3150 (*swylce giōmorgyd*, the only compound).—Three others have the second member of a compound in an unaccented position:

Wæs þū, Hrōðgār, hāl 407   sēcean wynlēas wīc 821

Hēr is ǣghwylc eorl 1228

b. Crossed alliteration, 5 examples:

Þǣr æt hȳðe stōd 32

lǣtað hildebord 397

þæs þe þincean mæg 1341

þæt hit scēadenmǣl 1939

and with the second member of a compound in an unaccented position,

Ond þū *Unferð* lǣt 1488

c. Alliteration on first stress alone, 70 examples:

þon[n]e yldo bearn 70

Đā se ellengǣst 86

ac ymb āne niht 135

Him þā hildedēor 312

and similarly 333 (Hwanon ferigeað gē), 340, 377, 457 (*For [g]ewy[r]htum þū*), 465, 500, 513, 605, 669, 778, 789, 791, 822, 834, 844, 859, 886, 910, 958, 988, 1004 (*ac gesēcan sceal*), 1009, 1032, 1035, 1039 (*þæt wæs hildesetl*), 1110, 1222, 1297, 1334, 1408, 1415, 1428, 1446, 1464, 1609, 1677, 1753, 1791, 1875 (*þæt h[ī]e seoððða(n) [nō]*), 1879,

2059, 2084, 2107, 2131, 2137, 2142, 2155, 2190, 2240, 2244, 2330, 2444, 2507, 2785, 2813, 2848, 2924, 2961, 2974, 2986, 3001, 3018, and 3134 (*Þā wæs wunden gold*), besides three verses with the second member of a compound in an un- accented position:

Ðone sīðfæt him 202   Ūre æghwylc sceal 1386

nealles inwitnet 2167

Two of the verses listed above, *ealne wīdeferhþ* 1222 and *hwīlum hildedēor* 2107, might be read as type D,

♩ ♩ | ♪ ♪ ♩ |, the first with transverse, the second with double alliteration.

3. | 𝄾 ♪ ♩ | ♪ ♪ ♩ |, with double, crossed, or single alliteration. Altogether, 4 examples:

a. Double alliteration, 1 example:

gebād wintra worn 264

b. Crossed alliteration, 1 example:

þæt hīe, þēoden mīn 365

c. Alliteration on first stress alone, 2 examples:

ond þā frēolīc wīf 615   forwrāt Wedra helm 2705

The *w* of *forwrāt* seems to me either accidental or merely supplementary, but this verse could be read as type D with anacrusis, ♪ | ♩ | ♪ ♪ ♩ |.

4. | 𝄾 ♩ ♩ ♩ | ♪ ♪ ♩ |, with double or single allitera- tion. Altogether, 14 examples:

a. Double alliteration, 2 examples:

hwæþere ic fāra feng 578   Swā hit oð dōmes dæg 3069

I think the first verse should be read with elision, or syncope (*hwæþre ic*), or both; any of these seems better than | ♪ ♪ ♪ ♪ | ♪ ♪ ♩ |, but see no. 7 below.

b. Alliteration on first stress alone, 12 examples:

> sē þe on handa bær 495   siðða hīe sunnan lēoht 648

and similarly 655 (*Næfre ic ǣnegum men*), 880, 909, 1056, 1106, 1308, 1356, 1915, 2114, and 2799.

5. | ♪ ♪ ♪ ♪ | ♪ ♪ ♩ |, with double or single alliteration. Altogether, 13 examples:

a. Double alliteration, 2 examples:

nē him þæs wyrmes wīg 2348   forðām hē manna mǣst 2645

b. Alliteration on first stress alone, 11 examples:

> þæt þone hilderǣs 300   Nē hūru Hildeburh 1071
> on mīnre ēþeltyrf 410   Gewāt þā twelfa sum 2401

and similarly 661, 1086, 1104, 1456, 1866, 2157, and 2184.

6. | ♪ ♪ ♪♪♪ | ♪ ♪ ♩ |, with double alliteration, 1 example:

> Gehwearf þā in Francna fæþm 1210

7. | ♪ ♪ ♪ ♪ | ♪ ♪ ♩ |, with double or single alliteration. Altogether, 3 examples:

a. Double alliteration, 1 example:

> þēah ðe hē his brōðor bearn 2619

b. Alliteration on first stress alone, 2 examples:

> swylce hīe æt Finnes hām 1156
> ðēah þe hine mihtig God 1716

(8. | ♪♪♪ ♪ ♪ | ♪ ♪ ♩ |, only in second half-line.)

(9. | ♩ | ♩ ♪ ♩ |, only in second half-line.)

10. | ♪ ♪ | ♩ ♪ ♩ |, with double, crossed, or single alliteration. Altogether, 28 examples:

a. Double alliteration, 9 examples:

Þā wæs eft swā ǣr 642, 1787   Þā se wyrm onwōc 2287
Þǣr wæs sang ond swēg 1063   Đā se gǣst ongan 2312
Þǣr wæs gidd ond glēo 2105   Ic ðæt mǣl geman 2633
geaf me sinc ond symbel 2431   ofer mīn gemet 2879

b. Crossed alliteration, 3 examples:

ðǣm tō hām forgeaf 374   swylce oft bemearn 907
            gif hē torngemōt 1140

c. Alliteration on first stress alone, 16 examples:

Him ðā Scyld gewāt 26   hū hē frōd ond gōd 279
Þæt fram hām gefrægn 194   þætte sūð nē norð 858

and similarly 1373, 1593, 1608, 1620, 1684, 1781, 2111,
2121, 2369, 2387, 2500, and 2948.

11. | ♩♩ |♩ ♪ ♩|, with alliteration on first stress
alone, 3 examples:

siþðan ic hond ond rond 656   Nō ðȳ ǣr ūt ðā gēn 2081
            þone ðe oft gebād 3116

12. | ♪ ♪ ♪|♩ ♪ ♩|, with alliteration on first stress
alone, 1 example:

þæt nǣron ealdgewyrht 2657

(13. | ♪ ♩♩ |♩ ♪ ♩| ,only in second half-line.)

(14. |♪ ♪ ♪ ♪|♩ ♪ ♩|, only in second half-line.)

†15. | ♩|♩♩ ♩| (no. 1 with resolution of first
stress), with double or single alliteration. Altogether,
3 examples:

a. Double alliteration, 2 examples:
      þus manige men 337   þurh wæteres wylm 1693

b. Alliteration on first stress alone, 1 example:
      Đǣm eafera wæs 12

16. |♪ ♪ ♪| ♪♩♩ ♩| (no. 2 with resolution of first stress), with double or single alliteration. Altogether, 10 examples:

a. Double alliteration, 7 examples:

under Heorotes hrōf 403	on swā hwæþere hond 686
under heofones hwealf 576, 2015	nē on gyfenes grund 1394
Ðǣr wæs hæleþa hleahtor 611	ofer fealone flōd 1950.

b. Alliteration on first stress alone, 3 examples:

ond on geogoðe hēold 466   Þū eart mægenes strang 1844
Oferhogode ðā 2345

(17. |♪ ♪ ♩| ♪♩♩ ♩| (no. 3 with resolution of first stress), only in second half-line.)

18. |♪ ♩♩♩| ♪♩♩ ♩| (no. 4 with resolution of first stress), with alliteration on first stress alone, 1 example:

þāra þe gumena bearn 878

19. |♪ ♪ ♪ ♪| ♪♩♩ ♩| (no. 5 with resolution of first stress), with crossed or single alliteration, 2 examples:

a. Crossed alliteration, 1 example:

forþan hīe mægenes cræft 418

b. Alliteration on first stress alone, 1 example:

ðæt hæfde gumena sum 2301

(20. |♪ ♪ ♩♩♩| ♪♩♩ ♩| (no. 6 with resolution of first stress), only in second half-line.)

21. |♪ ♪ ♪ ♪| ♪♩♩ ♩| (no. 7 with resolution of first stress), with double alliteration, 1 example:

nē hīe hūru heofena Helm 182

19

22. | ♩ | ♪ ♪ ♪ ♪ | (no. 1 with resolution of second stress), with double or single alliteration. Altogether, 5 examples:

a. Double alliteration, 2 examples:

    wið Grendles gryre 384   þurh sīdne sefan 1726

b. Alliteration on first stress alone, 3 examples:

    þurh rūmne sefan 278   ðæs morþorhetes 1105
        þurh hlēoðorcwyde 1979

23. | ♪ ♪ | ♪ ♪ ♪ ♪ | (no. 2 with resolution of second stress), with double, crossed, or single alliteration. Altogether, 17 examples:

a. Double alliteration, 8 examples:

    Wē þurh holdne hige 267   siþðan grimne gripe 1148
    hæfde māre mægen 518   sē ðe lengest leofað 2008
    Đā wæs hāten hreþe 991   wið his sylfes sunu 2013
    hire selfre sunu 1115   æfter billes bite 2060

b. Crossed alliteration, 1 example:

    æfter māþðumgife 1301

c. Alliteration on first stress alone, 8 examples:

    Þā wæs wundor micel 771   on swā geongum feore 1843
    sē þe secgan wile 1049   þæt hīe Gēata clifu 1911
    æfter dēofla hryre 1680   syððan Gēata cyning 2356
        æfter māððumwelan 2750

and with the second member of a compound in an unaccented position,

    nē þurh inwitsearo 1101

24. | ♩ ♩ | ♪ ♪ ♪ ♪ | (no. 4 with resolution of second stress), with alliteration on first stress alone, 1 example:

    oððe him Ongenðeowes 2475

25. |♪ ♪ ♪ ♪|♪ ♪ ♪ ♪| (no. 5 with resolution of second stress), with double or single alliteration, 2 examples:

a. Double alliteration, 1 example:

tō þǣre byrhtan byrig 1199

b. Alliteration on first stress alone, 1 example:

þæt hē wið attorsceaðan 2839

26. |♪ ♪ ♪ ♪|♪ ♪ ♪ ♪| (no. 7 with resolution of second stress), with alliteration on first stress alone, 3 examples:

næfre hē on aldordagum 718
swylce hē on ealderdagum 757
þæt hīo hyre (hēofun)g(da)gas 3153

†27. |♪ ♪ ♪|♪₃ ♪ ♪ ♪| (no. 10 with resolution of second stress), with double or single alliteration, 3 examples:

a. Double alliteration, 1 example:

þā wæs synn ond sacu 2472

b. Alliteration on first stress alone, 2 examples:

Hȳ on wīggetawum 368   Þanon eft gewiton 853
On the quantity of -getawum see below, group F, b.

(28. |♪ ♪ ♪ ♪|♪₃ ♪ ♪ ♪| (no. 12 with resolution of second stress), only in second half-line.)

†29. |♪ ♪ ♪ ♪|♪₃ ♪ ♪ ♪| (no. 14 with resolution of second stress), with alliteration on first stress alone, 1 example:

þæt wē him ðā gūðgetawa 2636
On the quantity of -getawa see below, group F, b.

†30. | ♩ ♪ ♪| ♩♩♩ ♪♪| (no. 2 with resolution of both stresses), with double alliteration, 2 examples:

> æfter hæleþa hryre 2052, 3005

> Probably also *under heofenes haðor* 414. See group F, no. 5.

(31. | ♪ ♪ ♪ ♪| ♩♩♩ ♪♪| (no. 5 with resolution of both stresses), only in second half-line.)

B2

32. | ♩ | ♪ ♫ ♪|, with double or single alliteration. Altogether, 9 examples:

a. Double alliteration, 2 examples:

> Ðām wīfe þā word 639   þurh hreðra gehygd 2045

b. Alliteration on first stress alone, 7 examples:

> Hē bēot ne ālēh 80   ond þegna gehwylc 1673
> on fēonda geweald 808, 903   ond þegna gehwām 2033
> æt nīða gehwām 882   wið Ēotena bearn 1088

> The last example might better have *Ēotna* and be read according to no. 1 above.

33. | ♪ ♪ ♪| ♪ ♫ ♪|, with double, crossed, or single alliteration. Altogether, 28 examples:

a. Double alliteration, 9 examples:

> æfre mærða þon mā 504   gē wið fēond gē wið frēond 1864
> sēcan dēofla gedræg 756   ofer borda gebræc 2259
> ond him fæste wiðfēng 760   ond æt gūðe forgrāp 2353
> þæt þec ādl oððe ecg 1763   ac in campe gecrong 2505

> and with the second member of a compound in an unaccented position,

> þæt wæs feohlēas gefeoht 2441

Cf. *sēcean wynlēas wīc* 821 under no. 2 above. One is tempted to read *feoht,* but cf. c below.

b. Crossed alliteration, 2 examples:

þæt hē dogora gehwām 88   Ðonne wēne ic tō þē 525

As authority for the elision in the second verse, see *Wēn' ic þæt gē for wlenco* 338 (under type A, no. 10 above) and *Wēn' ic þæt hē wille* 442 (under type A, no. 7 above).

c. Alliteration on first stress alone, 17 examples:

Ðā ic wīde gefrægn 74   ofer ȳða gewealc 464
Þā of wealle geseah 229 under swegles begong 860, 1773

and similarly 1040, 1365, 1469, 1872, 2006 (*swā begylpan* [*ne*] *þearf*), 2418, 2620 (*Hē* [*ðā*] *frætwe gehēold*), 2752, and 2870, besides *þæt hē Ēotena bearn* 1141 (*Ēotna?* Cf. no. 32b above), and two verses with the second member of a compound in an unaccented position:

Ðā him Hrōþgār gewāt 662   ond him Hrōþgār gewāt 1236

34. | ♩♪♪ | ♪ ♫ ♩ |, with double or single alliteration. Altogether, 5 examples:

a. Double alliteration, 1 example:

sē þe his wordes geweald 79

b. Alliteration on first stress alone, 4 examples:

Þā ic on morgne gefrægn 2484
Ðā ic æt þearfe [gefrægn] 2694
Ðā ic on hlǣwe gefrægn 2773
þēah ðe hē dǣda gehwæs 2838

35. | ♪ ♪ ♪ | ♪ ♫ ♩ |, with alliteration on first stress alone, 3 examples:

þæt ic on wāge geseah 1662 (*or like no. 34 above*)
forðām mē wītan ne ðearf 2741
forlēton eorla gestrēon 3166

(36. | ♪ ♩♪♪ | ♪ ♫ ♩ |, only in second half-line.)

(37. | ♪ ♪ ♪ ♪ | ♪ ♫ ♩ |, only in second half-line.)

(38. | ♫♩ ♪ ♪ | ♪ ♫ ♩ |, only in second half-line.)

(39. | ♪ ♪ ♫♩ | ♪ ♫ ♩ |, only in second half-line.)

(40. ♪ | ♪ ♪ ♪ ♪ | ♪ ♫ ♩ |, only in second half-line.)

41. | ⅍ ♪ ♪ | ♫ ♫ ♩ | (no. 33 with resolution of first stress), with double alliteration, 1 example:

ofer geofenes begang 362

†42. | ⅍ ♪ ♩ | ♫ ♫ ♩ | (cf. preceding), with alliteration on first stress alone, 1 example:

ond ðā Iofore forgeaf 2997

43. | ⅍ ♫♩ | ♫ ♫ ♩ | (no. 34 with resolution of first stress), with double alliteration, 1 example:

Swylce hē siomian geseah 2767

†44. | ⅍ ♪ ♪ ♪ | ♫ ♫ ♩ | (no. 35 with resolution of first stress), with alliteration on first stress alone, 1 example:

þurh hwæt his worulde gedāl 3068

†45. | ⅍ ♩ | ♪ ♫ ♪ ♪ | (no. 32 with resolution of second stress), with alliteration on first stress alone, 1 example:

wið fēonda gehwone 294

46. | ⅍ ♪ ♪ | ♪ ♫ ♪ ♪ | (no. 33 with resolution of second stress), with double, crossed, or single alliteration. Altogether, 5 examples:

a. Double alliteration, 2 examples:

    ond on healfa gehwone 800   under næssa genipu 1360

b. Crossed alliteration, 1 example:

    Swā hē nīða gehwane 2397

c. Alliteration on first stress alone, 2 examples:

    sē ðe mēca gehwane 2685   ofer flōda genipu 2808

47. | ♩ ♪ ♪ ♪|♪ ♫ ♪ ♪| (no. 35 with resolution of second stress), with crossed alliteration, 1 example:

    þæt næfre Gre[n]del swā fela 591

†48. ♪|♪ ♪ ♪ ♪|♪ ♫ ♪ ♪| (no. 40 with resolution of second stress), with double alliteration, 1 example:

    Mæg þonne on þæm golde ongitan 1484

(49. |♪ ♪ ♪|♫ ♫ ♪ ♪| (no. 33 with resolution of both stresses), only in second half-line.)

B3

†50. |♪ ♪ ♪|♪ ♫ ♪| (cf. 33), with alliteration on second stress alone, 1 example:

    hē is manna gehyld 3056

But probably this is a mistake for *hē is gehyld manna,* type C. For the grammatical sequence, compare *nē gemet mannes* 2533, *þē on land Dena* 242, *oððe gripe mēces* 1765.

†51. |♪ ♪ ♪|♪ ♫ ♪ ♪| (cf. 46), with transverse alliteration, 1 example:

    þæt hit ā mid gemete   (manna ænig) 779

Since it is hard to prove that transverse alliteration was consciously employed, this verse ranks with the preceding as an example of alliteration on the second stress. It would be possible, but I think unwise, to read the verse as the short form of type A3 which I have included under A4 (nos. 104-7)—that is, with the rhythm ♪ ♪ ♩♩♩ | ♪ ♩.| where *ā* receives only secondary accent. I think it unwise because the adverb ought to take precedence of the qualifying adverbial phrase of which *gemete* is a part. It seems probable that we ought rather to reverse the order of words in the second half-line. This would give us another instance of B2 no. 46, with crossed alliteration.

It will be seen from the preceding remarks that I do not believe in the legitimacy of type B3. The extreme rarity of the form is enough to render it suspect. In the present system it becomes doubly so because the alliteration is confined to a syllable that receives only secondary accent. This secondary accent is indeed a strong one, and its strength might conceivably lead careless scribes or even poets to forget its inferiority; but I do not think that careless workmanship can be associated with the composition of *Beowulf*. Where transpositions are as easy as in the two verses cited above, it is hard to believe that the author was responsible for the irregularity. — Two verses which are sometimes cited as examples of B3 (e. g. tentatively by Sievers, *Altgermanische Metrik* par. 85. 3), *þær him nǣnig wæter* 1514 and *geslōh þīn fæder* 459, will be found under type A, nos. 106, 107.

b. With anacrusis and a heavy stress in each measure.

B1

52. ♪| ♩ ♩ | ♩| (cf. 1), with double, crossed, or single alliteration. Altogether, 12 examples:

a. Double alliteration, 4 examples:

in fȳres fæþm 185	þurh hæstne hād 1335
on fāgne flōr 725	in Hrefnesholt 2935

b. Crossed alliteration, 1 example:

    ālēdon þā 34

c. Alliteration on first stress alone, 7 examples:

on ancre fæst 303   [Ge]grētte þā 652
ond ōðer swylc 1583   Gegrētte ðā 2516
Ymbēode þā 620   Gecyste þā 1870
          Geworhton ðā 3156

The last five verses, together with 34, under b, could be read

$| \begin{smallmatrix} \text{(s)} & \text{(N)} \end{smallmatrix} \; \begin{smallmatrix} \text{''} & \text{''} \end{smallmatrix} |$, because they introduce new sentences. Since, however, this involves the omission of both primary and secondary accents in the first measure, I have thought it safer to record them here.

53.   ♪| ♩. ♪| ♩| (cf. 9), with double alliteration, 2 examples:

nē lēof nē lāð 511   on hand gehwearf 2208

(54.   ♪| ♩ ♪ ♩| ♩| (cf. 15), only in second half-line.)

(55.   ♪| ♩ ♩ ♪| ♩| (cf. 54), only in second half-line.)

56.   ♪| ♩ ♩| ♩ ♩.| (cf. 22), with double or single alliteration, 3 examples:

a. Double alliteration, 1 example:

on Grendles gryre 478

b. Alliteration on first stress alone, 2 examples:

wið manna hwone 155   ymb aldor Dena 668

Verse 478 is very similar to 384, *wið Grendles gryre,* which I have included under no. 22 above. This is a good illustration of the dual potentiality of many of the verses that begin with one unimportant syllable. Only the context, about which I may well have erred in this and similar cases, can determine which of the two possible readings is to be adopted.

(57.   ♪| ♩ ♪ ♩| ♩ ♩.| (cf. 30), only in second half-line.)

B2

58.   ♪|♪♪♪ ♪|♪| (cf. 41), with double alliteration, 1 example:

geseted ond gesǣd 1696

TYPE C

a. First measure light, second heavy.

C1 (= Sievers' C1 + C2)

1. |♩ ♩|♩ ♩ ♪|, with double, crossed, or single alliteration. Altogether, 22 examples:

a. Double alliteration, 3 examples:

Oft Scyld Scēfing 4   of brȳdbūre 921
          geond sæl swingeð 2264

b. Crossed alliteration, 1 example:

bē ȳðlāfe 566 (*i. e.* bī; *Klaeber* be)

c. Alliteration on first stress alone, 18 examples:

hwæt swīðferhðum 173	swā dēorlīce 585
þǣr swīðferhþe 493	Swā manlīce 1046
mīn mondrihten 436	ond Hear[dr]ēde 2202
his unsnyttrum 1734	tō healdanne 1731
eal langtwīdig 1708	þā sēlestan 416
mid scipherge 243	ðǣm sēlestan 1685
on wælbedde 964	mid Wilfingum 461
on gylpsprǣce 981	for sc[ē]oten[d]um 1026
Him big stōdan 3047	wið hettendum 3004

I think the extra alliteration in 436 is accidental, but the verse could be read as type D.

2. |♩ ♪ ♪|♩ ♩ ♪|, with double, crossed, or single alliteration. Altogether, 133 examples:

a. Double alliteration, 8 examples:

swylce gīgantas 113	þæt hē mā mōste 735
æfter sǣsīðe 1149	þone hring hæfde 1202

ofer sǣ sīde 2394   geond þæt sæld swǣfun 1280
nē gemet mannes 2533   ofer sǣ sōhtan 2380

b. Crossed alliteration, 7 examples:

Þā wæs Hrōðgāre 64   æfter cearwælmum 2066
Swā wæs Bīowulfe 3066   ac hē mancynnes 2181
ond þā cearwylmas 282   ac for þrēanēdlan 2223
          þæt hē dæghwīla 2726

c. Alliteration on first stress alone, 118 examples:

ofer hronrāde 10   Þanon untȳdras 111
æfter wælnīðe 85   Þā wæs ēaðfynde 138

and with similar compounds in the second measure 159
((*ac se*) *ǣglǣca*), 163, 196, 200, 244 (*Nō hēr cūðlīcor*),
260, 273 (*swā wē sōþlīce*), 280 (*gyf him edwenden*), 378,
425, 434, 491, 509, 556, 571, 577, 796, 830, 832, 838, 893,
894, 899, 928, 932, 944, 1084, 1089, 1135 (*þā ðe syngāles*),
1269, 1315, 1345, 1457, 1486, 1638, 1655, 1796, 1818, 1827,
1850, 1900, 1936, 1955, 1986, 2087, 2203, 2232 (*in ðām
eorð(hū)se*), 2291, 2520, 2531, 2592, 2627, 2806, 2856,
2865, 2887, 2899 (*ac hē sōðlīce*), 2905, 2926, 2954, 2984,
3059, 3089 (*nealles swǣslīce*), and 3127;

þæt hīo Bēowulfe 623   þæt hē Hrōþgāres 717

and with similar proper names 1296, 1399, 1899, 2076
(*Þǣr wæs Hondsciô*), 2129, 2207, 2324, and 2375;

þæt ðā līðende 221   Him se yldesta 258
tō gecȳðanne 257   þæt mid Scyldingum 274

and with similar trisyllables in the second measure 363,
565, 634, 649, 708, 916, 1003 (*tō beflēonne*) 1076, 1309,
1406, 1640, 1828 (*swā þec het[t]ende*), 1829, 1851, 1922,
1956 (*þone sēlestan*), 1988, 2272, 2382, 2416, 2435, 2445,
2452, 2644, 2683, 2823, 2828, 2841, 2857, 2871, 2960
(*syððan Hrēðlingas*), and 3109; besides

oððe ā syþðan 283   Ðā cōm in gān 1644
þæt hīe oft wǣron 1247   þæt se secg wǣre 3071

3. |♪ ♪ ♩|♩ ♪ ♪|, with alliteration on first stress
alone, 2 examples:

Ond ðā Bēowulfe 1043   Ðā gȳt ǣghwylcum 1050

4. |♪ ♩♩♩|♪ ♪ ♪|, with double, crossed, or single alliteration. Altogether, 19 examples:

a. Double alliteration, 1 example:

sē ðe on hēa(um) h(æþ)e 2212

b. Crossed alliteration, 2 examples:

þonne him Hūnlāfing 1143   hwæþer him Alwalda 1314

c. Alliteration on first stress alone, 16 examples:

þāra þe tīrlēases 843   æfter þām wælrǣse 824
þonne hē Hrōðgāres 1580   sē þe ēow wēlhwylcra 1344
þā ðe mid Hrōðgāre 1592   Nō ðȳ ǣr fēasceafte 2373
oððe in Swīorīce 2495   oþ þæt hē fǣringa 1414
Nē ic te Swēoðēode 2922   þ(ēah) ð(e hē) slǣpende 2218
þæs þe him ȳþlāde 228   sende ic Wylfingum 471

besides four others in which the three preliminary syllables might better be allowed to fill the whole of the first measure, giving |♪ ♪ ♩| in 1756, |♩ ♪ ♪| in the others:

sē þe unmurnlīce 1756   þæt hē on Bīowulfes 2194
cwæð þæt se Ælmihtiga 92   cwæð, hē on mergenne 2939

In 2194 *þæt* is demonstrative and seems to need emphasis.

5. |♪ ♪ ♪ ♪|♪ ♪ ♪|, with alliteration on first stress alone, 15 examples:

mid þǣre wælfylle 125   þæt hē wið ælfylcum 2371
Nē þæt se āglǣca 739   *þæt* hē wið āglǣcean 2534
þæt hē þā wēalāfe 1098   þæt ūre mandryhten 2647
ond him tō Anwaldan 1272   on hyra mandryhtnes 2849
þæt hīe on bā healfa 1305   þæt hēo on ǣnigne 627
Ic hi*ne* hrædlīce 963   on þǣre wēstenne 2298
Forgeaf þā Bēowulfe 1020   ond nū æt sīðestan 3013
               Gewāt ðā byrnende 2569

In 1020 and 2569 the first syllable could be treated as anacrusis and the next two allowed to fill the whole of the first measure, giving the pattern of type D except for the light accentuation of the first measure (♪| ♩ ♩| ♩ ♪ ♪|).

6. |𝅘𝅥𝅮 𝅘𝅥𝅮 𝆺𝅥𝅮𝆺𝅥𝅮|𝅘𝅥 𝅘𝅥𝅮 𝅘𝅥𝅮|, with alliteration on first stress alone, 2 examples:

ne hȳrde ic cȳmlīcor 38   þē hine æt frumsceafte 45

The first of these could also be read with anacrusis,

𝅘𝅥𝅮|𝅘𝅥₃𝅘𝅥𝅮 𝅘𝅥𝅮|𝅘𝅥 𝅘𝅥𝅮 𝅘𝅥𝅮|.

7. |𝅘𝅥𝅮 𝅘𝅥𝅮 𝅘𝅥𝅮 𝅘𝅥𝅮|𝅘𝅥 𝅘𝅥𝅮 𝅘𝅥𝅮|, with alliteration on first stress alone, 5 examples:

þāra þe mid Bēowulfe 1051   þāra þe mid Hrōðgāre 1407
þæs þe hīe gewislīcost 1350   þāra ðe in Swīorīce 2383
þē hē ūsic gārwīgend 2641

(8. |𝆺𝅥𝅮𝆺𝅥𝅮 𝅘𝅥𝅮|𝅘𝅥 𝅘𝅥𝅮 𝅘𝅥𝅮|, only in second half-line.)

(9. |𝆺𝅥𝅮𝆺𝅥𝅮 𝅘𝅥𝅮 𝅘𝅥𝅮|𝅘𝅥 𝅘𝅥𝅮 𝅘𝅥𝅮|, only in second half-line.)

10. |𝄽 𝅘𝅥|𝅘𝅥𝅮 𝅘𝅥𝅮 𝅘𝅥𝅮 𝅘𝅥𝅮| (no. 1 with resolution of the first stress), with double or single alliteration, 6 examples:

a. Double alliteration, 1 example:

fram mere mōdge 855

b. Alliteration on first stress alone, 5 examples:

ond Higelāces 261   on Heaþo-Rǣmes 519
for herebrōgan 462   Wæs merefixa 549
his gædelinges 2617

11. |𝄽 𝅘𝅥𝅮 𝅘𝅥𝅮|𝅘𝅥𝅮 𝅘𝅥𝅮 𝅘𝅥𝅮 𝅘𝅥𝅮| (no. 2 with resolution of the first stress), with double, crossed, or single alliteration. Altogether, 49 examples:

a. Double alliteration, 5 examples:

ond tō Fæder fæþmum 188   ofer heafo healdan 2477
oððe atol yldo 1766   tō gescipe scyndan 2570
woldon (care) cwīðan 3171

b. Crossed alliteration, 1 example:

scolde herebyrne 1443

c. Alliteration on first stress alone, 43 examples:

þonne heoru bunden 1285	ond gehwæðer ōðrum 2171
oððe gripe mēces 1765	ac se maga geonga 2675

Nū ic suna mīnum 2729

ofer lagustrǣte 239	þæt wæs foremǣrost 309
ofer lagustrēamas 297	ac for higeþrymmum 339

and with similar compounds in the second measure 370, 396, 481, 526, 533, 804, 864 (*Hwīlum heaþorōfe,* where I think the extra alliteration is accidental), 1067, 1449, 1462, 1523, 1597, 1606, 1942, 1943, 2049, 2067 (*Þ̄y ic Heaðo-Bear[d]na*), 2257, 2428, 2581, 2605, 3020, and 3130 (*þæt hī ofostlīc(e)*);

wearþ hē Heaþolāfe 460	æfter Herebealde 2463
siððan Heremōdes 901	hæfde Higelāces 2952

hū ðā æþelingas 3, *similarly* 982, 1244, 1804, 2374

tō geþolianne 1419   ac hȳ scamiende 2850

†12. $\left|\begin{smallmatrix} {}^{\cap} \\ \gamma \end{smallmatrix} \right. \flat \; \rfloor \; | \; \flat \; \flat \; \flat \; \flat \; |$ (no. 3 with resolution of first stress), with alliteration on first stress alone, 1 example:

Onsend Higelāce 452

13. $\left|\begin{smallmatrix} {}^{\cap} \\ \chi \end{smallmatrix} \right. \overline{\rfloor\rfloor\rfloor} \; | \; \flat \; \flat \; \flat \; \flat \; |$ (no. 4 with resolution of first stress), with double or single alliteration, 6 examples:

a. Double alliteration, 1 example:

nō ðȳ ǣr suna sīnum 2160

b. Alliteration on first stress alone, 5 examples:

swylce ic maguþegnas 293	swā ðū on geoguðfēore 2664
nemne him heaðobyrne 1552	syððan hīe Hygelāces 2943

hraðe hēo æþelinga 1294

The last verse could be regarded as an example of type D with transverse alliteration, | ♪ ♪ ♩ | ♪ ♪ ♪ ♪ |. The second half is *ānne hæfde*.

14. | ⁊ ♪ ♪ ♪ | ♪ ♪ ♪ ♪ | (no. 5 with resolution of first stress), with double or single alliteration, 7 examples:

a. Double alliteration, 1 example:

in hyra gryregeatwum 324

b. Alliteration on first stress alone, 6 examples:

on þisse meoduhealle 638   þæt mon his winedryhten 3175
on þære medubence 1052   þæt hē fram Sigemunde[s] 875
ac ic ðær heaðufȳres 2522   þæt hig þæs æðelinges 1596

15. | ⁊ ♪ ♩♩♩ | ♪ ♪ ♪ ♪ | (no. 6 with resolution of first stress), with alliteration on first stress alone, 1 example:

nē hyne on medobence 2185

16. | ♪ ♪ ♪ ♪ | ♪ ♪ ♪ ♪ | (no. 7 with resolution of first stress), with alliteration on first stress alone, 4 examples:

Nō ic mē an herewæsmun 677   ðāra þe on Scedenigge 1686
Nē hīe hūru winedrihten 862   þonne hē on ealubence 2867

17. | 𝄽 ♪ ♪ | ♩ ♩♩♩ | (no. 2 with resolution of second stress), with alliteration on first stress alone, 1 example:

þæt hīo lēodbealewa 1946

The reading *-bealwa* would reduce this to no. 2.

(18. | 𝄽 ♩♩♩ | ♩ ♩♩♩ | (no. 4 with resolution of second stress), only in second half-line.)

†19. | ♩ | ♪♪ ♪♪♩ | (no. 1 with resolution of both stresses), with double alliteration, 1 example:

Swā fela fyrena 164

20. | ♪ ♪ | ♪♪ ♪♪♩ | (no. 2 with resolution of both stresses), with alliteration on first stress alone, 1 example:

sē þe wæteregesan 1260

C2(= Sievers' C3)

21. | ♩ | ♩ ♪ ♪ |, with double, crossed, or single alliteration. Altogether, 33 examples:

a. Double alliteration, 4 examples:

wið wrāð werod 319   ,geond wīdwegas 840
sē s[c]ynscaþa 707 (*Kl.* se) in fenfreoðo 851

b. Crossed alliteration, 3 examples:

tō līfwraþe 971   þæt mǣgwine 2479
of eorðsele 2515

c. Alliteration on first stress alone, 26 examples:

þæt healreced 68   tō West-Denum 383
Swā rīxode 144   þurh rūnstafas 1695
Swā bealdode 2177   ǣr swyltdæge 2798
mīn rūnwita 1325   on þǣm dæge 197, 790, 806
gē feor hafað 1340   on hēahstede 285
sceal hringnaca 1862   on ādfære 3010
eal bencþelu 486   on bēorsele 492, 1094
of feorwegum 37   in bīorsele 2635
of līchaman 3177   in *n*īdgripe 976
wið fǣrgryrum 174   in Frēswæle 1070
mid, for ārstafum 317, 382   in bǣlstede 3097

22. | ♪ ♪ | ♩ ♪ ♪ |, with double, crossed, or single alliteration. Altogether, 137 examples:

a. Double alliteration, 11 examples:

Swā sceal (geong g)uma 20   nē tō gnēað gifa 1930
Wæs sīo swātswaðu 2946   æfter dēaðdæge 187, 885
druncon wīn weras 1233   ofer wīd wæter 2473
Swylce ferhðfrecan 1146   on geflit faran 865
nō þȳ leng leofað 974   þone cwealmcuman 792

b. Crossed alliteration, 8 examples:

Hwæt, wē Gār-Dena 1   æfter waldswaþum 1403
sēo ðe bāncofan 1445   æfter lēodhryre 2030
syððan ðēodcyning 2970   æfter wīgfruman 2261
næfne goldhwæte 3074   on ðām feorhbonan 2465

c. Alliteration on first stress alone, 118 examples:

þē hīe ǣr drugon 15   Swā ðā drihtguman 99
būton folcscare 73   ðīnra gegncwida 367
þæt se ecghete 84   Hæfdon swurd nacod 539
ond gefrætwade 96   Hwæt, þū worn fela 530

and similarly 117, 170, 177, 189, 230, 242, 349, 373, 385, 437, 443, 458, 479, 647, 664 (*wolde wīgfruma,* where I think the extra alliteration is accidental), 695, 704, 738, 766, 793, 854, 866, 869, 873, 883, 979, 1007, 1010, 1064, 1066, 1192, 1213, 1253, 1258, 1317, 1320 (*æfter nēodlaðu*[*m*]), 1368, 1421, 1458, 1480, 1541, 1600, 1635, 1639, 1712, 1754, 1769, 1801 (*oþ þæt hrefn blaca*), 1823, 1841, 1894, 1907, 1920, 1928, 1938, 1981 (*geond þæt* heal*rɇced*), 1996, 2010, 2022, 2083, 2139 (*in ðām* [*gūð*]*sele*), 2144, 2152, 2176, 2197, 2278, 2318, 2321, 2333, 2340, 2344, 2363, 2366, 2391, 2407, 2561, 2637, 2688, 2718, 2735, 2753, 2775 (*him on bearm hladon*), 2786, 2830, 2835, 2840, 2844 (*hæfde ǣghwæðer*), 2846, 2858, 2873, 2877, 2884, 2900, 2903 (*him on efn ligeð*), 2918, 2963, 2985, 3008, 3028, 3042, 3046, 3053, 3077 (*Oft sceall eorl monig,* where I think the extra alliteration is accidental), and 3163, besides a series of questionable verses:

oferhīgian 2766   ond betimbredon 3159
oððe fe(o)r(mie) 2253   Swā begnornodon 3178
ond gebēotedon 536   Sē wæs wreccena 898

Sievers assigned these verses to type C, but pointed out that they would naturally have been accented on the final syllable rather than its predecessor, the later history of the language showing that only the preterite singular of weak verbs of the second class was regularly accented on the penultimate syllable, and the accentuation of the genitive plural *-ena* being doubtful. (See *Beiträge* 10.297 and 254.) Shifting the accent to the last syllable would produce verses of type B, except that the final accent would be much weaker than usual. It was for this reason that Sievers assigned these verses to type C (*Beiträge* 10.247). It seems best to classify them here, therefore, until more conclusive evidence can be offered. As for *wreccena,* the form *wrecna* is available (cf. *Genesis* 39, *Runic Poem* 20), which would convert the verse into type A3 (see A, nos. 64 and 65 above).

23. | ♪ ♪ 𝅘𝅥 | 𝅘𝅥 ♪ ♪ |, with alliteration on first stress alone, 4 examples:

þæt ðec, dryhtguma 1768	ond þā gyddode 630
Ond þā sīðfrome 1813	ond ðā folgode 2933

24. | 𝄽 ♪ 𝅘𝅥 𝅘𝅥 | 𝅘𝅥 ♪ ♪ |, with alliteration on first stress alone, 8 examples:

þone on gēardagum 1354	þāra þe lēodfruman 2130
swylce on næshleoðum 1427	þonne his ðīodcyning 2579
sē þe of flānbogan 1744	þǣr hyne Hetware 2916
syððan hē mōdsefan 2012	þenden hē burhwelan 3100

25. | ♪ ♪ ♪ ♪ | 𝅘𝅥 ♪ ♪ |, with double or single alliteration. Altogether, 21 examples:

a. Double alliteration, 2 examples:

beforan beorn beran 1024	mid mīnne goldgyfan 2652

b. Alliteration on first stress alone, 19 examples:

ond þē þā andsware 354	þæt hē his frēond wrece 1385
þæt hīe in bēorsele 482	þæt hē [in] nīðsele 1513
ac hē gefēng hraðe 740	nē him for hrōfsele 1515
þæt him se līchoma 812	þæt hire an dæges 1935
þæt hyre Ealdmetod 945	swā hȳ on gēardagum 2233

þæt hē for *mu*ndgripe 965   on hyra sincgifan 2311
ymb hyra sincgyfan 1012   tō ðyssum sīðfate 2639
on ðyssum windagum 1062   þē him se eorðdraca 2712
þē ðone [þēodcyning] 3086

and two verses with weak verbs of the second class, which might better be assigned to type B (see no. 22c above):

Gewāt ðā nēosian 115   Ful oft gebēotedon 480

†26. | ♪ ♪ ♩ | ♩ ♪ ♪ |, with alliteration on first stress alone, 2 examples:

ofer þǣm hongiað 1363   ðā ic ðē, beorncyning 2148

For the possibility that the first of these should be assigned to type B, see no. 22c above.—It would be possible to read both verses with initial rest, according to no. 24, but the reading here recommended seems more expressive.

†27. | ♩ ♪ ♪ | ♩ ♪ ♪ |, with alliteration on first stress alone, 2 examples:

Ðā hē him of dyde 671   Þā ymbe hlǣw riodan 3169

These verses also could be read with initial rest according to no. 24. I prefer the reading given because the emphasis on *Ðā* seems appropriate to a new stage of the narrative.

28. | 𝄾 ♪ ♩♩♩ | ♩ ♪ ♪ |, with alliteration on first stress alone, 2 examples:

þæt hē þone wīdflogan 2346 tō ðæs ðe hē eorðsele 2410

The first of these could be read according to no. 29 below.

29. | ♪ ♪ ♪ ♪ | ♩ ♪ ♪ |, with crossed or single alliteration, 4 examples:

a. Crossed alliteration, 1 example:

sē þe æfter sincgyfan 1342

b. Alliteration on first stress alone, 3 examples:

ðēah hīe hira bēaggyfan 1102   cwæð, hē þone gūðwine 1810
Hūru þæt onhōhsnod[e] 1944

> For *þæs wǣron mid Ēotenum* 1145, which as it stands
> might be read | ♩ ♫♩ | ♩ ♪♪ |, see type A, no. 72.

(30. | ♪♫ ♪ ♪♪ | ♪ ♪♪ |, only in second half-line.)

†31. ♪| ♪ ♪ ♪ ♪| ♪ ♪♪ |, with alliteration on first stress
alone, 1 example:

þæt ic wið þone gūðflogan 2528

b. WITH ANACRUSIS AND A HEAVY STRESS IN EACH MEASURE.

C1 (= Sievers' C1 + C2)

32. ♪| ♩| ♩ ♩ | (cf. 1), with double or single allitera-
tion, 3 examples:

a. Double alliteration, 1 example:
   wið þēodþrēaum 178

b. Alliteration on first stress alone, 2 examples:
   gerūmlīcor 139   in gumstōle 1952

†33. ♪ ♪| ♩| ♩ ♩ | (cf. 2), with crossed or single alliter-
ation, 2 examples:

a. Crossed alliteration, 1 example:
   ofer Bīowulfe 2907

b. Alliteration on first stress alone, 1 example:
   ofer hlēorber[g]an 304

> These exceptional readings are contingent on the assump-
> tion that the verses form single long phrases with those
> that precede them. Perhaps *þone sēlestan* 1406 might also
> be included, but I have assigned it to no. 2. See the dis-
> cussion in Part I above, pp. 61 ff.

34. ♪|♪♩.|♪ ♩| (cf. 10), with double or single alliteration, 13 examples:

  a. Double alliteration, 8 examples:

in worold wōcun 60	on sefa(n) sweorceð 1737
tō medo mōdig 604	on sefan sende 1842
on grames grāpum 765	gemyne mǣrþo 659
on weres wæstmum 1352	beloren lēofum 1073

  b. Alliteration on first stress alone, 5 examples:

on geogoðfēore 537	in ealobence 1029
æt heaðolāce 584	tō beadulāce 1561
on meodubence 1902	

†35. ♪ ♪|♪♩.|♪ ♩| (cf. 11), with double alliteration, 1 example:

  wið ðām gryregieste 2560

For this reading, see what is said under no. 33 above.

36. ♪|♪♩.|♪♪ ♩| (cf. 19), with double alliteration, 1 example:

  geboren betera 1703

C2(= Sievers' C3)

37. ♪|♩|♪♩.| (cf. 21), with double, crossed, or single alliteration. Altogether, 11 examples:

  a. Double alliteration, 4 examples:

on stefn stigon 212	forgrand gramum 424
geond wīdwegas 1704	ongēan gramum 1034

  b. Crossed alliteration, 1 example:

  tō ecgbanan 1262

  c. Alliteration on first stress alone, 6 examples:

in mōdsefan 180	of flānbogan 1433
on bearm nacan 214	his frēawine 2438
tō Gār-Denum 601	tō handbonan 2502

†38. ♪ ♪| ♩ | ♪ ♩.| (cf. 22), with alliteration on first stress alone, 1 example:

under stāncleofu 2540

For this reading, see what is said under no. 33 above. Two other verses that have been included above under no. 22 might be read in the same way, though less probably: *geond þæt* healr̯eced 1981 and *mid his handscale* 1317.

(39. ♪| ♪ ♩.| ♪ ♩.| (no. 37 with resolution of first stress), only in second half-line.)

TYPE D

D1

1. | ♩| ♩ ♪ ♪|, with double, crossed, or single alliteration. Altogether, 47 examples:

a. Double alliteration, 8 examples:

wīgweorþunga 176   [ea]l unhlitme 1129
heardhicgende 394, 799   wīs wēlþungen 1927
eallīrenne 2338   wearp wælfȳre 2582
          Wulf Wonrēding 2965

b. Crossed alliteration, 4 examples:

swīðhicgende 919, 1016   þanchycgende 2235
          hāmweorðunge 2998

c. Alliteration on first stress alone, 35 examples:

lindhæbbende 245   nīwtyrwydne 295
gūðfremmendra 246   gūðwērigne 1586

and with similar compounds 299, 861, 952, 1006, 1355, 1389 (*unlifgendum*), 744 (*unlyfigendes*), 1402, 1788, 1811, 2125, 2504, 2548, 2868, 2895, 3112, and 3158 ((*wǣ*)*g-līðendum*);

frēan Scyldinga 291, 351   wīg Hengeste 1083
Þēod-Scyldingas 1019   Wǣgmundinga 2814
lēod Scyldinga 1653, 2159

þegn Hrōðgāres 235   eorl Bēowulfes 795
cwēn Hrōðgāres 613   sīð Bēowulfes 872, 1971
torn unlȳtel 833   gold unrīme 3012

2. | ♪ ♩. | ♩ ♪ ♪ | (no. 1 with resolution of first stress),
with double, crossed, or single alliteration. Altogether,
49 examples:

a. Double alliteration, 23 examples:

fromum feohgiftum 21   wudu wælsceaftas 398
atol āngengea 165   etan unforhte 444

and similarly 449, 592, 598, 732, 816, 960, 2263, 2266, 2557,
2902, and 2915;

wado weallende 546   losað (li)figende 2062
wadu weallendu 581   nearo nēðende 2350
gifen gēotende 1690   hæleð hīofende 3142

heorohōcyhtum 1438   felafricgende 2106

b. Crossed alliteration, 1 example:

nefa Swertinges 1203

c. Alliteration on first stress alone, 25 examples:

merelīðende 255   mægenbyrþenne 1625
selerǣdende 1346   felamōdigra 1637

and similarly 1798, 1945, 2565, 2837, and 2955;

Heaðo-Scilfingas 63   Sige-Scyldingum 2004
            Merewīoingas 2921

wine Scyldinga 148, 1183, *similarly* 428, 663, 1418, 1601
mægen Hrēðmanna 445   sunu Ecglāfes 1808
sunu Bēanstānes 524   nefa Gārmundes 1962
reced sēlesta 412   segen gyldenne 1021
            duguð unlȳtel 498

3. | ♩ | ♪ ♪ ♪ ♪ | (no. 1 with resolution of second
stress), with double or single alliteration, 10
examples:

a. Double alliteration, 6 examples:

heall heorudrēore 487	weard winegeōmor 2239
betst beadorinca 1109	hæft hygegiōmor 2408
hild heorugrimme 1847	frōd felageōmor 2950

b. Alliteration on first stress alone, 4 examples:

mæg Higelāces 737, 914   feorh æþelinges 2424
sibæðelingas 2708

4. |♪ ♩.|♪ ♪ ♪ ♪| (no. 1 with resolution of both stresses), with double alliteration, 2 examples:

hladen herewǣdum 1897   hwatum Heorowearde 2161

(5. |♩|♩ ♩♩♩| (no. 1 with resolution of secondary stress), only in second half-line.)

†6. ♪|♩|♩ ♪ ♪| (no. 1 with monosyllabic anacrusis), with double alliteration, 2 examples:

gesægd sōðlīce 141   ābrēot brimwīsan 2930

†7. ♪|♪ ♩.|♩ ♪ ♪| (no. 2 with monosyllabic anacrusis), with double alliteration, 1 example:

gewrecen wrāðlīce 3062

†8. ♪|♩|♪ ♪ ♪ ♪| (no. 3 with monosyllabic anacrusis), with double alliteration, 2 examples:

onband beadurūne 501   gesēon sunu Hrǣdles 1485

†9. ♪|♪ ♩.|♪ ♪ ♪ ♪| (no. 4 with monosyllabic anacrusis), with double alliteration, 1 example:

gelocen leoðocræftum 2769

D2

10. | ♪ | ♪ ♪ ♪ | , with double or single alliteration. Altogether, 35 examples:

a. Double alliteration, 29 examples:

lēof landfruma 31	hēah Healfdene 57
lēof leodcyning 54	deorc dēaþscua 160

and similarly 288, 322, 551, 554, 936, 1409, 1845, 2025, 2042, 2090, 2226, 2271, 2315, 2368, 2563, and 2827;

heard hēr cumen 376	bāt bānlocan 742
beorht bēacen Godes 570	hīold hēahlufan 1954
eft eardlufan 692	(song) sorgcearig 3152
wong wīsian 2409	hēah hlīfian 2805
flōd fæðmian 3133	

Perhaps the last three should be assigned to D4. See above under type C, no. 22c.

b. Alliteration on first stress alone, 6 examples:

bearn Healfdenes 469	lēasscēaweras 253
frēan Ingwina 1319	feorh ealgian 2668
mǣg Ælfheres 2604	hord scēawian 2744

Again the last two might be assigned to D4.

11. | ♪ ♪. | ♪ ♪ ♪ | (no. 10 with resolution of first stress), with double or single alliteration. Altogether, 23 examples:

a. Double alliteration, 17 examples:

guma gilphlæden 868   frome fyrdhwate 1641, 2476

and similarly 1895, 1919, 1948, 2112, 2118, 2273, 2414, 2517, and 2642;

swutol sang scopes 90	eodor Ingwina 1044
brego Beorht-Dena 427, 609	hæleð Healf-Dena 1069

b. Alliteration on first stress alone, 6 examples:

mago Healfdenes 1867   suna Ōhtere[s] 2612
sunu Healfdenes 268, 645, 1699, 2147

12. | ♩ | ♪ ♪ ♪ ♪ | (no. 10 with resolution of second stress), with double or single alliteration, 2 examples:

    a. Double alliteration, 1 example:

      gold glitinian 2758.

      But perhaps this should be assigned to D4 (| ♩ | ♪♪♩ ♩ |).
      See no. 10a and type C, no. 22c.

    b. Alliteration on first stress alone, 1 example:

      Weard maþelode 286

13. ♪ | ♩ | ♩ ♪ ♪ | (no. 10 with monosyllabic anacrusis), with double alliteration, 3 examples:

    gewēold wīgsigor 1554   oflēt līfdagas 1622
           Gesyhð sorhcearig 2455

D3

According to Sievers, this subtype has the form ´ | �’ ˈ × , which would be interpreted as | ♩ | ♪ ♩ ♪ |. This rhythm is recommended by Heusler also, and may be correct; but I prefer to read the second measure | ♪ ♪ ♩ |. (Sievers would have marked this | ˘ × × .) It is true that the penultimate syllable is long in all well-attested examples of the form except the recurrent *andswarode* in the second half-line, and that when this long syllable receives quarter-note quantity it is held past the moment when the secondary accent of the measure is expected, thus producing a form of syncopation and adding some weight to an otherwise light verse. Nevertheless, this syncopated reading seems unnatural, not only because the penultimate syllable is never one that deserves emphasis, but because the final syllable, which is always enclitic as in *þeodcyninga*, is pushed closer to the following verse than to the syllable that precedes it, and thus assumes the rhythmic effect of a proclitic. It seems better, therefore, to adopt the natural accentuation *pĕodcýningà,* and to explain the preference for a long syllable in the penultimate position on grounds of burden rather than accent. That is, the effort required to pronounce a long syllable in the time of an eighth-note adds weight to the verse in one way just as the more forceful accentuation of it that attends syncopation does in another. (For Sievers, see *Altgermanische Metrik,* §§ 16.4, 84.6n., and 85.5; but note his earlier agreement with the accentual pattern that I have recommended, *Beiträge* 10.260 f. For Heusler, see *Deutsche Versgeschichte* 1. 152 and 161.)

14. | ♩ | ♪ ♪ ♩ | , once doubtfully with double alliteration, once with single—2 examples:

a. Double alliteration, 1 example:

hrēas [heoro]blāc 2488 (| ♩ | ♪ ♪ ♩ |)

This emendation is readable enough and should not offend modern ears, but it lacks the support of analogy. The alternative emendation [*hilde*]*'blāc,* though metrically unassailable (D4), seems less pregnant in meaning. Might we not read *hrēawblāc gehrēas?* This makes sense, accords with type E, and in addition explains the scribal error.

b. Alliteration on first stress alone, 1 example:

þēodcyninga 2

Perhaps also *Wuldurcyninge* 2795, which has been assigned to type A, no. 11c.

(15. | ♪ ♩. | ♪ ♪ ♩ | (no. 14 with resolution of first stress), only in second half-line.)

D4

16. | 𝅘𝅥 | 𝅘𝅥𝅮 𝅘𝅥𝅮 𝅘𝅥 | , with double or single alliteration.
Altogether, 25 examples.

    a. Double alliteration, 24 examples:

        wēold wīdeferhð 702   eal inneweard 998
        bād bolgenmōd 709   hār hilderinc 1307

    and similarly 1400, 1702, 1713, 1909, 2183, 2198, 2210,
2493, 2558, 2863 (*sec*[*g*] *sārigferð*), 2885, 2951 (*eorl
Ongenþīo*), 3063, and 3136 (*hār hilde*[*rinc*]) ;

        sweord swāte fāh 1286   holm heolfre wēoll 2138
        brim blōde fāh 1594   (sīd,) since fāh 2217
        segl sāle fæst 1906   frōd folces weard 2513

    b. Alliteration on first stress alone, 1 example:

        Flōd blōde wēol 1422

17. | 𝅘𝅥 𝅘𝅥. | 𝅘𝅥𝅮 𝅘𝅥𝅮 𝅘𝅥 | (no. 16 with resolution of first
stress), with double or crossed alliteration. Altogether, 28 examples:

    a. Double alliteration, 27 examples:

        micel morgenswēg 129   flota fāmīheals 218

    and similarly 298, 1022 (*hroden hildecumbor*), 1112, 1646,
1806, 1816 (*hæle hildedēor*), 2074, 2082, 3022, 3111, and
with the second member of a compound in an unaccented
position,

        ides āglǣcwīf 1259   atol inwitgǣst 2670

    and with two words in the second measure,

        maga māne fāh 978   fǣger foldan bearm 1137

    and similarly 1038, 1290, 1332, 1364, 1369, 1932, 1966, and
2178, besides three introduced by finite verbs,

        byreð blōdig wæl 448   warað wintrum frōd 2277
             swefeð sāre wund 2746

    b. Crossed alliteration, 1 example:

        bonan Ongenþēoęs 1968

18. |♩|♩ ₃♪ ♩| (like no. 16 except that the penultimate syllable is proclitic instead of enclitic), with double alliteration, 3 examples:

> Fyrst forð gewāt 210   eal ingesteald 1155
>
> born bord wið rond 2673 (*Klaeber* bord wið rond; *see Group F, no. 2, below.*)

(19. |♪ ♩.|♩ ₃♪ ♩| (no. 18 with resolution of first stress), only in second half-line.)

20. |♩|♪ ♫ ♩| , with double alliteration, 2 examples:

> sēon sibbegedriht 387   eald enta geweorc 2774

21. |♪ ♩.|♪ ♫ ♩| (no. 20 with resolution of first stress), with double alliteration, 3 examples:

> swefan sibbegedriht 729   atol ȳða geswing 848
> Metod manna gehwæs 2527

†22. |♩|♫♩ ♩| (no. 16 with resolution of second stress), with double alliteration, 2 examples:

> wlanc Wedera lēod 341   wræc Wedera nīð 423

(23. |♪ ♩.|♫♩ ♩| (no. 22 with resolution of first stress also), only in second half-line.)

24. |♩|♩ ₃♪ ♪♪| (no. 18 with resolution of secondary stress), with double alliteration, 1 example:

> wōm wundorbebodum 1747

†25. ♪|♩|♪ ♪ ♩| (no. 16 with monosyllabic anacrusis), with double alliteration, 4 examples:

> Ārīs, rīces weard 1390   forbarn brōdenmǣl 1616
> āwræc wintrum frōd 1724   forbarn brogdenmǣl 1667

†26. ♪| ♪́ ♩̆.| ♪́ ♪ ♪̀| (no. 17 with monosyllabic anacrusis), with double alliteration, 2 examples:

> ætwiton wēana dǣl 1150   onboren bēaga hord 2284

D*1

27. | ♩́ ♩̀| ♩́ ♪̀ ♪| , with double or single alliteration. Altogether, 33 examples:

a. Double alliteration, 27 examples:

> sīde sǣnæssas 223   rondas regnhearde 326

and similarly 770, 987 (*egl*[*u*] *unhēoru*), 1002, 1097, 1565, 1865, 1874, 1886, 2396, 2646 (*dǣda dollīcra*), 2648, 2725, 2810, and 3099;

> Setton sǣmēþe 325   secgað sǣlīðend 411

and similarly 1512, 1749, 2051, 2065, and 3031;

> Hwearf þā hrædlīce 356   miste mercelses 2439
> Scēotend Scyldinga 1154   yrre ōretta 1532

b. Alliteration on first stress alone, 6 examples:

> ceasterbūendum 768   ēþel Scyldinga 913
> ymbesittendra 2734   þēoden Scyldinga 1675, 1871
> brōðor ōðerne 2440

28. | ♩́.♪| ♩́ ♪̀ ♪| , with double alliteration, 1 example:

> lāc ond luftācen 1863

By reading *tācn* as a monosyllable, we could include this verse under type A, no. 36.

†29. | ♪́ ♪ ♩̀| ♩́ ♪̀ ♪| (no. 27 with resolution of first stress), with double alliteration, 3 examples:

> idese onlīcn*es* 1351   æðeling anhȳdig 2667
> gomela iōmēowlan 2931

(30. | ♪́ ♩̆ ♪| ♩́ ♪̀ ♪| (no. 28 with resolution of first stress), only in second half-line.)

†31. | ♩ ♪ ♪| ♩ ♪ ♪| , with double alliteration, 2 examples:

> sæcce tō sēceanne 2562   wrǣtlicne wundurmāððum 2173

I think Sievers was right in reading *sēcean,* type A, no. 5. Perhaps *māðm,* type A*, no. 60.

32. | ♪ ♪ ♪ ♪| ♩ ♪ ♪| , with double alliteration, 2 doubtful examples:

> Sorh is mē tō secganne 473   idese tō efnanne 1941

Again I think Sievers was right in reading *secgan, efnan,* type A no. 7.

33. | ♩ ♩| ♪ ♪ ♪ ♪| (no. 27 with resolution of second stress), with double alliteration, 24 examples:

> swylcra searonīða 582   eorlum ealuscerwen 769

and similarly 990, 1096, 1157, 1668, 2079 (*mǣrum maguþegne*), 2136 (*grimne gryrelīcne*), 2442, 2613 (*wrǣcca(n) winelēasum*), 2710 (*sīðas[t] sigehwīle*), 2749, 2755, 2819, 2829 (*hearde heaðoscearpe*);

scrīðan sceadugenga 703	hȳran heaðosīocum 2754
hwetton hige(r)ōfne 204	Hātað heaðomǣre 2802
mǣton merestrǣta 514	healdeð higemǣðum 2909
bǣdde byre geonge 2018	sōhte searonīðas 3067
eallum æþellingum 906	

†34. | ♩.♪| ♪ ♪ ♪ ♪| (no. 28 with resolution of second stress), with double alliteration, 1 example:

> brond nē beadomēcas 1454

†35. | ♪ ♪ ♩| ♪ ♪ ♪ ♪| (no. 27 with resolution of both stresses), with double alliteration, 2 examples:

> locene leoðosyrcan 1505, 1890

†36. ♪|♩ ♩|♩ ♪ ♪| (no. 27 with monosyllabic anacrusis), with double alliteration, 4 examples:

> befongen frēawrāsnum 1451   onwindeð wǣlrāpas 1610
> besette swīnlīcum 1453   Besæt ðā sinherge 2936

†37. ♫|♩ ♩|♩ ♪ ♪| (no. 27 with dissyllabic anacrusis), with double alliteration, 1 example:

> ne gefrægn ic frēondlīcor 1027

†38. ♪|♩ ♪ ♪|♩ ♪ ♪| (no. 31 with monosyllabic anacrusis), with alliteration on first stress alone, 1 doubtful example:

> Tō lang ys tō reccenne 2093

I think Sievers was right in reading *reccan,* type A no. 20.

†39. ♪|♩ ♩|♩ ♪ ♪ ♪| (no. 33 with monosyllabic anacrusis), with double alliteration, 6 examples:

> gesette sigehrēþig 94   ne sōhte searonīðas 2738
> wiðhæfde heaþodēorum 772   onbrǣd þā bealohȳdig 723
> āhyrded heaþoswāte 1460   Geseah ðā sigehrēðig 2756

D*2

40. |♩ ♩|♩ ♪ ♪|, with double or (once) single alliteration. Altogether, 42 examples:

a. Double alliteration, 41 examples:

> mǣre mearcstapa 103   aldor Ēast-Dena 392
> dēogol dǣdhata 275   sunne sweglwered 606

and similarly 616, 689, 986 (*hǣþenes handsporu*), 1212, 1231, 1298, 1339, 1348, 1410, 1468, 1568, 1678, 1793, 1969, 2123, 2205 (*hearde hildfrecan*), 2496, 2674, 2689, 2719, 2760, 2800, 2811, and 2847;

mearcað mōrhopu 450   burston bānlocan 818
grētte goldhroden 614   fērdon folctogan 839
scencte scīr wered 496   Fērdon forð þonon 1632
Meaht ðū, mīn wine 2047

licgean līfbysig 966   sto[n]dan stānbogan 2545
drēfan dēop wæter 1904   helpan hildfruman 2649

and with slightly heavier secondary stress in first measure,

lēoflīc lindwiga 2603   wundọrlīc wægbora 1440

  b. Alliteration on first stress alone, 1 doubtful example:

dennes nīosian 3045

Perhaps we should read *nīosan*, type A, no. 1.

41. | ♩. ♪ | ♩ ♪ ♪ | , with double alliteration, 6 examples:

flēon on fenhopu 764   eard ond eorlscipe 1727
bær on bearm scipes 896   lond ond lēodbyrig 2471
wīn of wundẹrfatum 1162   līf ond lēodscipe 2751

42. | ♪ ♪ ♩ | ♩ ♪ ♪ | (no. 40 with resolution of first stress), with double alliteration, 7 examples:

æþele ordfruma 263   eaforum Ecgwelan 1710
atole ecgþræce 596   æðeling unwrecen 2443
warigeað wulfhleoþu 1358   sigora Sōðcyning 3055

and with slightly heavier secondary stress in first measure,

egeslīc eorðdraca 2825

†43. | ♩ ♪ ♪ | ♩ ♪ ♪ | (no. 40 with resolution of a heavy secondary stress in the first measure, but cf. no. 44), with double alliteration, 3 examples:

fyrdsearu fūslicu 232   eahtodan eorlscipe 3173
sellice sædracan 1426

†44. | ♩ ♪ ♪ | ♩ ♪ ♪ | , with double alliteration, 4 examples:

word wæron wynsume 612   deorc ofer dryhtgumum 1790
mynte se mānscaða 712   wongas ond wīcstede 2462

21

45. |♩̷ ♩| ♪̷ ♪ ♪̷ ♪| (no. 40 with resolution of second stress), with double or single alliteration. Altogether, 26 examples:

a. Double alliteration, 1 example:

mōdges merefaran 502

b. Alliteration on first stress alone, 25 examples, all with compound proper names plus *maþelode*:

Wulfgār maþelode 348, 360   Hrōðgār maþelode 371

and similarly 405, 456, 499, 529, 631, 925, 957, 1215, 1321, 1383, 1473, 1651, 1687, 1817, 1840, 1999, 2425, 2510, 2631, 2724, 2862, and 3076.

†46. ♪| ♩̷ ♩| ♩̷ ♪̷ ♪| (no. 40 with monosyllabic anacrusis), with double alliteration, 1 example:

ālǣtan lǣndagas 2591

†47. ♫ | ♩̷ ♪ ♪| ♩̷ ♪̷ ♪| (no. 44 with dissyllabic anacrusis), with double alliteration, 1 example:

Ne gemealt him se mōdsefa 2628

†48. ♪| ♩̷ ♩| ♪̷ ♪ ♪̷ ♪| (no. 45 with monosyllabic anacrusis), with double alliteration, 1 example:

Ne sorga, snotor guma 1384

D*4

†49. |♩̷ ♩| ♪̷ ♪ ♩̷ |, with double alliteration, 19 examples:

ēode ellenrōf 358	mǣre māðþumsweord 1023
ēode yrremōd 726	ættren ellorgǣst 1617
grētte Gēata lēod 625	ǣnig yrfeweard 2731
ēode ēorla sum 1312	wǣpen wund[r]um heard 2687
ēode eahta sum 3123	Hēt ðā Hildeburh 1114
worhte wǣpna smið 1452	wearp ðā wundenmǣl 1531
sēcean sāwle hord 2422	brægd þā beadwe heard 1539
weaxan wonna lēg 3115	þǣr ic, þēoden mīn 2095

and with the second member of a compound in unaccented position,

eorres inwitfeng 1447

and with somewhat stronger secondary stress in first measure,

þrýðlíc þegna héap 400, 1627

†50. |𝅘𝅥𝅮 𝅘𝅥𝅮 𝅘𝅥|𝅘𝅥𝅮 𝅘𝅥𝅮 𝅘𝅥| (no. 49 with resolution of first stress), with double alliteration, 3 examples:

eaforan ellorsíð 2451   Eafores ánne dom 2964

and with the second member of a compound in unaccented position,

eatolne inwitscear 2478

†51. |𝅘𝅥 𝅘𝅥|𝅘𝅥₃𝅘𝅥𝅮 𝅘𝅥|, with double alliteration, 8 examples:

léoda landgeweorc 938	monnes módgeþonc 1729
frécne fengelád 1359	eorles ǽrgestréon 1757
enta ǽrgeweorc 1679	fíra fyrngeweorc 2286
sécan sundgebland 1450	lícað leng swá wél 1854

†52. |𝅘𝅥.𝅘𝅥𝅮|𝅘𝅥₃𝅘𝅥𝅮 𝅘𝅥|, with double alliteration, 1 example:

Héold on héahgesceap 3084

†53. |𝅘𝅥 𝅘𝅥|𝅘𝅥𝅮 𝅘𝅥𝅮𝅘𝅥𝅮 𝅘𝅥|, once with double alliteration, once very doubtfully with single—2 examples:

a. Double alliteration, 1 example:

oncýð eorla gehwǽm 1420 (|𝅘𝅥 𝅘𝅥|—)

b. Alliteration on first stress alone, 1 example:

stíð[r]a nægla gehwylc 985 (*MS.* steda)

But this rhythm conflicts with the grammar, according to which *stíðra nægla* should stand together against *gehwylc.* Therefore the only acceptable emendations are *stíðnægla gehwylc* (type E) and *stíðra nægla* (type A), with the omission of the redundant *gehwylc.* But *steda nægla gehwylc*, where "each of the places of the nails" means "each of the finger-tips," makes better sense than any of the proposed emendations, and can be read according to type E no. 7. For this interpretation see D. E. Martin Clarke, *MLR* 29.320, and Klaeber's note on the line.

(54. | ♩. ♪ | ♪ ♫ ♩ |, only in second half-line.)

†55. | ♩ ♩ | ♫♫ ♩ | (no. 49 with resolution of second stress), with double alliteration, 1 example:

> ȳðde eotena cyn 421

†56. ♪ | ♩ ♩ | ♪ ♪ ♩ | (no. 49 with monosyllabic anacrusis), with double alliteration, 3 examples:

> gehnægde helle gāst 1274   geþingeð þēodnes bearn 1837
> onginneð geōmormōd 2044

†57. ♫ | ♩ ♩ | ♪ ♪ ♩ | (no. 49 with dissyllabic anacrusis), with double alliteration, 2 examples:

> oferwearp þā wērigmōd 1543   oferfleôn fōtes trem 2525

†58. ♫ | ♩ ♩ | ♫ ♫ ♩ | (no. 53 with resolution of second stress and dissyllabic anacrusis), with double alliteration, 1 example:

> Oferswam ðā sioleða bigong 2367

TYPE E

1. | ♩ ♪ ♪ | ♩ |, with double, crossed, single, or transverse alliteration. Altogether, 68 examples:

a. Double alliteration, 50 examples:

> wonsǣlī wer 105   sorhfullne sīð 512, 1278, 1429
> sincfāge sel 167   flōdȳþum feor 542

and similarly 573, 636, 722, 734, 891 (*wrǣtlīcne wyrm*), 908, 1042, 1128 (*wælfāgne winter*), 1160, 1299, 1500,

1536, 1613 (*māðmǣhta mā*), 1889 (*hægstealdra [hēap]*), 1991 (*wīdcūðne wēan*), 2068, 2393, 2543, 2671, 2695, 2807 (*Bīowulfes biorh*), 2843, 2890, 2904 (*sexbennum sēoc*), 3052, and 3154 (*wælfylla worn*) ;

singāla sēað 190   dēaðfǣge dēog 850
synsnǣdum swealh 743   bānhringas brǣc 1567
     sorhwylmum sēað 1993

twelf wintra tīd 147   fīf nihta fyrst 545
     Ðȳs dōgor þū 1395

murnende mōd 50   Āgendes ēst 3075
nīpende niht 547   hǣþenra hyht 179
lifigende lāð 815   Hengestes hēap 1091
weallinde wæg 2464   sinnigne secg 1379 (MS. fela ⁓)
wæccendne wer 1268   sārigne sang 2447

b. Crossed alliteration, 2 examples:

gūðbilla nān 803   Gēatmecga lēod 829

c. Alliteration on first stress alone, 15 examples:

healærna mǣst 78   nihtlongne fyrst 528

and similarly 1158 (*drihtlīce wīf*), 1276, 1538 (*Gūð-Gēata lēod*), 1645, 2189 (*tīrēadigum menn*), 2285, 2740, and 3165 (*nīðhēdige men*) ;

slǣpendne rinc 741   oncerbendum fæst 1918 (E*?)
īren[n]a cyst 673, 1697   morgenlongne dæg 2894 (E*?)

d. Transverse alliteration, 1 example:

brūnfāgne helm (hringde byrnan) 2615

This is of course a very questionable example, because it would be easy to transpose the second half of the line and so produce crossed alliteration.

2. |♩ ♪♪|♩| (differing from no. 1 in that the secondary accent falls on a short syllable), with double alliteration, 1 example:

lāðlicu lāc 1584

This form is substantiated by several examples in the second half-line.

3. |♩̋ ♩̏ ♪ₐ♪|♩̋| (differing from no. 1 in that the third syllable is pro- rather than enclitic), with double alliteration, 6 examples:

sǣbāt gesæt 633
gumdrēam ofgeaf 2469
gūðhelm tōglād 2487

bānhūs gebræc 2508
Stīðmōd gestōd 2566
brēosthord þurhbræc 2792

4. |♩̋ ♪̏ ♫|♩̋|, with double or single alliteration, 6 examples:

a. Double alliteration, 4 examples:

Wēlandes geweorc 455
Wælsinges gewin 877

wīnærnes geweald 654
gumcyste ongit 1723

b. Alliteration on first stress alone, 2 examples:

ānfealdne geþōht 256   folcrihta gehwylc 2608

5. |♪̋‿♪ ♪̏ ♪|♩̋| (no. 1 with resolution of first stress), with double, crossed, or single alliteration. Altogether, 27 examples:

a. Double alliteration, 19 examples:

wlitebeorhtne wang 93   heresceafta hēap 335

and similarly 453, 644, 787, 1001, 1245, 1311, 1441 (*gryre-līcne gist*), 1974, 2153, 2317, 2352, 2547, 3119 (*fæðer-gearwum fūs*), and 3160 (*beadurōfes bēcn*);

searowundor sēon 920   medostigge mæt 924
Weder-Gēatum wēold 2379

b. Crossed alliteration, 3 examples:

lagucræftig mon 209   magorinca hēap 730
foresnotre men 3162

c. Alliteration on first stress alone, 5 examples:

Weder-Gēata lēod 2551   æþelinges bearn 888
winedryhten his 2722   æðelinga bearn 2597, 3170

6. |♪♪ ♩₃♪|♩| (no. 3 with resolution of first stress), with double alliteration, 2 examples:

heaðogrim ondhwearf 548   meotodsceaft bemearn 1077

7. |♪♪♪ ♫|♩| (no. 4 with resolution of first stress), with double alliteration, 2 examples:

Hafa nū ond geheald 658   heorogīfre behēold 1498

8. |♩ ♫♩|♩| (no. 1 with resolution of secondary stress), with double alliteration, 3 examples:

umborwesendum ǣr 1187   wundorsmiþa geweorc 1681
glēdegesa grim 2650

(9. |♩ ♫ ♫|♩| (no. 4 with resolution of secondary stress), only in second half-line.)

†10. |♪♪ ♫ ♫|♩| (no. 7 with resolution of secondary stress), with double alliteration, 1 example:

fæderæþelum onfōn 911

11. |♩ ♪ ♪|♪ ♩.| (no. 1 with resolution of second stress), with double alliteration, 9 examples:

healðegnes hete 142   gimfæste gife 1271
singāle sæce 154   ginfæstan gife 2182
sǣmanna searo 329   fyrnmanna fatu 2761
wynlēasne wudu 1416   hlāfordes (hry)re 3179
wuldortorhtan weder 1136

†12. |♩ ♩₃♪|♪ ♩.| (no. 3 with resolution of second stress), with double alliteration, 2 examples:

wīghēap gewanod 477   goldæht ongite 2748

13. | ♩ ♪ ♫ | ♪ ♩. | (no. 4 with resolution of second
stress), with double alliteration, 2 examples:

    fǣrniða gefremed 476   wīgspēda gewiofu 697

(14. | ♪ ♪ ♪ ♪ | ♪ ♩. | (no. 5 with resolution of second
stress), only in second half-line.)

†15. | ♪ ♪ ♩₃ ♪ | ♪ ♩. | (no. 6 with resolution of second
stress), with double alliteration, 1 example:

    seleweard āseted 667

†16. | ♪ ♪ ♪ ♫ | ♪ ♩. | (no. 7 with resolution of second
stress), with double alliteration, 2 examples:

    scaduhelma gesceapu 650   searoþoncum besmiþod 775

E*

(17. | ♪ ♪ ♪ ♪ | ♩ |, only (somewhat doubtfully) in
second half-line, unless we assign to this form two
verses in which the consonants *r* and *n* are usually
reckoned with the preceding syllable after suppression
of the intervening vowel:

    onc*e*rbendum fæst 1918   morgenlongne dæg 2894

> These have already been counted as examples of no. 1c, but
> I am not sure that the analogy of *tācn, wuldr,* etc., which
> were undeniably treated as monosyllables, ought to be
> extended to *oncer-* and *morgen-*.)

F. Unclassified Remainder

a. *Deficient Verses*

According to Klaeber's edition, the MS. contains eight
verses of the first half-line which, though grammatically

acceptable, are metrically deficient in number or length of syllables, or in stress. One of these has only two syllables, *hrēas blāc* 2488, with alliteration on the first. Such a verse can be read by allotting a separate measure to each syllable, but there is hardly even a remote chance of its authenticity. Klaeber rightly emends it, though the particular emendation he has chosen, *hrēas heoroblāc,* is itself irregular. This verse is discussed above under type D, no. 14. Four other verses have three syllables, *hægstealdra* 1889, *secg betsta* 947 and 1759, and *bord wið rond* 2673. Klaeber emends the first, rightly I think, to *hægstealdra hēap,* and I have listed it under type E, no. 1. The last is not the work of the scribe, but of modern editors, as I have explained below under no. 2. This leaves only the *secg betsta* verses, which are discussed below under no. 1. Still another verse, which Klaeber prints *bea(du)[we] weorces* 2299, seems to have a short syllable in the first measure, where a long is required; but this reading is inaccurate. The MS. had a word at the end of a line of which only the first three letters, *bea,* remain. Not even the earliest reader, Thorkelin, could distinguish more (see the facsimile edited by Zupitza, p. 108). It is therefore just as likely that the MS. had *beaduwe* or *beadwe* as that it had the metrically faulty *beadu,* and the verse should therefore be printed *bea(duwe),* or better *bea(dwe) weorces.* It is listed above under type A no. 3 in accordance with Klaeber's reading, though it might better be assigned to no. 1. Finally, there are the two verses *lissa gelong* 2150 and *þenden hē wið wulf* 3027, which are discussed below under nos. 3 and 4 respectively.

For other light verses which seem nevertheless acceptable, see type A nos. 64, 100, 101, 104-7, and type D no. 14.

1. $|\acute{\jmath}|\grave{\jmath}|\,\jmath|$, a trisyllabic form with alliteration on first stress alone, 2 examples:

secg betsta 947, 1759

The repetition of the same verse, together with the occurrence of *ðegn betstan* in the second half-line (1871), makes it almost impossible to deny the authenticity of the form. Sievers' emendation, *secga*, has been rightly abandoned by Klaeber because the weak adjective ought not to take a partitive genitive unless it is accompanied with the definite article. On the other hand, it is hard to believe that trisyllabic forms, even when they can be read as easily as these, were willingly employed by careful poets. Might we not solve this difficulty by reading *secg betesta*? The verses would then resemble *þēodcyninga* 2, type D no. 14.

(2. | ♩. ♪ | ♩ |, another trisyllabic form with alliteration on first stress alone, 1 traditional but incorrect example:

   bord wið rond 2673

Here the fault lies with modern editing. For what Klaeber prints as *Līgȳðum forborn / bord wið rond* the MS. has *lig yðū for born bord wið rond*, the space after *for* being greater than any other. The true reading, therefore, of lines 2669-2674 is as follows:

   Æfter ðām wordum   wyrm yrre cwōm,
   atol inwitgæst   ōðre sīðe
   fȳrwylmum fāh   fīonda nīos(i)an,
   lāðra manna;   līgȳðum fōr.
   Born bord wið rond,   byrne ne meahte
   geongum gārwigan   gēoce gefremman.

With *līgȳðum fōr* compare *ac mid bǣle fōr* 2308b. *Born bord wið rond* now becomes a perfectly normal verse of type D, no. 18, where I have ventured to include it.)

3. | ♩ ♪ ♪ | ♩ |, with double alliteration, 1 example:
   lissa gelong 2150

This differs from type E in that the secondary accent is very light. Holthausen's emendation, *mīnra lissa gelong* (type B), is very tempting, because in the sentence, *gēn is eall æt ðē / lissa gelong,* there is no mention of the speaker

(Beowulf) whose *liss* is in question. The verse will probably have to be accepted as it stands, however, because there is precisely the same rhythm and construction in *Guthlac* 313a (Krapp-Dobbie), where the sentence runs, *nis mē wiht æt ēow / lēofes gelong*. (None of the other emendations listed by Klaeber improves the sense as does Holthausen's, and each one has its peculiar weakness. Thus *gelong lissa* presents a wholly unnatural word-order, *lissa gelenge* has no idiomatic parallel, and *lissa gelongra*, which is not parallel to *unc sceal worn fela māþma gemǣnra* in 1783b-1784a, introduces a grammatical structure that spoils the meaning.)

4. | ♪ ♪ ♪ ♪ | ♩ |, with alliteration on the second stress alone, 1 example:

þenden hē wið wulf 3027

This cannot be compared to type E, because there is no syllable of any force in the first measure. Its nearest kin among orthodox verses is type A3, with which the dative form *wulfe* would identify it completely. Apparently *wið* means "together with" here, though the notion of rivalry may be latent. There is no precise parallel in *Beowulf* or other Old English verse, to judge by the references in Klaeber's glossary and Grein-Köhler's *Sprachschatz*, but in the two passages that show the closest resemblance we find once the accusative (*þæt hīe healfre geweald / wið Ēotena bearn / āgan mōston* 1087b-1088) and once a mixture of accusative and dative (*ond nū wið Grendel sceal, / wið þām āglǣcan / āna gehēgan / ðing wið þyrse* 424b-426a). The latter passage, together with the frequency of *wið* plus dative in general, would justify us in reading *wulfe* here, and I am inclined to think we should do so. The only reason for hesitating is the presence of five verses, *Wæs mīn fæder* 262, *þone þīn fæder* 2048, *Geslōh þīn fæder* 459, *Hwīlum hē on lufan* 1728, and *þær him nænig wæter* 1514 (all listed under A4, nos. 104-107), in which the penultimate syllable, carrying the alliteration, is short, so that one might argue the possibility of substituting a single long syllable for the last two. Nevertheless, types C and D show plainly that such substitutions cannot always be made. (Among the

very few closely parallel verses in other poems are *Hwæt,
ic þysne sang,* the opening verse of *The Fates of the
Apostles,* and *hwæðre ic þurh þæt gold,* 18a, in *The Dream
of the Rood.*)

b. *Overburdened Verses*

According to Klaeber's edition, the first half-line has
four verses which would belong to types B or D if their
penultimate syllables were short instead of long. As it is,
they look like hypermetric forms, but can hardly be so regarded because of their isolated position. Two of these
verses, however, can be accepted as normal representatives
of type B by the simple expedient of correcting a falsely
assigned quantity. They are *Hȳ on wiggetawum* 368 and
þæt wē him ðā gūðgetawa 2636, with which we may compare *in ēowrum gūðgetawum* (MS. *-geatawum*) in the
second half-line (395). Klaeber, in accordance with the
usual practice, marks *-getawe* with a long *a*. This quantity
rests on the apparent connection of the word with Gothic
tēwa. The related Old English verb *tawian,* however, comes
down into Modern English as *taw,* not *tow,* which indicates
a short *a* (see O. E. D. s. v. *taw* v.[1] and notice both the
opinion of the editors that the original verb had short *a* and
the citation of the form *tawwenn* from the *Ormulum*). In
Holthausen's *Altenglisches Etymologisches Wörterbuch*
both *getawe* and *tawian* are now recorded with short *a*.
(Sievers admitted the possibility of the short *a* in his
Angelsächsische Grammatik par. 57. 2a, but in *Beiträge* 10.
274 he recommended the substitution of *-geatwum, -geatwa*
in these verses—an emendation that is rendered improbable
by the fact that it would give us double alliteration in 395b,
the only place where the MS. suggests it by the reading
-geatawum.) All things considered, it seems almost certain
that the *a* was short, and I have therefore assigned the
verses to type B, nos 27 and 29. The two other verses, *under*

heofenes hādor 414 and *ealne ūtanweardne* 2297, though probably incorrect, are discussed under nos. 5 and 6 below.

†5. |♩ ♪ ♪| ♩♩♩ ♪ ♪|, with double alliteration, 1 very doubtful example:

> under heofenes hādor 414

> The word *hādor* offends not only by its quantity but also by failing to make sense. As Klaeber points out in his note on the line, *hādor* is elsewhere recorded only as an adjective, and Kock's effort (*Anglia* 45.110f.) to explain it as a noun meaning "brightness" and *heofones hādor* as "the clear sky" is therefore all the more dubious. The main objection to this interpretation, however, is that to say that the evening light is hidden under the clear sky is a singularly obscure way of announcing the coming of night. Surely we ought to return to Klaeber's earlier emendation, *haðor,* "enclosure," which is metrically sound because of its short vowel. The meaning would still be difficult, but heaven's enclosure could be taken as the firmament, and the expression viewed as a parallel to the modern statement that the sun is hidden under the horizon. (In the facsimile of the MS. edited by Zupitza I have noticed a very faint *ð* above the line between the *d* and *o* of *hador*. It has the same form as the *ð* normally employed by the scribe of this part of the MS., and may be evidence of his effort to correct the error. Unless the MS. itself shows that the *ð* is modern or non-existent, there should be no further doubt of the correct reading. Apparently neither Zupitza nor anyone else has noticed it previously. This observation also precludes the suggestion that we omit *under* and take *heofones hādor* as a variation of *ǣfenlēoht.*)

†6. |♩ ♩| ♪ ♪ ♪ ♪|, with double alliteration, 1 doubt-ful example:

> ealne ūtanweardne 2297

> The four emendations that have been proposed for this troublesome verse (see Klaeber's footnote on the line) are all somewhat questionable. Sievers first suggested *eal*

ūtanweard (*Beiträge* 10.306) in the belief that *hlǣw,* which
these words modify, might be neuter; but although it is
referred to by the neuter pronoun *hit* in line 2806, all immediate modifiers show the word as consistently masculine.
Sievers' later suggestion, *ealne ūtweardne* (*Altgermanische
Metrik* par. 85 n. 8) is more plausible, but still doubtful
because the precise meaning is conveyed by *ūtan* rather than
ūt, and this distinction seems to be uniformly observed in
the poetry. Sedgefield's reading in his edition, *ealne ūtan,*
seems dangerously far from the MS. On the whole, the
best emendation seems to be *ealne ūtanweard* in Trautmann's edition and the sixth edition of Holthausen. Here
ūtanweard would rank as an adverb. Even this is doubtful,
however, because while unaccompanied *weard* is frequently
treated adverbially, Grein-Köhler's *Sprachschatz* indicates
a consistently adjectival use of the various comparable
compounds. (The MS. at this point is peculiarly corrupt.
Fol. 181ʳ, on which this verse occurs, has at least four mistakes, *hlæwum* for *hlæw, hilde* for *wiges, fela ða* for *se
laða, læg* for *leng.* Some of these may be due to incorrect
freshening of faded letters. There is even a little support
for *ūtanweard.* The second line on the page has *weard ne
neðær ænigmon,* and between *ne* and *ne* are the faint traces
of an *ð.* Perhaps the scribe originally wrote *weard ne ðær,*
where *ne* would belong to the following verse, then tried
to correct what he thought was a mistake and produced the
present ungainly reading. His general confusion at this
point might also explain why the ensuing verse lacks a verb,
for we should expect *ne wæs ðær ænig mon.* Where possibilities are so numerous, however, it may be wise to refrain
from emendation.)

(7. |♩. ♪|♪ ♪ ♪ ♪|, only in second half-line.)

II. SECOND HALF-LINE

TYPE A

A1

1. |𝅘𝅥 𝅘𝅥|𝅘𝅥 𝅘𝅥|, 460 examples:

hȳran scolde 10	lange āhte 31
æfter cenned 12	hringedstefna 32
aldor(lē)ase 15	lēofne þēoden 34, etc.

Here are included (a) 16 verses requiring syncope of medial vowels:

ōþres dōgores 219, 605	lēoda ǣnigum 793
forman dōgore 2573	secga ǣnegum 842

Grendeles mǣgum 2353, *similarly* 2006, 2118, 2139
nǣnegum ārað 598   ǣnige þinga 791, 2374, 2905
ǣnige hwīle 2548   windige næssas 1358
blōdigan gāre 2440

(b) 2 verses with infinitives of the first weak class where i = j:

snyttrum styrian 872   herian þorfte 1071

(c) 1 verse with a contracted form that must be read as two syllables:

nêan bīdan 528

(d) a number of emended verses:

ræste [sōhte] 139	(āna) þrītig 2361
ōðre [sīðe] 3101	(lǣded) weorðan 3177
eorðan worh(te) 92	(hyr)stedgolde 2255

(Gē)at(isc) mēowle 3150

and with various minor restorations or changes, 84, 418, 466, 1104, 1106, 1318, 1354, 1602, 2044, 2363, 2961, 3151, 3170.

2. | 𝅘𝅥. 𝅘𝅥𝅮 | 𝅘𝅥 𝅘𝅥 |, 134 examples:

þrym gefrūnon 2	Men ne cunnon 50
forð onsendon 45	fēond on helle 101
healsgebedda 63	ūt of healle 663
	helm ond byrnan 1022, etc.

Here are included *setl getǣhte* 2013 (which could be read like no. 4), *nēan ond feorran* 2317 (which, with dissyllabic *neân,* could be read like no. 5), and *man geþēon* 25, besides three emended verses, *br[ē]ost geweorðod* 2176, *handgesteallan* 2596, and *brȳd āhredde* 2930.

3. | 𝅘𝅥𝅮 𝅘𝅥𝅮 𝅘𝅥 | 𝅘𝅥 𝅘𝅥 |, 61 examples:

sceaþena þrēatum 4	sweotolan tācne 141
	mægenes strengest 196, etc.

Here are included *Denigea freân* 1680, *gumena ǣnigum* 2416, and the emended verse *weoroda rǣswa[n]* 60.

4. | 𝅘𝅥𝅮 𝅘𝅥 𝅘𝅥𝅮 | 𝅘𝅥 𝅘𝅥 |, 13 examples:

cuman ongunnon 244	nacan on sande 295
ofost is sēlest 256	geador ætsomne 491

and similarly 614, 1183, 1360, 1609, 2775, 2951, 2970, 3047, and 3086.

5. | 𝅘𝅥 𝅘𝅥𝅮 𝅘𝅥𝅮 | 𝅘𝅥 𝅘𝅥 |, 237 examples:

gōde gewyrcean 20	niht ofer ealle 649
sunnan ond mōnan 94	fēond oferswȳðeþ 279
hēold þenden lifde 57	Sōð is gecȳþed 700
	dōð swā ic bidde 1231, etc.

In 210 of these verses the first measure consists of a dissyllable and a proclitic monosyllable or prefix, as in the first two examples. A few verses with trisyllables in the first measure might have been included. They will be found under A2, no. 30 below.—Here are included *herian ne cūþon* 182, *weorcum geferian* 1638, *ǣnige gefremman* 2449, *feorran ond neân* 839, *beorh þone heân* 3097, and five verses which could be assigned to no. 2 by treating the first two syllables as one: *māþðum gesealde* 1052, *bearhtm ongēaton* 1431, *ealdorgewinna* 2903, *hleahtor ālegde* 3020, and *Wundur hwār þonne* 3062. The last might even be assigned to type D by stressing *hwār* (| ♩ | ♩ ♪ ♪ |).—Emended verses are *mīn[n]e gehȳrað* 255, *frēcne ne meahte* 1032, *īrne gemunde* 1141, *māþme þȳ weorþra* 1902, *fȳra gehwylcne* 2250, *mīne bebohte* 2799, *hilde genǣgdon* 2916, *Sw[ē]ona ond Gēata* 2946, *forð oferēodon* 2959, *grimme gecēa(þo)d* 3012, *s(w)īðe geneahhe* 3152, *hearde (ondrē)de* 3153, and *wīde g(e)sȳne* 3158.

6. | ♩ ♪ ♩ | ♩ ♩ |, 5 examples:

    Ūþe ic swīþor 960   wisse hē gearwe 2339, 2725
              hindeman sīðe 2049, 2517

Perhaps also *myndgiend wǣre* 1105, *swīgedon ealle* 1699, and *Gēotena lēode* 443, which have been included under no. 30 below, besides the eleven verses like *Grendeles mǣgum* under no. 1.

7. | ♪ ♪ ♪ ♪ | ♩ ♩ |, 35 examples:

  a. With long first syllable, 8 examples:

    Sægde sē þe cūþe 90, *similarly* 1003, 1387, 2766
    ealle ofercōmon 699   sægde ofer ealle 2899
    Yrre wǣron bēgen 769   sibbe oððe trēowe 2922

  b. With short first syllable (so always when first word is trisyllabic), 27 examples:

    Metod hīe ne cūþon 180   manegum gecȳðed 349
    flota wæs on ȳðum 210   seonowe onsprungon 817
    wæter oferhelmað 1364   wunode mid Finne 1128, etc.

Like the first column are 1060, 1176, 1303, and 3093. The rest are all like the second column (20 in all). There is one emended verse, *hamere geþrūen* 1285.

†8. | ♩ ♩♩♩ | ♩ ♩ |, 2 examples:

    brūc þenden þū mōte 1177 Wes þenden þū lifige 1224

9. | ♪ ♪ ♩♩♩ | ♩ ♩ |, 1 example:

sealde þām ðe hē wolde 3055

(10. | ♩♩♩ ♪ ♪ | ♩ ♩ |, only in first half-line.)

11. | ♩ ♩ | ♪ ♪ ♩ |, 23 examples:

ellen fremedon 3   folce Den*i*ga 465
feorran cumene 361   georne truwode 669

and similarly 226, 378, 677, 728, 1011, 1019, 1091, 1253,
1341, 1419, 1606, 1781, 1823, 1847, 1935, 2529, 2558, 2667,
and 2840.

12. | ♩. ♪ | ♪ ♪ ♩ |, 17 examples:

eft gewunigen 22   ealdgesegena 869
torn geþolode 147   Sōð ic talige 532

and similarly 135, 165, 585, 940, 1428, 1583, 1845, 1946,
1988, 2190, 2212, 2478, and 3130.

13. | ♪ ♪ ♩ | ♪ ♪ ♩ |, 4 examples:

mægenes Deniga 155   hafelan werede 1448
hæleða monegum 3111   werudes egesan 3154

14. | ♪ ♩ ♪ | ♪ ♪ ♩ |, 6 examples:

Dena ond Wedera 498   gryra gefremede 591
samod ætgædere 329, 387, 729, 1063

15. | ♩ ♪ ♪ | ♪ ♪ ♩ |, 19 examples:

gēoce gefremede 177   sīðe ne truwode 1993

and similarly 551, 938, 1135, 1187, 1514, 1533, 1552, 1796,
2004, 2322, 2370, 2540, 2645, 2924, 2931, 2953, and 3109.

16. | ♪ ♪ ♪ ♪ | ♪ ♪ ♩ |, 3 examples, all with short first
syllable:

duguþe ond geogoþe 160   duguða biwenede 2035
wætere gelafede 2722

(17. | ♪♪♩ ♪ ♪|♪♪ ♩|, only in first half-line.)

18. ♪| ♩.♪| ♩ ♩|, 3 examples:

swā sǣ bebūgeð 1223   ðurhfōn ne mihte 1504
hȳ eft gemētton 2592

19. ♪| ♪♩ ♪|♩ ♩|, 5 examples:

swā wæter bebūgeð 93   gesacan ne tealde 1773
swā guman gefrungon 666   forberan ne mehte 1877
nū hæleð ne mōstan 2247

20. ♪| ♩ ♪ ♪|♩ ♩|, 1 doubtful example:

his ealdre gebohte 2481

Klaeber assigns *his* to the first half-line, but see the remarks on the latter under A3, no. 64 above.

(21-27, other forms with anacrusis, only in first half-line.)

A2a

28. | ♩ ♪| ♩ ♩|, 21 examples:

ombihtþegne 673	foldweg mǣton 1633
ǣghwǣr sēlest 1059	hringnet bǣron 1889
anwīggearwe 1247	þrēo hund wintra 2278
mandrēam fleôn 1264	Hordweard sōhte 2293
dēaþwīc scôn 1275	morþorbed strêd 2436

Ecgþēow hāten 263, *and similarly with proper names* 339, 373, 664, 1216, 1646, 1758, 1816, 2010, 2155, *and* 2389.

I follow Sievers in reading *anwīggearwe* instead of Klaeber's *an wīg gearwe*. It is true that the compound does not occur elsewhere, but it is perfectly intelligible, and is demanded by the alliterative scheme (the first half-line is *þæt hīe oft wǣron,* where *oft* must take precedence of *wǣron*).—Several of these examples are doubtful. Thus the proper names need not receive strong secondary stress, and further composition might well reduce the force of the

second syllable in *ombihtþegne* and *anwīggearwe*. Sievers
suggested *āwer* or *ōwer* for *ǣghwǣr*, and *beran* for *bǣron*
(*Beiträge* 10.224). He was inclined at first to read 2436 as
type E (*Beiträge* 10.267), but later included it here (*Altgermanische Metrik*, p. 132).

29. | ♪ ♪ ♩ | ♩ ♩ |, 2 examples:

Higelāc Gēata 1202   meduseld būan 3065

30. | ♩ ♪ ♪ | ♩ ♩ |, 6 examples:

holtwudu sēce 1369	myndgiend wǣre 1105
weardode hwīle 105	swīgedon ealle 1699
fundode wrecca 1137	Gēotena lēode 443

Only the first example is certain. The rest need not have
strong secondary stress, and those in the second column
might even be read according to no. 6 above. The last
should really be *Gēotna* or, as everywhere else, *Gēata*.

(31. | ♪ ♪ ♪ ♪ | ♩ ♩ |, only in first half-line, unless
gladum suna Frōdan 2025 be considered an example.
Sievers classified it here, but the analogy of *swutol
sang scopes* 90a and *beorht bēacen Godes* 570a
suggests that it should belong to type D, where
accordingly I have placed it.)

(32. | ♩ ♩ | ♪ ♪ ♩ |, only in first half-line.)

(33. | ♪ ♪ ♩ | ♪ ♪ ♩ |, only in first half-line.)

34. | ♩ ♪ ♪ | ♪ ♪ ♩ |, 2 examples:

healwudu dynede 1317   sundwudu þunede 1906

A2b

35. | ♩ ♩ | ♩ ♩ |, 3 examples:

monna ǣghwylc 2887   lēofa Bēowulf 1854, 1987

(36. | ♩. ♪ | ♩ ♩ |, only in first half-line.)

37. | ♪ ♪ ♩ | ♩ ♩ |, 4 examples:

　　wine mīn Bēowulf 457, 1704　　wine mīn Unferð 530
　　　　　gumena nāthwylc 2233

Perhaps the first three should be assigned to A2ab.

(38. | ♪ ♩ ♪ | ♩ ♩ |, only in first half-line.)

(39. | ♩ ♪ ♪ | ♩ ♩ |, only in first half-line.)

40. | ♪ ♪ ♪ ♪ | ♩ ♩ |, 1 example:

　　sceaðona ic nāt hwylc 274

(41. | ♪ ♪ ♩♩♩³ | ♩ ♩ |, only in first half-line.)

†42. | ♩♩♩³ ♪ ♪ | ♩ ♩ |, 1 example:

　　Gyrede hine Bēowulf 1441

(43. | ♩♩♩³ ♩♩♩³ ♩ ♩ |, only in first half-line.)

44. | ♩ ♩ | ♪ ♪ ♩ |, 1 example:

　　dryhten Higelāc 2000

(45. | ♩. ♪ | ♪ ♪ ♩ |, only in first half-line.)

(46. | ♪ ♩ ♪ | ♪ ♪ ♩ |, only in first half-line.)

47. | ♩ ♪ ♪ | ♪ ♪ ♩ |, 4 doubtful examples:

　　Gēat unigmetes wēl 1792　　þegn ungemete till 2721
　　wyrd ungemete nēah 2420　　dēað ungemete nēah 2728

These four examples, all deriving their peculiar form from the use of *ungemete,* were assigned to type D by Sievers. This would give us the reading | ♩ | ♩♩ ♩♩ ♩ |, which is barely possible if, following the suggestion of the spelling in 1792, we treat *un-* as a short syllable. I have preferred to avoid the haste of this reading, however, by letting *-mete* take precedence of *un-* in accent.

(48. | ♪ ♪ ♪♪♪ | ♪ ♪ ♪ |, only in first half-line.)

(49-52, forms with anacrusis, only in first half-line.)

A2ab

53. | ♩ ♩ | ♩ ♩ |, 1 example:
  glædman Hrōðgār 367

(54. | ♪ ♪ ♩ | ♩ ♩ |, only in first half-line, unless one assigns to this form the three verses cited under no. 37 above.)

(55-58, only in first half-line.)

A*

(59. | ♩ ♩ ♪ | ♩ ♩ |, only in first half-line.)

60. | ♩ ♩ ♪ | ♩ ♩ |, 1 example:
  Gūðlāf ond Ōslāf 1148

(61-62, the preceding forms with resolution of the first stress, only in first half-line.)

(A3)

(63-97, only in first half-line.)

A4(= A1, A2 with short ending)

Short A1

†98. | ♩̋ ♩̀ | ♪̋ ♪̰ ♩. |, 6 examples:

hwīlum dydon 1828	Hrunting nama 1457
rīdend swefað 2457	Hrunting beran 1807
feormynd swefað 2256	Hrēðel cyning 2430

While the other five examples remain unchallenged, it seems unnecessary to follow Sievers and others in reading *dǣdon* or *dēdon* for *dydon,* though that is a possibility.

†99. | ♪̋ ♪ ♩̀ | ♪̋ ♪̰ ♩. |, 2 examples:

æþeling manig 1112   æþelin*g* boren 3135

(100. | ♩̋ ♪ ♪ | ♪̋ ♪̰ ♩. |, only in first half-line.)

(101. | ♪̋ ♪ ♪ ♪ | ♪̋ ♪̰ ♩. |, only in first half-line.)

Short A2

102. | ♩̋ ♩̀ | ♪̋ ♪̰ ♩. |, 27 examples:

gūðrinc monig 838	andweard scireð 1287
Goldfāg scinon 994	heardecg togen 1288

and similarly 1289, 1510, 1731, 1834, 1896, 1914, 1964, 2007, 2060, 2110, 2174 (*þrīo wicg somod*), 2334, 2417, 2460, 2663 (*lǣst eall tela*), 2754, 2969, 2972, 3019, and 3081, besides three with proper names:

Bēowulf fetod 1310   Wēohstā*n* bana 2613
Wīglāf siteð 2906

103. | ♪̋ ♪ ♩̀ | ♪̋ ♪̰ ♩. |, 8 examples:

herespēd gyfen 64	sunu *dēoð* wrecan 1278
Eoforlīc scionon 303	bregorōf cyning 1925
sigerōf kyning 619	Bealocwealm hafað 2265
snotor ceorl monig 908	Hiorogār cyning 2158

(Short A3, nos. 104-107, only in first half-line.)

TYPE B

a. First measure light, second heavy.

B1

1. | ♩ | ♪ ♪ ♩ |, 21 examples:

ymb þīnne sīð 353	Hīe dȳgel lond 1357
Hȳ bēnan synt 364	ðǣr fyrgenstrēam 1359
on morgentīd 484	ond hālig God 1553
þurh mīne hand 558	Oft seldan hwǣr 2029
þæt syðþan nā 567	hē fyrmest læg 2077
ond icge gold 1107	him Grendel wearð 2078
Ic mīnne can 1180	Næs hearpan wyn 2262
ond wunden gold 1193	Swā Wedra helm 2462
bē(*i. e.* bī) wǣpnedmen 1284	on Frēsna land 2915
[swā] gegnum fōr 1404	

and with the second member of a compound in unaccented position,

þǣr Hrōðgār sæt 356	Næs Bēowulf ðǣr 1299

2. | ♪ ♪ | ♪ ♪ ♩ |, 222 examples:

syððan ǣrest wearð 6	þǣr geneh[h]ost brægd 794
[Hwæt, ic hwī]le wæs 240	þā ðǣr sōna wearð 1280

and similarly with adverb and verb in the second measure, 1281, 1617, 1748, 1901, 1947, 1994, 2009, 2175, 2214, 2225 (*ond ðǣr inne feal*h), 2238, 2310, 2423, 2525 (*ac unc* [*furður*] *sceal*), 2743, 2816, 3082, 3108, and 3168 (*swā hi*(*t ǣro*)*r wæs*);

swā hē selfa bæd 29	him on bearme læg 40

and similarly with adjective or noun and verb in the second measure, 103, 144, 145, 151, 251, 286, 352, 384, 405, 421, 445, 472, 527, 553, 726, 753, 816, 905, 913, 925, 1002, 1037, 1077, 1133, 1170, 1171, 1190, 1207, 1235, 1239 (*hit geond-brǣded wearð*), 1243, 1255 (*Þæt gesȳne wearþ*), 1261 (*siþðan Cāin wearð*), 1333, 1349, 1435, 1547, 1698, 1719, 1775, 1784, 1786, 1811, 1815, 1855, 1863, 2024 (*Sīo gehāten* (*is*)), 2048, 2103, 2124, 2179, 2199, 2303, 2308, 2327, 2354,

2404, 2474, 2535, 2568, 2612, 2676 (*þā his āgen w(æs)*),
2692 (*hē geblōdẹgod wearð*), 2709, 2732, 2736, 2739, 2852,
2919, 2944, 2978, 3009, 3098, 3124, and 3140;

 ðǣr gelȳfan sceal 440 gif hē wealdan mōt 442

and similarly with infinitive and auxiliary in the second
measure, 636, 942, 977, 1378, 1852, and 2275;

 (þ)ǣr hē meahte swā 762 gif ic wiste hū 2519

and similarly with verb and adverb in the second measure,
797, 2091, 2648 (*wutun gongan tō*), 2855, and 2990 (*ond
gelǣste swā*) ;

 þǣr wæs hearpan swēg 89 Næs hit lengra fyrst 134

and similarly with two words or a compound of the noun-
adjective class in the second measure, 330, 348, 381, 409,
413, 437, 454, 510, 604, 637, 702, 705, 765, 781 (*nymþe
līges fæþm*), 807, 836 (*under gēapne hr(ōf)*), 850, 917, 934,
1147, 1208, 1232, 1283, 1372, 1393, 1432, 1463, 1527, 1529,
1559 (*þæt [wæs] wǣpna cyst*), 1607, 1621, 1666, 1691,
1692, 1717, 1764, 1765, 1812, 1844, 1873, 1927, 2016, 2023
(*þǣr hīo (næ)gled sinc*), 2128 ((*un)der firgenstrēam*),
2264, 2269, 2276, 2297, 2325 (*þæt his sylfes hām*), 2405,
2415, 2428 (*þā mec sinca baldọr*), 2458, 2470, 2477, 2493,
2508, 2532, 2553, 2555, 2580, 2625, 2626, 2628 (*nē his
mǣges lāf*), 2642 (*þēah ðe hlāford ūs*), 2744, 2755, 2759,
2791, 2910, 3023, 3024 (*ac se wonna hrefn*), 3031, 3035,
3045, 3066, and 3173;

 þē him elles hwǣr 138 sē þe longe hēr 1061

and similarly with two adverbs, or adjective and adverb in
the second measure, 1951, 2135, 2412, 2923, 3006, and with
a compound 937 (*þæt hīe wīdeferhð*) ; and with noun and
adverb,

 ond his mōdor ēac 1683 nō on wealle læ[n]g 2307
 næs mid Gēatum ðā 2192 Næs ðæs wyrmes þǣr 2771

besides a number from these classes with the second member
of a compound (sometimes hardly recognized as such) in an
unaccented position,

hine fyrwyt bræc 232

hyne fyrwet bræc 1985, 2784

nē him inwitsorh 1736

under inwithrōf 3123

þonne edwītlīf 2891

hwīlum syllīc spell 2109

swā sceal æghwylc mon 2590

Ic þæs Hrōðgār mæg 277

þonon Ēomēr wōc 1960

þonan Bīowulf cōm 2359

Nū ic, Bēowulf, þec 946

syððan Heardrēd læg 2388

Ēode Wealhþēow forð 612

þā cwōm Wealhþēo forð 1162

3. | ♪ ♩ | ♪ ♪ ♩ |, 13 examples:

geseah stēapne hrōf 926

gecēas ēcne rǣd 1201

Ne mæg byrnan hring 2260

Ne scel ānes hwæt 3010

forðām [secgum] wearð 149

forðām Offa wæs 1957

þē þus brontne cēol 238

nē gē lēafnesword 245

þæt ðǣr ænig mon 1099

ond nū ōþer cwōm 1338

scealt nū dǣdum rōf 2666

tō hwan syððan wearð 2071

of ðām lēoma stōd 2769

Several of these are questionable. A slightly different interpretation of their meaning would allow us to include them under no. 2.

4. | ♩ ♩ ♩ | ♪ ♪ ♩ |, 59 examples:

sē þe in þȳstrum bād 87   þæs þe hē Ābel slōg 108

and similarly with a word of the noun-adjective class and a verb in the second measure, 369, 419, 561, 573, 588, 601, 693, 723 (*ðā (hē ge)'bolgen wæs*), 733, 755 (*wolde on heolster flēon*), 1041, 1079 (*þær hē[o] ǣr mǣste hēold*), 1234, 1442, 1508 (*nō he þæs mōdig wæs*), 1537, 1539, 1670, 1714, 1839, 1883, 2220 (*þæt hē gebolge(n) wæs*), 2378, 2409, 2480, 2550, 2595, 2599, 2696, 2698 (*þær hē his mǣges healp*), 2756, 2782, 2880, 2983, 3026, 3088, 3125, and 3174 (*swā hit gedē(fe) bið*);

sealde his hyrsted sweord 672

and similarly with two words of the noun-adjective class in the second measure, 887, 1475, 1579, 1835, 1949, 2433, 2524, 2527, 2675, 2876, and with pronoun, 248 (*ðonne is ēower sum*); besides the following miscellaneous assortment:

nū ic þus feorran cōm 430   sē þe ǣr feorran cōm 825
þone ic longe hēold 2751

þone ðe Grendel ǣr 1054   swā ic þē wēne tō 1396
swylce on horde ǣr 3164   hēt hyne brūcan well 2812

It should be observed that the line between this and the
following group is not always clear. When a verse begins
with a monosyllable it can often be read according to either
of the two rhythms.

5. | ♪ ♪ ♪ ♪ | ♪ ♪ ♪ |, 59 examples:

ðā him gebēacnod wæs 140   on þǣm se rīca bād 310

and similarly with a word of the noun-adjective class and a
verb in the second measure, 424, 438, 1053, 1178, 1219,
1293, 1295, 1434, 1506, 1532, 1544, 2019, 2146 (*ac hē mē
(māðma)s geaf*), 2362 (*þā hē tō holme (st)āg*), 2384,
2498, 2635, 2640, 2704, 2724, 2865, and 3078;

þā him wæs manna þearf 201   ne sceal þǣr dyrne sum 271

and similarly with two words of the noun-adjective class in
the second measure, 503, 660, 685, 716, 1150, 1191, 1217,
1266, 1918, 1967, 2014, 2040, 2147 (*on (mīn)ne sylfes
dōm*), 2399, 2541, 2546, 2586, 3011, 3049 (*swā hīe wið
eorðan fæðm*), and with a compound, 75 and 1771 (*geond
þisne middangeard*); besides the following miscellaneous
assortment:

ne wæs his drohtoð þǣr 756   ac hē þæs fæste wæs 773
Ne wæs þǣm ōðrum swā 1471   ond him tōgēanes fēng 1542
gif hē gesēcean dear 684   ac him tōgēanes rād 1893
ond ēowic grētan hēt 3095   þæt hine syðþan nō 1453
ond þæt geæfndon swā 538   ne meahte horde nēah 2547

and with the second member of a compound in unaccented
position,

Ne bið swylc cwēnlīc þēaw 1940
þæt wit on gārsecg ūt 537

6. | ♩ ♪ ♩♩ | ♪ ♪ ♩ |, 4 examples:

ne wiston hīe Drihten God 181
þā hine on morgentīd 518
Ne wæs þæt gewrixle til 1304
nō ymbe ðā fæhðe spræc 2618

7. | ♪ ♪ ♪ ♪ | ♪ ♪ ♩ |, 7 examples:

ðonne ǣnig ōþer man 534
þā him swā geþearfod wæs 1103
Nū is þīnes mægnes blǣd 1761
sægde him þæs lēanes þanc 1809
þonne hē tō sæcce bær 2686
þone þe him hringas geaf 3034

and with the second member of a compound in unaccented
position,

ðone þe him Wealhðēo geaf 2173

†8. | ♩♩♩ ♪ ♪ | ♪ ♪ ♩ |, 1 example:

Hwæþere him on ferhþe grēow 1718

The reading *Hwæþre* would change this to the preceding
form.

†9. | ♩ ♩ | ♩ ♪ ♩ |, 2 examples:

hīe wyrd forswēop 477   him wiht ne spēow 2854

10. | ♩ ♪ ♪ | ♩ ♪ ♩ |, 89 examples:

Him on mōd bearn 67   oð ðæt ān ongan 100

and similarly with a monosyllable of the noun-adjective
class plus prefix (or *ne*) plus verb in the second measure,
107, 115, 488, 579, 618, 622, 628, 653, 654, 730, 749, 852,
890, 1121, 1205, 1263, 1274, 1398, 1512, 1522, 1524, 1528,
1555, 1568, 1605, 1665, 1667, 1679, 1689, 1696, 2005, 2041,
2042 (*sē ðe eall gem(an)*), 2046, 2108, 2116, 2127, 2165,
2210, 2219 (*þæt sīe ðīod (onfand)*), 2323, 2427, 2439,
2467, 2492, 2526, 2567, 2577, 2629 (*þæt se wyrm onfand*),

2690, 2697, 2700, 2701, 2711, 2723 (*ond his hel(m) onspēon*), 2814 (*ealle wyrd forswēop*), 2898, 3058, 3061, and 3087;

     hē þæs ǣr onðāh 900   (sē þe nē)h gefe(al)g 2215

and similarly with adverb plus prefix (or *ne*) plus verb in the second measure, 1466, 1587, 2289, and 3064;

     wæs tō fæst on þām 137   he [wæs] fāg wið God 811

and similarly with noun or adjective plus proclitic plus noun, adjective, or pronoun in the second measure, 1008, 1700, 1723, 1742, 2149, 2591, 2684, 2845, 3157, and with a compound, *Nō his līfgedāl* 841; besides the following miscellaneous assortment:

    Nō hē wiht fram mē 541   Nō ic wiht fram þē 581
         Hwæt, hyt ǣr on ðē 2248

næs hīo hnāh swā þēah 1929   Ðū þē lǣr be þon 1722
ond sē ān ðā gēn 2237   ond ongan swā þēah 2878
Næs hē forht swā ðēh 2967   þæt ðē feor ond nēah 1221

11. | ♪ ♩ ♩ | ♩ ♪ ♩ |, 19 examples:

hē him ðæs lēan forgeald 114   oþ þæt unc flōd todrāf 545

and similarly with noun plus prefix plus verb in the second measure, 575, 632, 1436, 1584, 2236, 2299, 2403, 2872, and 2992; besides the following:

oþ þæt him eft onwōc 56   syþðan hē eft āstōd 1556
swā him ful oft gelamp 1252   þone ðe ǣr gehēold 3003
       nō þȳ ǣr in gescōd 1502
Nū is se rǣd gelang 1376   þūhte him eall tō rūm 2461
      ūrum sceal sweord ond helm 2659

12. | ♪ ♪ ♪ | ♩ ♪ ♩ |, 13 examples:

wæs þæt gewin tō strang 133   wæs þæt gewin tō swyð 191
      Ne wæs þæt wyrd þā gēn 734

ðā hīe se fǣr begeat 1068   ond hyre sea*x* getēah 1545
Ic þē þæs lēan geman 1220   ac hyne ecg fornam 2772
þæt hēo on flet gebēah 1540   þē him *tō* sār belamp 2468
      gif hē þæt eal gemon 1185

þē hē him ǣr forgeaf 2606   hē hine eft ongon 2790
     ond hē þā forðgesceaft 1750

†13. | ♩ ♪ ♩ ♩ ♩ | ♩ ♪ ♩ |, 1 example:

þā hyne sīo þrāg becwōm 2883

†14. | ♪ ♪ ♪ ♪ | ♩ ♪ ♩ |, 5 examples:

ac hē hine feor forwræc 109   oð ðæt hyne ān ābealch 2280
þær hē hine ær forlēt 2787   þāra ðe ðær gūð fornam 1123
þāra ðe þis [līf] ofgeaf 2251

Verses 109 and 2787 could be read like the preceding.

Verses 1123 and 2251 could be read | ♩ ♩ ♩ ♩ | ♩ ♪ ♩ |.

(15. | ♩ ♩ | ♩ ♩ ♩ ♩ |, only in first half-line.)

16. | ♩ ♪ ♪ | ♩ ♩ ♩ ♩ |, 30 examples:

swylcum gifeþe bið 299   þær se snotera bād 1313
æfter *æþel*um frægn 332   swā mē gifeðe wæs 2491
sē æt Heorote fand 1267   þær se gomela læg 2851
Ðā se æðeling gīong 2715

wið þæs recedes weal 326   Hwīlum cyninges þegn 867
ofer wæteres hrycg 471   þæt þær gumena sum 1499
þær wæs hæleða drēam 497   þæs sig Metode þanc 1778
Git on wæteres æht 516   ofer ganotes bæð 1861
Syððan heofones gim 2072

is his eafor*a* nū 375   þær mē gifeðe swā 2730
hine fyren onwōd 915   þætte wrecend þā gȳt 1256
þē him foran ongēan 2364

and with the second member of a compound name in an unaccented position,

ðā wæs Heregār dēad 467   syððan Wiðergyld læg 2051
swā mē Higelāc sīe 435

and similarly with *Higelāc,* 2151, 2201, 2355, 2372, 2434, and 2914.—The rhythm of this last group would more accurately be described as | ♩ ♪ ♪ | ♩ ♪ ♩ |.—The three verses 915, 1256, and 2364 represent no. 10 with resolution of the first stress, the others no. 2, but the resultant rhythm is the same.

†17. | ♪ ♩ | ♫ ♩ |, a minor variant of the preceding, 1 example:

> Ne wearð Heremōd swā 1709

Like the last group above, this would more accurately be

described as | ♪ ♩ | ♫ ♪ ♩ |.

18. | ♫♩ | ♫♩ ♩ |, 7 examples:

oðð þæt sēo geogoð gewēox 66   hwæþre mē gyfeþe wearð 555
cūþe hē duguðe þēaw 359   Hē æfter recede wlāt 1572
ðā hine *Wede*ra cyn 461   sē þe oft manegum scōd 1887
þæt hyt on heafolan stōd 2679

19. | ♪ ♪ ♪ | ♫ ♩ |, 5 examples:

ne wæs him Fitela mid 889   þæt þū on Heorote mōst 1671
ond þǣre idese mid 1649   ond þā þās worold ofgeaf 1681
æt mīnum fæder genam 2429

†20. | ♪ ♫♩ | ♫♩ ♩ |, 1 example:

hēo fore þǣm werede spræc 1215

21. | ♪ ♪ ♪ ♪ | ♫ ♩ |, 1 example:

þæt hē ēower æþelu can 392

22. | ♩ | ♪ ♪ ♪ ♪ |, 2 examples:

tō aldorceare 906   Him Bēowulf þanan 1880

23. | ♪ ♪ | ♪ ♪ ♪ ♪ |, 19 examples:

þǣr wæs mādma fela 36   sōhte holdne wine 376
ofer landa fela 311   þonne Grendel hine 678
þǣr hē worna fela 2003   þæt wæs tācen sweotol 833
sē ðe worna fela 2542   nalles fācenstafas 1018
þǣr wæs swylcra fela 2231   Ðā wæs winter scacen 1136
him wæs geōmor sefa, 49, 2419

hwæt mē Grendel hafað 474   þæt wē rondas beren 2653
þēah þæt wǣpen duge 1660   þæt hē āna scyle 2657
scolde Grendel þonan 819   him se ōðer þonan 2061
Ic genēðde fela 2511

Verses 833, 1018, 1136, and 1660 would belong to type C2 with monosyllabic treatment of *tācn, fācn, wintr,* and *wǣpn.*

24. |♩ ♩♩♩|♪ ♪ ♪ ♪|, 2 examples:

hæbbe ic mǣrða fela 408   nemne wē ǣror mægen 2654

25. |♪ ♪ ♪ ♪|♪ ♪ ♪ ♪|, 3 examples:

ac hē mē habban wile 446   þæt hē mec fremman wile 1832
ond þone māðþum byreð 2055

Monosyllabic *māðm* would convert the last into type C2.

26. |♪ ♪ ♪ ♪|♪ ♪ ♪ ♪|, 3 examples:

gif hē ūs geunnan wile 346   ac hig him geþingo budon 1085
swā ic giō wið Grendle dyde 2521

(27. |♪ ♪ ♪|♩ ♪ ♪ ♪|, only in first half-line.)

†28. |♪ ♪ ♪ ♪|♩ ♪ ♪ ♪|, 1 example:

in ēowrum gūðgetawum (*MS.* -geatawum) 395
On the quantity of *-getawum* see first half-line, Fb.

(29. |♪ ♪ ♪ ♪|♩ ♪ ♪ ♪|, only in first half-line.)

(30. |♪ ♪ ♪|♩♩♩ ♪ ♪|, only in first half-line.)

†31. |♪ ♪ ♪ ♪|♩♩♩ ♪ ♪|, 1 example:

þæt hē þā geogoðe wile 1181

B2

32. | 𝄽 ♩ | ♪ ♫ ♩ |, 3 examples:

> þū wāst, gif hit is 272   Sum sāre angeald 1251
> swylc Æschere wæs 1329

33. | 𝄽 ♪ ♪ | ♪ ♫ ♩ |, 50 examples:

> hē þæs frōfre gebād 7   hwā þǣm hlæste onfēng 52

and similarly with dissyllabic noun plus prefix plus verb in the second measure, 76, 122, 143, 420, 696, 775, 1198, 1254, 1337, 1470, 1770, 1975, 1977, 2134, 2138, 2258, 2298 (*hwæðre wīges gefeh*), 2614, 2819 (*him of hræðre gewāt*), 2834, and with a slight difference, *swā him wyrd ne gescrāf* 2574 and *hē þæt wyrse ne con* 1739;

> mid his eorla gedriht 357   þæt hīe healfre geweald 1087

and with two similar words of the noun-adjective class in the second measure, 1497, 1622, 1727, and 1826; besides the following miscellaneous assortment:

> hine gearwe geman 265   ond him fægre gehēt 2989
> hē þæt sōna onfand 2300, 2713

> wæron bēgen þā gīt 536   Ond his mōdor þā gyt 1276
> nō þǣr ænige swā þēah 972   næs ic fǣge þā gyt 2141
> him bebeorgan ne con 1746   næs hē fǣge þā gīt 2975
> næs him wihte ðē sēl 2687   sceolde hwæðre swā þēah 2442
> gyf þū ǣr þonne hē 1182

> Gǣð ā wyrd swā hīo scel 455   wæs þæt blōd tō þæs hāt 1616

and with long, normally stressed medial syllable in unaccented position,

> wæs him Bēowulfes sīð 501   þæt ic ænigra mē 932

and with short medial syllable (which should almost certainly be dropped),

> Hē mid Ēotenum wearð 902   swā hē Frēsena cyn 1093
> oððe ēagena bearhtm 1766

With *Ēotnum* (still better *Ēotum*), *Frēsna, ēagna*, these three verses would belong to no. 2. There is nothing against

23

treating *bearhtm* as a monosyllable, as one must do in order to make 1766 a normal verse; but the sense would be greatly improved and the rhythm eased by deleting *oððe* (which may have crept in once too often at the end of a long series) and reading simply *ēagna bearhtm*, type A. The sentence would then run, *oððe atol yldo / ēagna bearhtm / forsiteð ond forsworceð*, or, if we must continue to regard the verbs as intransitive, we could start a new sentence with *ēagna*. In either case the darkening of the eyes would assume its proper significance as a symptom of approaching death, instead of being associated with such causes of death as fire, sword, and old age.

34. | ♪ ♩♩ | ♪ ♫ ♩ |, 23 examples:

Næfre ic māran geseah 247   þæt hē for eaxlum gestōd 358

and similarly with dissyllable of the noun-adjective class plus prefix (or *ne*) plus verb in the second measure, 366, 401, 404 (*þæt hē on heo[r]ðe gestōd*), 891, 929, 1209, 1302, 1467, 2222, 2471, 2624, 450, 595, and 2332; besides the following miscellaneous assortment:

wiste his fingra geweald 764   Scolde his aldorgedāl 805
nē hē þæt syððan (bemāð) 2217   āhte ic holdra þȳ lǣs 487
Wæs him se man tō þon lēof 1876

and with short medial syllable in unaccented position,

þēah ðe hīo ǣnlicu sȳ 1941   wes þū ūs lārena gōd 269

The last, however, should almost certainly have *lārna* and thus be read according to no. 4.

35. | ♪ ♪ ♪ ♪ | ♪ ♫ ♩ |, 16 examples:

þē on ðā lēode becōm 192	þæt hē his selfa ne mæg 1733
þæt ic mid sweorde ofslōh 574	ond þē þæt sēlre gecēos 1759
þæt hē on hrūsan ne fēol 772	ond hē him helpe ne mæg 2448
þæt ic ðȳ wǣpne gebrǣd 1664	þæt hē on eorðan geseah 2822
[ond] mīnra eorla gedryht 431	mid þīnra secga gedryht 1672
mid mīnra secga gedriht 633	þæt ic on holma geþring 2132
ne wæs hit lenge þā gēn 83	ne byð him wihte ðȳ sēl 2277

and with elision,

    hē þē æt sunde‿oferflāt 517

and with long medial syllable in unaccented position,

    Ne bið þē [n]ǣnigre gād 949

†36. |♪ ♪ ♩♩♩ | ♪ ♫ ♩|, 4 examples:

    þā hine se brōga ongeat 1291
    ond hine þā hēafde becearf 1590
    þæt þū him ondrǣdan ne þearft 1674
    þæt hē hyne sylfne gewræc 2875

†37. |♪ ♪ ♪ ♪ | ♪ ♫ ♩|, 8 examples:

    nō ic him þæs georne ætfealh 968
    nǣfre hit æt hilde ne swāc 1460
    sē þe ǣr æt sæcce gebād 1618
    þæs ðe ic on aldre gebād 1779
    oþ þæt hine yldo benam 1886
    nō hē him þā sæcce ondrēd 2347
    þām ðe ǣr his elne forlēas 2861
    ðȳ hē þone fēond ofercwōm 1273

†38. |♪ ♪ ♩♩♩ | ♪ ♫ ♩|, 3 examples:

    þæs ðe hire se willa gelamp 626
    syþðan hē hire folmum (æthr)ān 722
    Ðē hē ūsic on herge gecēas 2638

†39. |♩♩♩ ♪ ♪ | ♪ ♫ ♩|, 3 examples:

    Hwæþere hē his folme forlēt 970
    þone ðe hēo on ræste ābrēat 1298
    þāra þe hit mid mundum bewand 1461

†40.   ♪ |♪ ♪ ♪ ♪ | ♪ ♫ ♩|, 1 example:

    tō ðæs þe hē on ræste geseah 1585

41. |♪ ♪ ♪ | ♫ ♫ ♩|, 8 examples:

    mid his hæleþa gedryht 662   Him þæt gifeðe ne wæs 2682
    þā ðæs monige gewearð 1598   wæs þæt gifeðe tō swīð 3085
    þæt him Onela forgeaf 2616   ic on ofoste gefēng 3090

and with the second member of a compound name in unaccented position,

Ic on Higelāce wāt 1830

and with substitution of the short form *ðon* for MS.
ðonne,

sē wæs betera ðon ic 469

Concerning the last example, see p. 71.

(42. [♪ ♩ | ♫ ♫ ♩], only in first half-line.)

43. [♫♩ | ♫ ♫ ♩], 1 example:

þēh hē þǣr monige geseah 1613

(44. [♪ ♪ ♪ | ♫ ♫ ♩], only in first half-line.)

(45. [♩ | ♪ ♫ ♪♪], only in first half-line.)

46. [♪ ♪ | ♪ ♫ ♪♪], 1 example:

þæt wæs geōmuru ides 1075

But probably we should read *geōmru* and count the verse
with no. 23.

47. [♪ ♪ ♪ | ♪ ♫ ♪♪], 1 example:

ac hine wundra þæs fela 1509

(48. ♪ | ♪ ♪ ♪ ♪ | ♪ ♫ ♪♪ |, only in first half-line.)

†49. [♪ ♪ | ♫ ♫ ♪♪], 1 example:

būton Fitela mid hine 879

Perhaps we should read *Fitla* and include this under no. 46.

(Type B3, nos. 50, 51, only in first half-line.)

b. WITH ANACRUSIS AND A HEAVY STRESS IN EACH MEASURE.

B1

52. ♪ | ♩ ♩ | ♩ | (cf. 1), 10 examples:

ond Hālga til 61	on sweordes hād 2193
ond norþanwind 547	wið stēapne rond 2566
on Finna land 580	ond dȳre swyrd 3048
on elran men 752	on brēostum læg 552
ond Grendles hond 927	on lande stōd 1913

53. ♪ | ♩. ♪ | ♩ | (cf. 9), 1 example:

on flēam gewand 1001

†54. ♪ | ♪ ♪ ♩ | ♩ | (cf. 15), 1 example:

ond hæleþa bearn 1189

†55. ♪ | ♪ ♩ ♪ | ♩ | (no. 53 with resolution of first stress, cf. 15), 4 examples:

tō, on, *or* in sele þām hēan 713, 919, 1016, 1984 (heân?)

56. ♪ | ♩ ♩ | ♪ ♩. | (cf. 22), 3 examples:

tō wīdan feore 933   on Hrefnawudu 2925
              of hlīðes nosan 1892

But the quantities in the last are by no means certain. Perhaps we should read *of hliðes nōsan,* type C.

†57. ♪ | ♪ ♪ ♩ | ♪ ♩. | (cf. 30), 2 examples:

on nicera mere 845   wið hæleþa brego 1954

B2

58. ♪ | ♪ ♪ ♪ ♪ | ♩ | (cf. 41), 1 example:

tō Heorute ātēah 766

TYPE C

a. First measure light, second heavy.

C1 (= Sievers' C1 + C2)

1. | 𝄽 ♩ | ♩ ♪ ♪ |, 7 examples:

> wið þē mōton 365   on þā healfe 1675
> hāt in gân 386   nē mægð scȳne 3016
> Ic þē nū ðā 426   þā sēlestan 3122
> mid Hruntinge 1659

2. | 𝄽 ♪ ♪ | ♩ ♪ ♪ |, 74 examples:

> þone God sende 13   þæt ic þē sōhte 417

and similarly with noun or pronoun plus verb in the second measure, 72, 233, 318, 383, 485, 522, 563, 731, 930, 1116 (*ond on bǣl dôn*), 1172 & 1534 (*swā sceal man dôn*), 1271, 1375, 1482, 1702, 2166 (*Swā sceal mǣg dôn*), 2182, 2490, and 2649 (*þenden hyt sȳ*); and with adjective plus verb, *þæt hē slēac wǣre* 2187;

> tō gescæphwīle 26   Nū gē feorbūend 254

and with similar compounds, 16 (*him þæs Līffreâ*), 335 (*Ic eom Hrōðgāres*), 393, 433, 856 (*Ðǣr wæs Bēowulfes*), 904, 989, 1000, 1157, 1186, 1636, 1711, 1910, 1934 (*nefne sinfrêa*), 1978, 1990 (*Ac ðū Hrōðgāre*), 2064 ((*syð*)*ðan Ingelde*), 2274, 2379, 2911 (*syððan under*[*ne*]), 3161, and with a compound verb, *ic ðē fullǣstu* 2668; and with tri-syllables,

> tō gefremmanne 174   sē ðe Waldendes 2292

and similarly 644, 2329, 2634, 2807, and 2964;

> þā him mid scoldon 41   sē þe wēl þenceð 289

and similarly with adverb plus verb in the second measure, 881, 1134 (*swā nū gȳt dêð*), 1371, 1476, 1821, 2585, and 2601; besides the following miscellaneous assortment:

> þonne hē sylfa 505   nefne God sylfa 3054
> swylce þȳ dōgore 1797   nemne fēaum ānum 1081
> nefn(e) mīn ānes 2533   Ðā wæs hord rāsod 2283

būton þē nū ðā 657   ond his cwēn mid him 923
þæt gebearh fēore 1548   hē gewræc syððan 2395
Ūs wæs ā syððan 2920

3. |♪ ♪ ♩|♩ ♪ ♪|, 1 example:

be ðē lifigendum 2665

4. |♪ ♩♩♩|♩ ♪ ♪|, 23 examples:

þēah hē him lēof wǣre 203   oþðe on wæl crunge 635
þēah ðe hē rōf sîe 682   nymðe mec God scylde 1658
þēah ðe hē geong sŷ 1831   hwæðre him God ūðe 2874
þēah hē him hold wǣre 2161   swā him gemet þince 687
nō ic fram him wolde 543   swā him gemet ðūhte 3057

nō þŷ ǣr fram meahte 754   þæt ic þē wēl herige 1833
hēt hine wēl brūcan 1045   swylce ðǣr iū wǣron 2459
swā hē nū gīt dêð 1058   swā hē nū gēn dêð 2859

nalles for wræcsīðum 338   sum[e] on galgtrēowu[m] 2940
wiste þǣm āhlǣcan 646   syððan hē Hrōðgāres 2351
þonne tō sǣlāde 1139   swylce hē þrŷdlīcost 2869
          oþ þæt hŷ [s]æl timbred 307

5. |♪ ♪ ♪ ♪|♩ ♪ ♪|, 14 examples:

      ǣr hē on weg hwurfe 264   þā wit on sund reôn 539
      þā git on sund reôn 512   þē ic geweald hæbbe 950
            tō hire frēan sittan 641

   þæt hīe him tō mihton 313   þē þū hēr tō lōcast 1654
   þæt ðū mē ā wǣre 1478   þē gē þǣr on standað 2866

   Ne seah ic elþēodige 336   wit unc wið hronfixas 540
         geseah his mondryhten 2604

   ic mē mid Hruntinge 1490   þæt ic mē ǣnigne 1772

6. |♪ ♪ ♩♩♩|♩ ♪ ♪|, 1 example:

gehŷrde on Bēowulfe 609

7. |♪ ♪ ♪ ♪| ♪ ♪ ♪|, 7 examples:

swā hȳ nǣfre man lȳhð 1048   swā hē hyra mā wolde 1055
þæt hē mē ongēan sléâ 681

þonne ǣnig man ōðer 1353   ðonne ǣnig mon ōðer 1560
nō hē þǣre feohgyfte 1025   swylce hira mandryhtne 1249

†8. |♩ ♩ ♩ ♪| ♩ ♪ ♪|, 2 examples:

þāra þe hē cēnoste 206   þæs þe him ǣr God sealde 1751

†9. |♩ ♩ ♩ ♪ ♪| ♩ ♪ ♪|, 1 example:

þāra þe hē him mid hæfde 1625

10. |𝄽 ♩| ♪ ♪ ♪ ♪|, 2 examples:

of gomenwāþe 854   [ond] kyning mǣnan 3171

I am not at all sure that *ond* in the latter verse should be
regarded as a pure emendation. The ultra-violet photo-
graph of the last page of the MS. recently published by
A. H. Smith (" The Photography of Manuscripts," *London
Mediæval Studies* 1 (1938), Plate VI following p. 200),
shows more distinctly than Zupitza's facsimile the upright
of what has always been taken for *k,* but it also reveals a
horizontal stroke to the left, which joins the upright at just
the level of the abbreviation for *ond* (7). I believe, therefore, that *kyning* has been made out of an original *ond
cyning*, either in an attempt at restoration or by some
accident. The MS. itself may lead to a more definite conclusion if it is studied with this possibility in mind. Sievers
(*Beiträge* 10. 232) made the same suggestion on the basis of
Zupitza's facsimile.

11. |𝄽 ♪ ♪| ♪ ♪ ♪ ♪|, 43 examples:

þā wið Gode wunnon 113   nē his myne wisse 169

and similarly with noun and verb in the second measure,
411, 490, 593, 777, 947, 1042, 1355, 1362 (*þæt se mere
standeð*), 2445, 2608, 2633, and with infinitive, 707, 1862
(*ofer heafu bringan*), and 2294;

nē gehwæþer incer 584   Bēo þū suna mīnum 1226

and similarly with two words of the noun-pronoun-adjective class in the second measure, 814, 1248, 1282, 2059, 2455, 2632, and 3096; besides the following miscellaneous assortment:

þæt hē þanon scolde 691   ac hē hraþe wolde 1576
uton hraþe fēran 1390   þæt ðū geare cunne 2070
þonne hniton fēþan 1327   þonne hnitan fēðan 2544
sē þe fela æror 809   ic bēo gearo sōna 1825
               nē gesacu ōhwær 1737 (*Sievers* ōwer?)

syððan æðelingas 2888   mid his gædelingum 2949
Wē synt Higelāces 342   mid his heteþancum 475
Ic eom Higelāces 407   Hæfde Kyningwuldor 665
tō his winedrihtne 360   wæs tō foremihtig 969
               mīnum magoþegnum 1480

(12. | ♪ ♪ ♩ | ♪ ♪ ♪ ♪ |, only in first half-line.)

13. | ♪ ♩♩♩ | ♪ ♪ ♪ ♪ |, 8 examples:

þāra ðe cwice hwyrfaþ 98   þonne hē fela murne 1385
sē þe wið Brecan wunne 506   þonne his sunu hangað 2447
nō ic þæs [fela] gylpe 586   þonne his myne sōhte 2572
sume on wæle crungon 1113   oð ðæt his byre mihte 2621

14. | ♪ ♪ ♪ ♪ | ♪ ♪ ♪ ♪ |, 5 examples:

þā hīe tō sele furðum 323   þær hyre byre wæron 1188
swā ðone magan cende 943   þær hyne Dene slōgon 2050
               þæt him his winemāgas 65

15. | ♪ ♪ ♩♩♩ | ♪ ♪ ♪ ♪ |, 1 example:

ne hȳrde ic snotorlīcor 1842

16. | ♪ ♪ ♪ ♪ | ♪ ♪ ♪ ♪ |, 5 examples:

næfne him his wlite lēoge 250   þæt þū ðē for sunu wolde 1175
hwanan ēowre cyme syndon 257   þæt hīe ær tō fela micles 694
               þæt hīe heora winedrihten 1604

17. | ♩ ♪ ♪ | ♩ ♩♩♩ |, 1 example:

    Hē on weg losade 2096

†18. | ♩ ♩♩♩ | ♩ ♩♩♩ |, 1 example:

    þē ic hēr on starie 2796

(19. | ♩ ♩ | ♩ ♪ ♩♩♩ |, only in first half-line.)

20. | ♩ ♪ ♪ | ♩ ♪ ♩♩♩ |, 3 examples:

    Ic þæs wine Deniga 350   ond on mere staredon 1603
           Wæs se fruma egeslīc 2309

C2(= Sievers' C3)

21. | ♩ ♩ | ♩ ♩ ♪ |, 15 examples:

in gēardagum 1	on land Dena 253
ond frēondlaþu 1192	on dēop wæter 509
ðǣr Hring-Dene 1279	Wæs þēaw hyra 1246
ond swyrdgifu 2884	nē gōd hafoc 2263
þon þā dydon 44	Hī sīð drugon 1966
Nū scealc hafað 939	ic lȳt hafo 2150
heald forð tela 948	hēold mīn tela 2737
Ic wāt geare 2656	

22. | ♩ ♪ ♪ | ♩ ♩ ♪ |, 166 examples:

    Hēt him ȳðlidan 198   nis þæt seldguma 249

and with similar compounds, 116 (*hū hit Hring-Dene*), 199, 380, 476, 640, 710, 737, 771, 801, 820, 828 (*Hæfde Ēast-Denum*), 993, 1033, 1073 (*æt þām lindplegan*), 1138, 1325, 1351, 1388, 1420, 1493, 1853, 1963, 1992, 2018, 2039, 2065, 2122, 2335, 2341 (*Sceolde lǣndaga*), 2622, 2733, 2747, 2893, 2999, 3036, 3040, 3112, and with syncope of a medial vowel, *on þǣm meðelstede* 1082;

    þæt hē þrītiges 379   Ic him þēnode 560

and less certainly (see no. 22c under first half-line),

ic ēow wīsige 292, 3103   þæt wē fundiaþ 1819

besides a large number with two separate words in the second measure,

þæt wæs gōd cyning 11, 2390   scōp him Heort naman 78

and similarly with two words of the noun-adjective class, 146, 178, 223, 331, 698, 918, 920, 1109, 1151 (*Ðā wæs heal roden*), 1152, 1153, 1250, 1306, 1439, 1495, 1575, 1611, 1738, 1745, 1783, 1814, 1885, 1989, 2043, 2180, 2209, 2306, 2314, 2506, 2727, 2762, 2913, 2957, 2981, 3007 (Nū *is ofǫst betost*), and 3105;

þonne wīg cume 23   lēton holm beran 48

and similarly with noun or adjective plus verb (finite or infinitive), 439, 447, 452, 589, 594, 599, 680, 953, 954 (*þæt þīn [dōm] lyfað*), 1343, 1366, 1370, 1374, 1430, 1481, 1610, 1802, 1808, 1846, 1923, 2027, 2031, 2058, 2126, 2252, 2530, 2536, 2742, 2745, 2818, 2982, 3014, 3015, 3114, 3126, 3132, and 3172 (*ond ymb w(er) sprecan*);

þenden þǣr wunað 284   oþ ðæt eft byreð 296

and similarly with adverb plus verb, 400, 444, 831, 944, 1381, 1676, 1858, 1891, 2069, and 3070;

ond on weg þanon 763   þǣr wæs eal geador 835

and similarly with noun or adjective plus adverb, 1211, 1614, 1668, 2062, 2099, 2196, 2343, 2408, and 2987;

þanon up hraðe 224   ǣr gē fyr heonan 252

and similarly with two adverbs, 1292, 1361, 1805, 1820, 1921, and 2117; besides the following:

hē onfēng hraþe 748   ic ne wāt hwæðer 1331
ond geþēoh tela 1218   hē gehēold tela 2208
Ic þē an tela 1225   ac forgeald hraðe 2968

ond onsǣl meoto 489   þanon wōc fela 1265
ðā gebēah cyning 2980   nē mē swōr fela 2738
    hē ne lēag fela 3029
    hē mæg þǣr fela 1837

23. |♪ ♪ ♩|♩ ♪♪|, 3 examples:

    þā gēn gūðcyning 2677   þā gēn sylf cyning 2702
        ond nō mearn fore 136

24. |𝄽 ♩♩♩ | ♩ ♪ ♪|, 29 examples:

    ǣr hē on bed stige 676   būtan his līc swice 966

and similarly with noun plus verb in the second measure, 1074, 1328 (*Swy(lc) scolde eorl wesan*), 1392, 1491, 1536, 1741, 1749, 2446, 2453, 2499, 2518, 2708, 2976, 3000 (*ðæs ðe ic [wēn] hafo*), and 3073 (*sē ðone wong strude*);

    swā hē nū gȳt dyde 956   þonne ðū forð scyle 1179

and similarly with adverb plus verb, 1238, 1735, 1824, 3106, 3167, and 3176; besides the following:

ymb hine rinc manig 399   hū i(c ð)ām lēodsceaðan 2093
Nū is sē dæg cumen 2646   oððe tō Gār-Denum 2494

25. |𝄽 ♪ ♪ ♪ | ♩ ♪ ♪|, 26 examples:

    þæt mīne brēost wereð 453   ac wit on niht sculon 683

and similarly with noun plus verb in the second measure, 798, 975, 1367, 1382, 1849, 2598, and 3021; besides the following:

ne mihte snotor hæleð 190   ac þæt wæs gōd cyning 863
þæt þis is hold weorod 290   wæs hira blǣd scacen 1124
      on ðǣm wæs ōr writen 1688

    Gewītaþ forð beran 291   þæt ic ðȳ sēft mæge 2749
    ond hine ymb monig 689   Gewāt him on naca 1903
      forðon hē ǣr fela 2349

      gewāt him hām þonon 1601

þæt hit wearð ealgearo 77   swā hine fyrndagum 1451
þæt hīe sint wilcuman 388   gif mec se mānsceaða 2514
æt þǣre bēorþege 617   þæt mīnne līchaman 2651

(26. |♪ ♪ ♩ | ♩ ♪ ♪|, only in first half-line, unless *swā hīe oft ǣr dydon* 1238, which is included under no. 24 above.)

(27. |♩ ♪ ♪ | ♩ ♪ ♪|, only in first half-line, unless *Swylc scolde eorl wesan* 1328 or *swylc sceolde secg wesan* 2708, which are included under no. 24.)

28. | ♪ ♪ ♩ ♩ ♩ | ♩ ♪ ♪ |, 3 examples:

> tō þæs þe hē wīnreced 714   forðon ic mē on hafu 2523
> ne mæg ic hēr leng wesan 2801

29. | ♪ ♪ ♪ ♪ | ♩ ♪ ♪ |, 6 examples:

> sē þe hine dēað nimeð 441   wolde hyre mǣg wrecan 1339
> þāra þe on swylc starað 996   wolde hire bearn wrecan 1546
> sē ðe wyle sōð specan 2864
> ðonne wē on orlege 1326

†30. | ♩ ♩ ♩ ♪ ♪ | ♩ ♪ ♪ |, 1 example:

> þonne hē on þæt sinc starað 1485

(31. ♪ | ♪ ♪ ♪ ♪ | ♩ ♪ ♪ |, only in first half-line.)

Note: C2 with resolution of the first stress seems to have been avoided rather
carefully. The only possible examples are *on þǣm meðelstede* 1082,
Nū is ofost betost 3007, and *ne mihte snotor hæleð* 190, which have
been reduced by syncope, in accordance with the usual practice, to conformity with nos. 22 and 25. See also Cb2, no. 39 below.

b. WITH ANACRUSIS AND A HEAVY STRESS IN EACH MEASURE.

C1 (= Sievers' C1 + C2)

32. ♪ | ♩ ♩ | ♩ ♩ | (cf. 1), 40 examples:

> gebūn hæfdon 117   gesēon mihte 571

and similarly with prefix plus participle or infinitive plus
finite verb, 511, 648, 910, 961, 1078, 1140, 1277, 1462,
1535, 1628, 1875, 1998, 2090, 2186, and 2630; besides the
following:

> gefēan hæfdon 562   gefēan habban 2740
> gehwǣr dohte 526

> on Frēan wǣre 27   on hrēon mōde 1307
> on twā healfa 1095   on hrēoum mōde 2581
> on bā healfe 2063

on sǣ wǣron 544   on flet teôn 1036
ymb hord wīgan 2509   on flett gǣð 2034, 2054
be sǣm twēonum 858, 1297, 1685, *and* (*with* bī) 1956
ond orcnêas 112   on seglrāde 1429
æt Wealhþeôn 629   ond mon(ðw)ǣrust 3181
ond grīmhelmas 334   ond lofgeornost 3182

For Klaeber's *an wīg gearwe* 1247, read *anwīggearwe,* type
A2, no. 28 above.

(33.   ♩ ♪|♪̋|♩ ♩|, only in first half-line.)

34.   ♪|♪̋ ♩.|♩̋ ♩| (cf. 10), 74 examples:

forscrifen hæfde 106   ongyton mihton 308

and similarly with prefix plus participle or infinitive plus
finite verb, 220, 804, 1472, 1599 (*ābroten hæfde*), 2145,
2397, 2726, 3147, 2104, 2707, 3165, 1196, 1928, 780, 1350,
1496, 1561, 1911, 1919, 2770, 2954, 738, 990, 2588, 355, 414,
2218 (besyre(d wur)de), and 2400; and a few other combinations after a prefix,

beforan gengde 1412   gehroden golde 304
beforan wolde 2497   getrume micle 922
ongeador sprǣcon 1595   tōbrocen swīðe 997
        gebogen scrīðan 2569

besides a large number in which the first syllable is a separate word (preposition or conjunction), most of which could
be read according to no. 10:

on fæder (bea)rme 21   tō ban*an* folmum 158

and similarly with proclitic plus two words of the noun-
adjective class, 473, 483, 1114, 1236, 1507, 1479, 1836, 1950,
2088, 2320, and 2549;

ymb Brecan sprǣce 531   tō banan wurde 587

and similarly with proclitic plus noun plus verb, 706, 967,
1130, 1342, 1640, 1648, 1857, 1895, 1974, 2203, 2485, 2892,
and 2960;

ond heaðowǣdum 39   tō Wedermearce 298

and similarly with proclitic plus compound, 1437, 2204,
2805, 2815, 2993, 3083, and 3136.

(35. ♪ ♪ | ♪̏ ♪̋ ♩. | ♪̋ ♩ |, only in first half-line.)

36. ♪ | ♪̏ ♩̋. | ♪̏ ♪ ♩ |, 6 examples:

tō brimes faroðe 28	tō scypon feredon 1154
ond feorum gumena 73	tō Denum feredon 1158
mid ofermægene 2917	on sele wunian 3128

C2(= Sievers' C3)

37. ♪ | ♩̋ | ♪̋ ♩̋. |, 28 examples:

mid ǣrdæge 126	æt *hærgtrafum* 175

and similarly with proclitic plus compound, 460, 1330, 1578, 1856, 2079, 2437, 2896, and 2932;

on bearm scipes 35	on hand gyfen 1678
on bid wrecen 2962	on wǣn hladen 3134
on flet boren 1647	on tȳn dagum 3159
tō hām faran 124	on bearm dyde 1144
on wang stigon 225	on holm wliton 1592
ymb sund flite 507	for wiht dyde 2348

on lāst faran 2945

þū nū hafast 1174	on weg þanon 844
gescād witan 288	geþyld hafa 1395

ābredwade 2619

(38. ♪ ♪ | ♩̋ | ♪̋ ♩̋. |, only in first half-line.)

†39. ♪ | ♪̋ ♩̋. | ♪̋ ♩̋. | 1 doubtful example:

æt brimes nosan 2803

For the quantity of *nosan*, see the references in Klaeber's glossary. It seems to me far more likely that we should read *nōsan* and assign the verse to no. 34 above. This would involve changing *of hlīðes nosan* 1892 (type B no. 56) to *of hlīðes nōsan* (type C no. 34).

TYPE D

D1

1. $|\tilde{\vphantom{l}}\!\!\downarrow|\ \tilde{\vphantom{l}}\!\!\downarrow\ \downarrow\ \downarrow|$, 78 examples:

ymbsittendra 9 (MS. þara ⌣)   unmurnlīce 449
foldbūendum 309   fylwērigne 962

and similarly with a single compound, 377, 468 (*unlifigende*), 568, 1013, 1227, 1308 (*unlyfigendne*), 2015, 2022, 2716, 2908 (*unlifigendum*), 3113, 3138, 2089, 1518, 2778, 3017, and with proper names, 464, 1710, 2607, and 2927;

Wiht unhǣlo 120   fēond mancynnes 164

and similarly with monosyllabic noun plus compound noun or adjective, 621, 727, 885, 1111, 1498, 1769, 2076, 2120, 2123, 2223 (*þ(ēow)nāthwylces*), 2413, 2483, 2767, and with compound adverb, 2881, and with compound proper names, *bearn Ecgþēowes* 529, 631, 957, 1383, 1473, 1651, 1817, 1999, 2177, 2425, *mǣg Hȳlāces* 1530, and *sweord Bīowulfes* 2681;

weard Scildinga 229   [h]of mōdigra 312

and similarly with monosyllabic noun and trisyllabic noun or adjective, 371, 456, 1321, 500, 1069, 521, 1096, 2381, 2603 (all these have proper names), 847, 2484, 2537, 2538, 2809, 2889, 2985, 2994, 3002, 3080, 3107, and with monosyllabic possessive, *mīn ǣrende* 345; besides the following:

slāt unwearnum 741   bāt unswīðor 2578
folc tō sǣgon 1422

2. $|\downarrow\ \tilde{\vphantom{l}}\!\!\downarrow.|\ \tilde{\vphantom{l}}\!\!\downarrow\ \downarrow\ \downarrow|$, 60 examples:

wine Scyldinga 30, 170, 2026   Heaðo-Scilfingas 2205

and with similar proper names, 58, 597, 620, 778, 1108, 1563, 2052, and 2101;

sunu Ecglāfes 590, 980   sele Hrōðgāres 826

and with similar proper names, 1456, 1465, 1550, 1884, 2367, 2398, 2587, 2752, 2907, 2971, 3110, and 3120;

selerǣdende 51   higeþīhtigne 746

and with similar compounds, 95, 237, 1142 (w[e]orodræ-
dende), 1780, 1888, 2720, 2781, and 3091;

    segen g(yl)denne 47   micel ærende 270

and with similar combinations, 216, 294, 652, 1851, 1860,
2195, and 2259 (bite īren[n]a);

    gumum undyrne 127   fela missēra 153, 2620

and with similar combinations, 316, 406, 502, 1932, 2053,
2068, 2821 (guman unfrōdum), and 3148; besides the
following:

    Guman ōnetton 306   scaþan ōnetton 1803
          weras on sāwon 1650

3. | ♩ | ♪ ♪ ♪ ♪ |, 3 examples:

    mǣg Higelāces 758   mǣg Hygelāces 813
         segn Higelāce[s] 2958

4. | ♪ ♩. | ♪ ♪ ♪ ♪ |, 4 examples:

  hroden ealowǣge 495   nefan Hererīces 2206
  gladum suna Frōdan 2025 (A31?)   sunu Hygelāces 2386

†5. | ♩ | ♩ ♩♩♩ |, 1 example:

  milts ungyfeðe 2921

This could be read as type A, | ♩ ♩ | ♪ ♪ ♩ |.

(6-9, the preceding forms with anacrusis, only in first half-
line.)

D2

10. | ♩ | ♩ ♪ ♪ |, 64 examples:

    secg wīsade 208   feo þingode 470

and similarly with third person singular preterite of weak
verbs of the second class, 320, 611, 725, 901, 951, 1204,
1206, 1407, 1566, 1687, 1721, 1898, 2084, 2085, 2164, 2285,

24

2383, 2793, 3027, and preceded by adverbs, 1795, 1916, and 2897;

lāst scēawedon 132   rǣd eahtedon 172

and similarly with third person plural preterite of weak verbs of the second class (which may belong under D4— see first half-line, C 22c), 204, 423, 983, 1212, 2075, and preceded by adverbs, 639 and 3050;

fēa þingian 156   rinc sīðian 720

and similarly with infinitive of weak verbs of the second class (which may likewise belong under D4), 787, 796, 971, 1391, 1413, 1426, 1444, 2168 (*dēað rēn(ian)*), 2589, 2605, 2655, 2658, 2773, and preceded by adverbs, 451, 808, and 3008; and with first person singular present, 1380 and 2652; and with third person plural present, 3104;

b*ear*n Healfdenes 1020	Beorh eallgearo 2241
þēod ealgearo 1230	grim andswaru 2860
word ūt faran 2551	strēam ūt þonan 2545
Wyrd oft nereð 572	gid oft wrecen 1065
bōt eft cuman 281	
bēah eft þonan 2956	

Sievers somewhat hesitantly assigned the last four and 1230 and 2241 (where he read *eal gearo* as separate words) to type A2k (which I have called A4). See *Beiträge* 10. 230 and 255. For 1230 and 2241 the reading *ealgearo* seems preferable and necessitates the assignment of these verses to type D. The rhythm of the others depends on one's interpretation of their meaning. They seem to me more expressive when read according to type D.

11. $|\text{♩}\ \text{♩.}|\ \text{♩}\ \text{♩}\ \text{♪}|$, 54 examples:

Sele hlīfade 81   Heorot eardode 166

and similarly (cf. no. 10 for this and the following distinctions), 625, 770, 843, 1090, 1117, 1237, 1397, 1589, 1630, 1799, 2098, 2102, 2336, 2352, 2594, and with the first word an adverb, 370 and 1500;

Gode þancedon 227   wada cunnedon 508

and similarly 570, 1102, 1440, and 1626;

    freoðo wilnian 188   Heorot fǣlsian 432

and similarly 1662, 1843, 2045, 2211 (*draca rīcs[i]an*), 2402, and 3025;

    weras ehtigað 1222   gearco scēawige 2748

and certainly the following:

    maga Healfdenes 189   suna Ōhteres 2380

and with the same proper names, 1474, 2011, 2143, 344, 1040, 1652, 2394, and 2928;

Godes andsacan 786	hwate scild*wigan* 3005
Godes andsaca 1682	mægenfultuma 1455
hider wilcuman 394	Samod ǣrdæge 1311, 2942 (somod)
guman ūt scufon 215	dracan ēc scufun 3131

12. | ♩ | ♪ ♪ ♪ ♪ |, 1 example:

    hord openian 3056

Perhaps this should be assigned to D4, like the other similar verses under nos. 10 and 11.

13.   ♪ | ♩ | ♩ ♪ ♪ |, 1 example:

    þā secg wīsode 402

Probably *þā* should be omitted; cf. 208 under no. 10.

D3

14. | ♩ | ♪ ♪ ♩ |, 13 examples:

hēahcyninges 1039	sǣcyninga 2382
eorðcyninges 1155	Frēscyning[e] 2503
	þēodcyninges 2694
feorh cyninges 1210	fyll cyninges 2912
umborwesende 46	cnihtwesende 372, 535
	sāwlberendra 1004

and with short penultimate syllable,

        andswarode 258, 340

†15. | ♪ ♩. | ♪ ♪ ♩ |, 2 examples:

woroldcyninga 1684   wyruldcyning[a] 3180

D4

16. | ♩ | ♪ ♪ ♩ |, 27 examples:

blǣd wīde sprang 18   word æfter cwæð 315

and similarly with noun plus adverb plus verb, 341, 478, 496, 569, 761, 1423, 1570, 1588, 1800, 2154, 2213, 2331, and 2764;

blōd ēdrum dranc 742   holm storme wēol 1131
swāt ǣdrum sprong 2966   gǣst yrre cwōm 2073
swāt ȳðum wēoll 2693   wyrm yrre cwōm 2669

hond (wǣge nam) 2216   ferh ellen wrǣc 2706
            sceft nytte hēold 3118
            From ǣrest cwōm 2556

Heort innanweard 991   flet innanweard 1976

In 2073 and 2669 I take *yrre*, though it is probably an adjective, in an adverbial sense. Otherwise these verses would belong to type E.

17. | ♪ ♩. | ♪ ♪ ♩ |, 20 examples:

fæder ellor hwearf 55   wæter under stōd 1416
flota stille bād 301   hreðer inne wēoll 2113
Heorot innan wæs 1017   dug(uð) ellor s[c]eōc 2254
wala ūtan hēold 1031   Bona swylce læg 2824

geofon ȳþum wēol 515   hreðer ǣðme wēoll 2593
draca morðre swealt 892   Metod eallum wēold 1057
          Heofon rēce swe(a)lg 3155

gearo sōna wæs 121   hraþe seoþðan wæs 1937

Denum eallum wearð 767, 823   Denum eallum wæs 1417

          foran ǣghwylc wæs 984

          eafor hēafodsegn 2152

In verses 767, 823, and 1417 the grammatical agreement of

Denum and *eallum* would suggest type E, but *wearð* and *wæs* do not deserve primary accent. I feel less certain about 121 and 1937. The latter especially would sound right as type E.—Verse 984 has the second member of a compound in an unaccented position, and seems rather awkward. Perhaps we should follow John Ries (*Die Wortstellung im Beowulf*, Halle a. S., 1907, p. 378 f.) in reading *foran wæs æghwylc* (type A2b), which is certainly smoother, but the verse is expressive as it stands and not really abnormal, and if we retain the next verse unchanged (*steda nægla gehwylc*) it is almost imperative to keep this also, for otherwise both would end with *-hwylc* and an already embarrassing repetition would become painful.

18. |♩|♩♪ ♩|, 23 examples:

holm up ætbær 519	cēol up geþrang 1912
Swēg up āstāg 782	Hond up ābrǣd 2575
stefn in becōm 2552	
secg eft ongan 871	sweord ǣr gemealt 1615
Fin eft begeat 1146	Sweord ǣr gebrǣd 2562
hord eft gescēat 2319	Bill ǣr gescōd 2777
lȳt eft becwōm 2365	helm ǣr gescer 2973
Frōfor eft gelamp 2941	Weard ǣr ofslōh 3060
helm oft gescær 1526	
wēan oft gehēt 2937	
Scyld wēl gebearg 2570	
hond rond gefēng 2609	feor eal gemon 1701
wyrm hāt gemealt 897	Bēot eal wið þē 523
Forð nēar ætstōp 745	

Sievers somewhat hesitantly placed the verses with *eft, oft, ǣr, wēl,* and *eal* under type E (see *Beiträge* 10. 257 ff.). But all the adverbs, including *ǣr,* which Sievers thought especially unemphatic, take precedence of verbs in types B and C. I do not think this a conclusive argument, but I cannot avoid the feeling that the verses in question are more expressive when read according to type D. Doubtless there must always be disagreement in this matter. Comparison of the list under type E no. 3 will show that I have not treated all verses with *eal* in the same fashion.—I agree with Sievers that *hāt* in 897 has adverbial force and so belongs here.

†19. |♪ ♩.| ♩ ₃♪ ♩ |, 8 examples:

Monig oft gesæt 171   Gamen eft āstāh 1160
monig oft gecwæð 857   wæter up þurhdēaf 1619

þanon eft gewāt 123   nyðer eft gewāt 3044

hider ūt ætbær 3092

sunu dēað fornam 2119

On the verses with *oft* and *eft* see the discussion under no. 18.

20. |♩| ♪ ♫ ♩ |, 12 examples:

Þegn nytte behēold 494   hrōf āna genæs 999
Heal swēge onfēng 1214   Wīg ealle fornam 1080
secg weorce gefeh 1569   Līg ealle forswealg 1122
            hond sweng ne oftēah 1520
            winter ȳþe belēac 1132

word inne ābēad 390   hring ūtan ymbbearh 1503
            sibb' æfre ne mæg 2600
            hlǣw oft ymbehwearf 2296

Very likely we should read *ymbhwearf* in 2296 and include the verse under no. 18. It will be noticed that if we read this as type E we shall be faced with double alliteration—another argument to add to those under no. 18.

21. |♪ ♩.| ♪ ♫ ♩ |, 2 examples:

Duru sōna onarn 721   cyning ealdre binēat 2396

(22. |♩| ♪³♩♩ ♩ |, only in first half-line.)

†23. |♪ ♩.| ♪³♩♩ ♩ |, 1 example:

cyning æþelum gōd 1870

24. | ♩ | ♩ ₃ ♪ ♪ ♪ |, 1 example:

wōp up āhafen 128

(25, 26, forms with anacrusis, only in first half-line.)

D*1

27. | ♩ ♩ | ♩ ♪ ♪ |, 3 examples:

Bēowulf Scyldinga 53   lāðra ōwihte 2432
dohtor Hrōðgāres 2020

The first two are doubtful, because we should probably read *Bēow* for *Bēowulf* and *ōhte* for *ōwihte*.

28. | ♩. ♪ | ♩ ♪ ♪ |, 1 example:

seah on unlēofe 2863

(29. | ♪ ♪ ♩ | ♩ ♪ ♪ |, only in first half-line.)

†30. | ♪ ♩ ♪ | ♩ ♪ ♪ |, 1 example:

Gode ic þanc secge 1997

(31. | ♩ ♪ ♪ | ♩ ♪ ♪ |, only in first half-line.)

32. | ♪ ♪ ♪ ♪ | ♩ ♪ ♪ |, 1 very doubtful example:

Wundor is tō secganne 1724

I think Sievers was right in reading *secgan,* type A.

33. | ♩ ♩ | ♪ ♪ ♪ ♪ |, 1 example:

ðēod*ne* Heaðo-Beardna 2032

(34-39, only in first half-line.)

D*2

40. | ♩ ♩ | ♩ ♪ ♪ |, 6 examples:

    wundor scēawian 840   wīca nēosian 1125
    wundur scēawian 3032   fīonda nīos(i)an 2671
    oftost wīsode 1663   snūde eft cuman 1869

The first four are doubtful, because we could read *wundr* and *nēosan*. Sievers wanted to read 1869 with elision as type A2k, but see nos. 10 and 18 above.

41. | ♩.♪ | ♩ ♪ ♪ |, 2 examples:

    Dēad is Æschere 1323   him on andsware 1840

42. | ♪ ♪ ♩ | ♩ ♪ ♪ |, 1 example:

    ðolode ǣr fela 1525

This rather strange combination is explained, I think, by the fact that *fela* is tied very closely to the next verse, *hond-gemōta*.

(43. | ♩ ♪ ♪ | ♩ ♪ ♪ |, only in first half-line.)

(44. | ♩ ♪ ♪ | ♩ ♪ ♪ |, only in first half-line.)

45. | ♩ ♩ | ♪ ♪ ♪ ♪ |, 1 example:

    wǣpen hafenade 1573

We could, of course, read *wǣpn*.

(46-48, forms with anacrusis, only in first half-line.)

D*4

(49-53, only in first half-line.)

†54. | ♩.♪ | ♪ ♫ ♩ |, 1 example:

    seah on enta geweorc 2717

(55-58, only in first half-line.)
```
```

TYPE E

1. | ♩ ♪ ♪ | ♩ |, 147 examples:

weorðmyndum þāh 8   lofdǣdum sceal 24

and similarly with compound plus verb, 130, 131, 161, 241, 287, 305, 321, 719, 818, 846, 1051 (*brimlāde tēah*), 1072, 1269, 1332, 1352, 1365 (*nīðwundor sēon,* perhaps *nīðwundr sêon,* type A2), 1401, 1513, 1631, 1657, 1774 (*edwenden cwōm*), 1777, 1782 (*symbelwynne drēoh*), 1822, 1838, 1881, 1882, 1908, 1931 (*Mōdþrȳðo wǣg*), 1959, 1982, 2097 (*līfwynna br(ēa)c*), 2136, 2188, 2268 (*unblīðe hwe(arf)*), 2270, 2281, 2360, 2377, 2385, 2392, 2414, 2482, 2501, 2510, 2564, 2672 (*līgȳðum fōr,* see first half-line F 2), 2842, 2886, 2894, 3037 (*wundordēaðe swealt*), and 3043;

undyrne cūð 150, 410   nihtbealwa mǣst 193

and similarly with compound plus noun or adjective, 104 (*fīfelcynnes eard*), 207, 276, 302, 314, 322, 499, 550, 675, 921, 928, 955 (*Alwalda þec*), 998 (*īrenbendum fǣst*), 1066, 1119, 1169, 1194 (*earm[h]rēade twā*), 1195, 1229 (*mandrihtne hol[d]*), 1240, 1316, 1459 (*ātertānum fāh*), 1489, 1582, 1623, 1752, 1776, 1917, 1958, 2028, 2115, 2245 (*hordwyrðne dǣl*), 2279, 2387 (*Ongenðīoes bearn*), 2406, 2611, 2768, 2783, 2811, 2820, 2833 (*māðmǣhta wlonc*), 2901, 2938, 3038 (*syllīcran wiht*), 3072, 3143, and 3149 (*mondryhtnes cw(e)alm*);

mancynne fram 110   sǣgrunde nēah 564

and similarly with compound plus preposition or adverb, 602, 1642, 1715, 1924, 2357, 2411, 2826, and 2831;

ēhtende wæs 159   yrringa slōh 1565

and similarly with trisyllable plus verb, 1581, 1767, 1953 (*lifigende brēac*), 1973 (*lifigende cwōm*), 2789, 2832, and 3028;

wīgendra hlēo 429, 899, 1972, 2337

and similarly with trisyllable plus noun or adjective, 802, 1690, 1944 (*Hemminges mǣg*), 1961 (*Hem[m]inges mǣg*), 2817, 2979, 3127, and 3145 (*swōgende lēg*);

word ōþer fand 870   Frēan ealles ðanc 2794
fēa worda cwæð 2246, 2662   frēan eaxlum nēah 2853
lȳt manna ðāh 2836   Hygd swīðe geong 1926
        lȳt ænig mearn 3129

fēhð ōþer tō 1755   geong sōna tō 1785
Brūc ealles well 2162   eft sōna bið 1762

Verse 870 belongs here if it means, " he found other words."
If it means " one word found another," it belongs under D4.
See Klaeber's note on the line.

2. | ♩ ♪♪ | ♩♪ |, 4 examples:

Sūð-Dena folc 463   Norð-Denum stōd 783
bēaghroden cwēn 623   mundbora wæs 2779

3. | ♩ ♩ ♪ | ♩♪ |, 45 examples:

wordhord onlēac 259   wældēað fornam 695

and similarly with compound plus prefix plus verb, 736,
759, 815, 874, 895, 987, 1024 (*Bēowulf geþāh*), 1044,
1118, 1494, 1501, 1516, 1521, 1541 (*andlēan forgeald*),
1549, 1564, 1720, 1789, 1890, 2092, 2094 (*ondlēan forgeald*), 2221 (*wyrmhord ābræc*), 2249, 2288, 2302, 2554,
2559, 2584, 2929 (*ondslyht āgeaf*), 3146, and with infinitive,
Hrōðgār gesēon 396, and *Frȳsland gesēon* 1126;

                uncūð gelād 1410
Nægling forbærst 2680   Hengest ðā gȳt 1127

bil eal ðurhwōd 1567   līc eall forswealg 2080
flet eall geondhwearf 2017   worn eall gespræc 3094

līf ēac gesceōp 97   segn ēac genōm 2776
        Eard gīt ne const 1377

        God wāt on mec 2650

Possibly some of those with *eal, ēac,* and *gīt* belong under
D4, no. 18, which should be consulted for a discussion of
the confusion between the two forms.

4. | ♩ ♪ ♫ | ♩ |, 12 examples:

sundornytte behēold 667	sǣlāce gefeah 1624
hlēorbolster onfēng 688	gūðrǣsa genæs 2426
Nihtweorce gefeh 827	wæll-seaxe gebrǣd 2703
fletræste gebēag 1241	feorhsweng ne oftēah 2489
	heals ealne ymbefēng 2691

gīganta geweorc 1562   Wergendra tō lȳt 2882
fæstrǣdne geþōht 610

For *Līgȳðum forborn* 2672 read *Līgȳðum fōr,* no. 1 above, and see first half-line, F 2. In 2691 either elision or the substitution of *ymb-* is obligatory.

5. | ♪ ♪ ♪ ♪ | ♩ |, 57 examples:

heaðowylma bād 82   hetenīðas wæg 152

and similarly with compound plus verb, 236, 422, 659, 849, 935, 1047, 1200 (*searonīðas flēah*), 1405, 1511, 1643, 1669, 1965, 1970, 1980, 2021, 2169, 2224, 2282, 2313, 2326, 2358, 2539, 2576, 2678, 2714 (*bealonīð(e) wēoll*), and 2988;

Higelāces þegn 194, 1574, 2977   sigedrihten mīn 391

and similarly with compound plus noun or adjective, 1007, 1492, 1557, 1612, 1634, 1740, 1878, 1905, 2086, 2243, and 2328;

Scedelandum in 19   wæterȳðum nēah 2242

widerræhtes þær 3039

æþelinges fær 33	æþelinga bearn 1408
Godes yrre bær 711	bona swīðe nēah 1743
sume worde hēt 2156	′nefa swȳðe hold 2170
fela þǣra wæs 992	Raþe æfter þon 724
dracan hēafde nēah 2290	Breca nǣfre gīt 583
	nioðor hwēne slōh 2699

6. | ♪ ♪ ♩ ♪ | ♩ |, 13 examples:

heaþorǣs fornam 557	mægenrǣs forgeaf 1519
medoful ætbær 624	meregrund gefēoll 2100
eotonweard' ābēad 668	wud(u)rēc āstāh 3144
	Higelāc ongan 1983

Werod eall ārās 651   Dena land ofgeaf 1904
Duguð eal ārās 1790   Godes lēoht gecēas 2469
Weorod eall ārās 3030   gomel swyrd getēah 2610

7. | ♪ ♪ ♪ ♫ | ♩ |, 11 examples:

meodosetla oftēah 5   selereste gebēah 690
fyrenðearfe ongeat 14   Sigemunde gesprong 884
woroldāre forgeaf 17   Higelāce onsend 1483
            oferhȳda ne gȳm 1760

Heaða-Bear[d]na gestrēon 2037   æþelinga gedriht 118
searo[gimma] geþræc 3102   æþelinga gestrēon 1920

8. | ♩ ♫♩ | ♩ |, 2 examples:

wīgheafolan bær 2661   līgegesan wæg 2780

†9. | ♩ ♫ ♫ | ♩ |, 1 example:

Hrēðsigora ne gealp 2583

(10. | ♪ ♪ ♫ ♫ | ♩ |, only in first half-line.)

11. | ♩ ♪ ♪ | ♪ ♩. |, 15 examples:

uncūþes fela 876   gūðrǣsa fela 1577
wundorsīona fela 995   wordrihta fela 2631
gummanna fela 1028   māððumsigla fealo 2757
wyrmcynnes fela 1425   earmbēaga fela 2763
Folcwaldan sunu 1089
Wēoxstānes sunu 2602, 2862 (Wēoh-), 3076 (Wīh-)

Brōsinga mene 1199   unsōfte þonan 2140

and with the second syllable short (cf. no. 2),

Healfdenes sunu 1009

(12. | ♩ ♩ ♪ | ♪ ♩. |, only in first half-line.)

13. | ♩ ♪ ♫ | ♪ ♩. |, 2 examples:

Bēowulf is mīn nama 343   gumcynnes gehwone 2765

†14. |♪ ♪ ♪ ♪|♪ ♩.|, 1 example:

nicorhūsa fela 1411

(15. |♪ ♪ ♩ ₃♪|♪ ♩.|, only in first half-line.)

(16. |♪ ♪ ♪ ♫|♪ ♩.|, only in first half-line.)

E*

†17. |♪♪♪♪|♩|, 4 examples, all properly |♪ ♪ ♩ ₃♪|♩|:

Wā biŏ þæm ŏe sceal 183   Gǣþ eft sē þe mōt 603
Wēl biŏ þæm ŏe mōt 186   Fēþa eal gesæt 1424

The last verse may be included under no. 3 by elision. The
others are really a law unto themselves, and are examples of
the occasional failure of a series of monosyllables to fit
patterns designed for longer and more imposing words. See
also 998 and 2387, which have been included under no. 1.

F. Unclassified Remainder

a. *Deficient Verses*

If the MS. has been read correctly, there are four verses
in the second half-line which could be accepted grammatically but are metrically deficient. They are *ŏegn betstan*
1871, *rǣhte ongēan* 747, *gegnum fōr* 1404, and *kyning
mǣnan* 3171. The first two are retained by Klaeber and will
be discussed below under nos. 1 and 3. Klaeber has emended
the others to *swā gegnum fōr* and *ond kyning mǣnan*. These
emendations seem entirely reasonable (though *swā hēo* or
þǣr hēo gegnum fōr would make the meaning still clearer),
and I have catalogued the two verses in accordance with
them, the first under type B no. 1, the second under type C
no. 10, where I have mentioned the possibility that the
original reading of the MS. was *ond cyning mǣnan*.

1. $|\, \mathbf{J}\,|\, \mathbf{J} \,\, \mathbf{J} \,|$, 1 example:

ðegn betstan 1871

Under the corresponding number in the first half-line I have suggested the possibility of reading *ðegn betestan,* type D no. 14.

(2. $|\, \mathbf{J}.\, \mathbf{\flat}\,|\, \mathbf{J} \,|$, only in first half-line, and there by a modern error.)

3. $|\, \mathbf{J} \,\, \mathbf{\flat} \,\, \mathbf{\flat}\,|\, \mathbf{J} \,|$, 1 example:

ræhte ongēan 747

This verse is metrically the same as the equally dubious *lissa gelong* in the first half-line. It is not by any means clear, however, that this is the reading of the MS. In his facsimile edition, Zupitza reports that some five letters were erased at the end of a line, immediately preceding *ræhte,* which begins a new line. Traces of the letters are plainly visible in the facsimile, though they cannot be read with certainty. I strongly doubt that they were erased intention-ally, because corresponding places on the two sides of the preceding leaf are likewise obscured, as if something had been spilled there. It should be legitimate, therefore, to fill in the gap. Zupitza said of the damaged letters, " the first seems to have been *h,* the second possibly was *a.*" As I have said, the facsimile cannot be read with certainty, but it seems possible that the traces still visible represent the five letters *him sw* (the *s* high, only the lower half of its stem visible, the *w* showing quite plainly below the line). A final letter in the now missing margin would give us the two words *him swa,* which make excellent sense. The MS. itself must be checked before this can be accepted as the true reading, but even if the damaged word or words must remain in doubt, I think we can be sure that the scribe did not present us with *ræhte ongēan* as a complete verse. The verse which I have suggested, *him swā ræhte ongēan,* would belong to type B, no. 33.

(4. $|\, \mathbf{\flat} \,\, \mathbf{\flat} \,\, \mathbf{\flat} \,\, \mathbf{\flat}\,|\, \mathbf{J} \,|$, only in first half-line.)

b. *Overburdened verses.*

I have already discussed *in ēowrum gūðgetawum* 395 in the corresponding section of the first half-line, and in accordance with the quantity of *-getawum* there postulated have assigned the verse to type B no. 28. The only other overburdened verse is discussed below.

(5. | ♩ ♪ ♪| ♫♩ ♪ ♪|, only in first half-line.)

(6. | ♩ ♩|♪ ♪ ♪ ♪|, only in first half-line, but cf. the following.)

†7. |♩.♪|♪ ♪ ♪ ♪|, 1 example:

> ungedēfelīce 2435

This verse resembles *ealne ūtanweardne* 2297a in that the long penultimate syllable prevents it from being included in type D. Two easy remedies were proposed by Sievers (*Altgermanische Metrik* par. 85 n. 8). We can either regard the *i* of *-lice* as short (apparently its quantity fluctuated with the degree of emphasis it received), or we can read simply *ungedēfe*. The latter is metrically preferable.

SUMMARIES

Type A

		FIRST HALF-LINE								SECOND HALF-LINE					
		A₁	A₂			A*	A*	A₃	A₃	A₁	A₂			A*	A*
Catalogue Number[1]	Rhythm		a	b	ab						a	b	ab		
1 28 35 53		371	53	18	11			2		460	21	3	1		1
63		144		23						134					
2															
36															
64		60	21	7	1			4		61	2	4			
3 29 37 54															
65		29		7				4		13					
4															
38															
5		275	51	24				58	3	237	6				
39															
66 67															
30															
55					10										
59 60						2	3								
6		1		2				26	2	5		1			
68 69															
7		40	4	2				90	11	8					
40		44		2						27					
70 71															
31						2	5								
61 62															
8								2		2		1			
72															
73								1							
74 75								8	1						
		964	129	83	22	4	8	195	17	947	29	8	1	0	1

[1] The two halves of the line are numbered alike. To use this table as an index, first find the desired rhythm, then the accentual scheme in one of the eight columns for the first half-line or in one of the six for the second, then find the corresponding catalogue number at the left.

Type A—Continued

Catalogue Number			Rhythm	FIRST HALF-LINE								SECOND HALF-LINE					
				A₁				A*		A₃		A₁	A₂			A*	
					a	b	ab						a	b	ab		
9	41	76	(musical notation)	3	.	.	.	.	.	.	11	.	.	.	.	.	.
10	42	77	(musical notation)	4	.	2	.	.	.	.	17	1	.	1	.	.	.
	43	78	(musical notation, with anacrusis)	.	.	1	.	.	.	.	6	.	.	.	.	.	.
18			(musical notation)	3	.	.	.	.	.	.	.	3	.	.	.	.	.
19			(musical notation)	3	.	.	.	.	.	.	5	5	.	.	.	.	.
20	89		(musical notation)	16	.	.	.	.	.	.	.	1	.	.	.	.	.
21			(musical notation)	1	.	1	.	.	.	.	17	.	.	.	.	.	.
22	49	90	(musical notation)	3	.	.	.	.	.	.	1	.	.	.	.	.	.
23		91	(musical notation)	3	.	.	.	.	.	.	1	.	.	.	.	.	.
		92	(musical notation)	2	.	.	.	.	.	.	1	.	.	.	.	.	.
		93	(musical notation)	.	.	.	.	.	.	.	.	23	.	1	.	.	.
24			(musical notation)	1	15	3	3	.	.	.	.	17	.	.	.	.	.
11 32 44 56			(musical notation)	27	15	3	3	.	.	.	.	.	.	.	.	.	.
12	45	79	(musical notation)	11	.	7	.	.	.	.	2	.	.	.	.	.	.
13 33	57		(musical notation)	4	2	2	1	.	.	.	4	.	.	.	.	.	1
14	46		(musical notation)	2	.	.	.	.	.	.	6	.	29	.	.	.	.
Brought Forward				83	17	16	4	0	0	0	60	2	0	0	0	
				964	129	83	22	4	8	17	947	8	29	1	0	1
				1047	146	99	26	4	8	17	1007	10	29	1	0	1
										62						
										195						
										257						

TYPE A—CONTINUED

	RHYTHM	FIRST HALF-LINE								SECOND HALF-LINE						
CATALOGUE NUMBER		A₁	A₂ a	A₂ b	A₂ ab	A*	A*	A₃	A₃	A₁	A₂ a	A₂ b	A₂ ab	A*	A*
15 47 34 58	*(rhythm notation)*	30	10	6				10	1	19		4			
16 80 81 82 83 84	*(rhythm notation)*	1 5			2			1 8	1		2				
85	*(rhythm notation)*							1		3					
86	*(rhythm notation)*			1				1							
17 48 87	*(rhythm notation)*	1						1	1						
88	*(rhythm notation, With anacrusis)*														
25 50 51	*(rhythm notation)*	1		1 1				2	1						
26 52	*(rhythm notation)*	1			2			1							
27 94 95 96 97	*(rhythm notation)*	3		2				1							
Brought forward		42 1047	10 146	11 99	2 26	0 4	0 8	26 257	4 17	22 1007	2 29	4 10	0 1	0 0	0 1
		1089	156	110	28	4	8	283	21	1029	31	14	1	0	1
Total each half		1699								1076					

TYPE A—CONCLUDED

		FIRST HALF-LINE	A4 Short		SECOND HALF-LINE	A4 Short	
CATALOGUE NUMBER	RHYTHM	A1	A2	A3	A1	A2	A3
98 102 104		·	17	1	6	27	·
99 103 105		·	8	1	2	8	·
100		2	·	·	·	·	·
101 106		1	·	2	·	·	·
107		·	·	1	·	·	·
		3	25	5	8	35	0

Total each half   33   43

Plus above totals   1699   1076

TOTAL TYPE A   1732   1119

TOTAL BOTH HALVES   2851

TYPE B

a. First measure light, second heavy

No.	RHYTHM B₁	HALF-LINE I	II
1		18	21
2		98	222
3		4	13
4		14	59
5		13	59
6		1	4
7		3	7
8		.	1
9		.	2
10		28	89
11		3	19
12		1	13
13		.	1
14		.	5
15		3	.

No.	RHYTHM B₁	HALF-LINE I	II
16		10	30
17		.	1
18		1	7
19		2	5
20		.	1
21		5	1
22		.	2
23		17	19
24		1	2
25		2	3
26		3	3
27		3	.
28		.	1
29		1	.
30		2	.
31		.	1
		234	591

TYPE B—Continued

a. First measure light, second heavy

No.	RHYTHM B₂	HALF-LINE I	II
32		9	3
33+50*		28+1*	50
34		5	23
35		3	16
36		·	4
37		·	8
38		·	3
39		·	3
40		·	1
41		1	8
42		1	·
43		1	1
44		1	·
45		·	·
46+51*		5+1*	1
47		1	1
48		1	·
49		·	1
		57+2*	123

b. Anacrusis—heavy stress both measures

No.	RHYTHM B₁	I	II
52		12	10
53		2	1
54		·	1
55		·	4
56		3	3
57		·	2
		17	21

No.	RHYTHM B₂	I	II
58		1	1
		18	22

TOTAL TYPE B   309+2*   736

BOTH HALVES COMBINED   1047

* The illegitimate B₃ with alliteration on second stress.

TYPE C

a. First measure light, second heavy

RHYTHM C₁

No.	HALF-LINE I	HALF-LINE II
1	22	7
2	133	74
3	2	1
4	19	23
5	15	14
6	2	1
7	5	7
8	.	2
9	.	1
10	6	2
11	49	43
12	1	.
13	6	8
14	7	5
15	1	1
16	4	5
17	1	1
18	.	1
19	1	.
20	1	3
	275	199

RHYTHM C₂

No.	HALF-LINE I	HALF-LINE II
21	33	15
22	137	166
23	4	3
24	8	29
25	21	26
26	2	.
27	2	.
28	2	3
29	4	6
30	.	1
31	1	.
	214	249

b. Anacrusis—heavy stress both measures

RHYTHM C₁

No.	HALF-LINE I	HALF-LINE II
32	3	40
33	2	.
34	13	74
35	1	.
36	1	6
	20	120

RHYTHM C₂

No.	HALF-LINE I	HALF-LINE II
37	11	28
38	1	.
39	.	1
	12	29

TOTAL TYPE C BOTH HALVES COMBINED 521 597 1118

Type D

Rhythm D₁

No.	HALF-LINE I	HALF-LINE II
1	47	78
2	49	60
3	10	3
4	2	4
5	.	1
6	2	.
7	1	.
8	2	.
9	1	.
	114	146

Rhythm D₂

No.	HALF-LINE I	HALF-LINE II
10	35	64
11	23	54
12	2	1
13	3	1
	63	120

Rhythm D₃

No.	HALF-LINE I	HALF-LINE II
14	2	13
15	.	2
	2	15

Rhythm D₄

No.	HALF-LINE I	HALF-LINE II
16	25	27
17	28	20
18	3	23
19	.	8
20	2	12
21	3	2
22	2	.
23	.	1
24	1	1
25	4	.
26	2	.
	70	94

TOTAL SUB-TYPE D

	249	375

Type D—Continued

Rhythm D*₄

No.	HALF-LINE I	HALF-LINE II
49	19	·
50	3	·
51	8	·
52	1	·
53	2	·
54	·	1
55	1	·
56	3	·
57	2	·
58	1	1
	40	1

	HALF-LINE I	HALF-LINE II
SUB-TYPE D*	211	18
SUB-TYPE D	249	375
TOTAL TYPE D	460	393
BOTH HALVES COMBINED	853	

Rhythm D*₁

No.	HALF-LINE I	HALF-LINE II
27	33	3
28	1	1
29	3	·
30	·	1
31	2	·
32	2	1
33	24	1
34	1	·
35	2	·
36	4	·
37	1	·
38	1	·
39	6	·
	80	7

Rhythm D*₂

No.	HALF-LINE I	HALF-LINE II
40	42	6
41	6	2
42	7	1
43	3	·
44	4	1
45	26	·
46	1	·
47	1	·
48	1	·
	91	10

TYPE E

RHYTHM E

No.	HALF-LINE I	II
1	68	147
2	1	4
3	6	45
4	6	12
5	27	57
6	2	13
7	2	11
8	3	2
9	.	1
10	1	.
11	9	15
12	2	.
13	2	2
14	.	1
15	1	.
16	2	.
	132	310

RHYTHM E*

No.	HALF-LINE I	II
17	.	4
	0	4

TOTAL TYPE E 132 314

BOTH HALVES COMBINED 446

Group F—Remainder

RHYTHM

No.	HALF-LINE I	II
1	2	1
2	.	.
3	1	1
4	1	1
5	1	.
6	1	.
7	.	1
	6 + 3	= 9

GRAND TOTALS

Type	First Half-Line	Second Half-Line	Combined
A	1732	1119	2851
B	311	736	1047
C	521	597	1118
D	460	393	853
E	132	314	446
Group F	6	3	9
	3162	3162	6324
Not catalogued, Hypermetric	11_1	11_1	22
Missing or conjectural	9_2	9_3	18
	3182	3182	6364

1 Lines 1163-8, 1705-7, 2005-6.   2 Lines 62a, 200.   403b, 2226-30b, 2792b.